THE SECOND
ARAB AWAKENING

THE SECOND ARAB AWAKENING

Revolution, Democracy, and the Islamist
Challenge from Tunis to Damascus

ADEED DAWISHA

W. W. Norton & Company

New York • London

For information about permission to reproduce selections from this book,
write to Permissions, W. W. Norton & Company, Inc.,
500 Fifth Avenue, New York, NY 10110

For information about special discounts for bulk purchases, please contact
W. W. Norton Special Sales at specialsales@wwnorton.com or 800-233-4830

Manufacturing by Courier Westford
Production manager: Anna Oler

Library of Congress Cataloging-in-Publication Data

Dawisha, A. I.
The second Arab awakening : revolution, democracy,
and the Islamist challenge from Tunis to Damascus / Adeed Dawisha.
pages cm
Includes bibliographical references and index.
ISBN 978-0-393-24012-2 (hardcover)
1. Arab Spring, 2010– 2. Arab countries—Politics and government—
21st century. 3. Islam and state—Arab countries. 4. Islam and politics—
Arab countries. 5. Islamic fundamentalism—Arab countries.
6. Democratization—Arab countries. 7. Revolutions—Arab countries. I. Title.
JQ1850.A1D38 2013
909'.097492708312—dc23

2012049831

W. W. Norton & Company, Inc.
500 Fifth Avenue, New York, N.Y. 10110
www.wwnorton.com

W. W. Norton & Company Ltd.
Castle House, 75/76 Wells Street, London W1T 3QT

1 2 3 4 5 6 7 8 9 0

To the three people who have been
my biggest cheerleaders:
Karen, Nadia, and Emile

CONTENTS

PREFACE

While of course we can always look back and rewrite history (and experts and academics are not immune to such proclivities), the truth is that by the dawn of the new millennium most of us Middle East watchers had given up hope that any meaningful political reform would occur in the Arab world, enveloped as it was by a seemingly impenetrable iron wall of dogged and unshakable tyranny. Not that these Arab autocrats could be credited with other redeeming features; they presided over countries that had some of the worst unemployment figures in the world, that suffered from rampant corruption, that provided little or no services, and that allowed large chunks of their populations to live in abject poverty. But these very same despots, failures at governance, exhibited astonishing talents when it came to the business of controlling and holding on to the levers of political power. Such was their pervasive and palpable dominion that only the hopelessly romantic believed that meaningful change was in the air.

Then the self-immolation in December 2010 of an impoverished street vendor in an out-of-the-way Tunisian town rendered all firmly held beliefs and conclusions obsolete. I for one was mesmerized and enthralled by the extraordinary happenings in the Arab world in late 2010 and early 2011, and immediately felt the need to chronicle and evaluate the unfolding events. I began researching this book as bloody clashes between protestors and entrenched dictators dominated the airwaves and filled television screens every day.

My partiality for the young and courageous demonstrators was in fact tinged with doubts and fears, for in the back of my mind were the revolutions that had swept the Arab world fifty to sixty years earlier. Similarly initiated by young and idealistic revolutionaries, and led by visionary leaders, these eruptions carried so much promise, so much hope, but ended up producing the batch of cruel and thoroughly ghastly dictators against whom the present protests were launched. *The Second Arab Awakening*, evaluating the present through understanding the failures of the past, was well on its way.

During the fall 2011 semester, I was helped in my research by four bright and industrious Miami undergraduates: Katharine Davies, Nicholas Jenkins-Neary, Stacey Mighton, and Benjamin Richards, and I thank them for their excellent work. The spring semester, January to May 2012, was spent at the Woodrow Wilson International Center for Scholars in Washington, DC. It was there that the bulk of the book was written. In addition to providing an ideal ambience for research and writing, the Center was a lively hub for truly exciting intellectual and policy discourse with a host of American and international scholars in myriad fields and specialties. I am particularly indebted to Haleh Esfandiari, the director of the Middle East Program at the Center. It was due primarily to her efforts that I was able to join the center as a Public Policy Scholar, and she and her efficient and hardworking staff made my stay there not just productive but very pleasant. I also would like to offer my thanks to Michael Van Dusen and Rob Litwak for facilitating my appointment, and for the many congenial lunches we had, together with other colleagues, at the center's cafeteria. My research assistant at the Center, Oren Auslin, helped me greatly keep up with the rapid developments in the Arab world.

I owe a great debt to my editor at W. W. Norton, Alane Salierno Mason. From the moment she read the proposal, she became a singular champion of the project. She is not just a acquiring editor; she is an editor in the full sense of the term. She meticulously went through every single sentence, made adjustments, suggested improvements, and tightened arguments. There is little doubt that, due to her, this is a better book. My thanks also go to Denise Scarfi, the assistant editor, who worked tirelessly to shepherd the manuscript through the many stages of the production process; to Ann Adelman, a wonderful copyeditor; and to Elisabeth Kerr, the foreign rights director who, though she may not remember it, was the first person I contacted about the possibility of publishing the book with Norton. Actually, I got Elisabeth's name from my very good friend Avi Shlaim, who through the years has been a constant source of support and wise counsel.

My wife, Karen, author of many books on Soviet and Russian politics, took valuable time off writing her own book on Vladimir Putin and methodically read through the first proofs, picking up mistakes that had escaped me. My two children, Nadia and Emile, themselves no strangers to writing, but in ways that reflect the norms and styles of their generation,* always asked about the book's progress, offered encouragement, and took pride in any good news I related to them. To this wonderful family of mine, I dedicate this book.

*http://listengirlfriends.wordpress.com and www.chicagonow.com/greater-good

THE SECOND
ARAB AWAKENING

Daily clashes between protestors and security forces
during the winter of Arab discontent. *Associated Press / Ben Curtis*

Chapter One

THE WINTER OF THEIR
DISCONTENT

As the first light of dawn broke through the night, ushering in Friday, December 17, 2010, no one in the North African Arab country of Tunisia, awake or still asleep, thought that this would be anything but just another uneventful, run-of-the-mill day. In the city of Sidi Bouzid, situated in the arid middle of the country, way out on the neglected margins of Tunisia's northern and coastal cultural and economic hub, people woke up, and readied themselves for the day's events and its chores—Friday prayer at the mosque, a visit to the market, maybe a walk down the city's boulevards. For most of them, wretchedly poor and without hope, promenading along the city's main boulevard was the most "fun" they could squeeze out of their day. No one could anticipate the momentous happenings that would sweep through Tunisia and other parts of the Arab world: happenings that would be triggered by one macabre act of self-sacrifice in Sidi Bouzid itself; an act that would make Muhammad Bouazizi, one of the thousands of down-trodden and anonymous street vendors who suffuse Arab markets, into an iconic hero, imprinting his name into not only Tunisian but Arab and international consciousness.

Muhammad Bouazizi did not start the day of December 17 anticipating that what he would end up doing would be the stuff of legends, and that he would be identified reverently as the instigator of the revolutionary waves that erupted across the Arab world by no lesser personage than the president of the United States of America.[1] Bouazizi was in fact no revolutionary; he had no political agenda, no grand ideas about institutional changes. He was a twenty-six-year-old man concerned with little more than providing a living, meager as it was, to elderly parents and younger siblings. His was a hard life that began every day in the early hours of the morning when he would take his cart to local producers, fill it with fruit and vegetables, and then push it for some distance to the town center, where he would hope to make a small profit. Once there, however, he was constantly harassed, bullied, and humiliated by the local police, who more often than not were looking for the customary bribe.

On Friday, December 17, for some unexplained reason, Bouazizi stood his ground and refused to bend to this petty tyranny. A loud argument ensued and his cart was confiscated. Deprived of his only source of livelihood, he spent the morning feverishly trying to retrieve the cart, but to no avail, having been given the runaround from one governmental office to the other. Finally, he went to the governor's office and pleaded to see him, but he was laughed off by the guards and summarily dispatched. Enveloped by the suffocating arbitrariness of authoritarian rule, where ordinary people had little recourse to due process or justice, Bouazizi this time had reached the end of his tether. He walked to a nearby store, bought a can of gasoline, went back in front of the governor's mansion, doused his body with the petrol, and set himself alight. And so began the winter of their discontent—Tunisians first, to be followed by other Arabs.

Bouazizi's self-immolation was a horrific statement that echoed the pervasive despair of his generation—a generation that saw every avenue of political and economic hope closed to it; a generation that had lived under no other system but that of tyranny. Demonstrations would erupt almost immediately, first in Sidi Bouzid and soon after in other central and southern cities and towns. In the days to come, unemployed Tunisian youth would be joined by university students, unionized workers, lawyers and members of other professions. They demanded an end to corruption and better economic opportunities, but most of all they called for an end to the twenty-three-year autocracy of the country's president, Zine al-Abidin Ben Ali, and the immediate institution of democratic rule. By the time Bouazizi died in hospital on January 4, 2011, the entire country was in open rebellion. Still, the state would not budge, and the security forces were out in force responding harshly, and with live bullets, to the escalating popular uprising.

Ben Ali and Tunisia's ruling elites, who had dealt successfully with upheavals in the past, no doubt hoped that the energy and seeming determination of the demonstrators soon would be spent; people would get tired, give the whole affair a shrug, and go back to what they were doing before the minor inconvenience of Bouazizi's self-immolation. They of course grossly miscalculated. On Friday, January 14, four weeks to the day after Bouazizi set himself on fire, the capital, Tunis, was flooded by people from all over the country, and in their hundreds of thousands they overwhelmed the police and other security, repeating their demands for Ben Ali's removal and for universal political suffrage. That day, the now beleaguered president, along with his commonly detested family, fled the country to Saudi Arabia, the only state that would have them and give them protection from eager human rights prosecutors.

If Tunisia's revolt was the first in the Arab world, Egypt's, which began on January 25, 2011, was the most consequential. For over two centuries, Egypt constituted the intellectual center, cultural pacesetter, and political role model among Arab countries. Political developments in Egypt have always had, and will always have, palpable impact on the length and breadth of Arab lands. So while the Egyptian autocrat, Muhammad Hosni Mubarak, along with other entrenched Arab kings and presidents, watched the Tunisian events with mounting concern, they still felt reasonably confident that, unlike that small and compact North African country, Egypt with its sprawling population and huge security forces would prove to be a bulwark against any fanciful demands for democracy and political participation.

But this did not come to pass; indeed, it was Egypt's president and the other Arab leaders who were the ones entertaining fanciful aspirations about building immunity against the virus of liberation. Egypt was to succumb—and pretty quickly, as it turned out. On January 25, demonstrators took to the streets throughout the country, demanding Mubarak's ouster, and this would be followed on a daily basis by bigger and louder protests. Without an organizing body, the protestors depended on the social media to transmit messages and directives. Appeals for support, calls for demonstrations, directions to gather at particular locations, and intelligence about police concentrations were all transmitted via Facebook and Twitter. From the very outset, the protestors insisted on the nonviolent nature of the revolt, and they would carry this commitment successfully throughout the uprising.

The same restraint was not evident in the regime's response

to the protestors. The reviled Central Security Forces unleashed a series of attacks against the unarmed demonstrators, and soon they would use hired thugs (a tactic that had proved successful in the past when utilized in elections against opponents) to beat up, intimidate, and occasionally shoot at protestors. The main targets were the demonstrators in Tahrir Square in the center of Cairo, which very quickly became the single most visible site of the uprising. There thousands camped day and night, venting their anger at the Mubarak regime in full view of the international media. Mubarak's goal was to drive them out of the square, and by doing so, create the impression that things were back to normal. Well aware that the square had become the symbol of the revolution, the protestors fought tooth and nail to stay put, chanting what in many ways became the anthem of the revolution: *mush ha nimshi, huwa yimshi*, we're not leaving, he's leaving. When the effort to clear the square failed, the regime withdrew the police and security forces from the streets and almost simultaneously opened up the prisons and let convicts out, resulting in widespread looting. The regime obviously was presenting citizens with a stark choice: authoritarian stability or the chaos that comes with freedom.

For the colliding humanity that overwhelmed the main streets and squares of Cairo and Egypt's other major cities, the choice was predetermined. They already had embarked on the journey to freedom, and turning back was no longer an option. Indeed, the determination and ever-mounting confidence of the revolutionaries was evident in the series of concessions that Mubarak began to offer. He initially dismissed his government and appointed a vice president (the first in his thirty-year rule) and a new prime minister. He then promised not to be a candidate in the upcoming presidential election, scheduled for September 2011. He also allowed his party, the ruling National Democratic Party (NDP), to dismiss his

The protestors' many demands in February 2011 included the ousting of
Mubarak, free elections, and trials for those stealing the country's wealth.
Mona Sosh

son Gamal, along with a few other scions of the regime, from their senior party positions. All this while the government-controlled media continued to speak of dark conspiracies against Egypt from motley groups that ranged from Iran and al-Qaeda to Israel and the United States.

But Mubarak's days were numbered, and he realized this when the top brass of the army, which had replaced the detested security and police forces—and which, by virtue of having no history of malevolence against citizens, was respected among the ranks of demonstrators—declared its steadfast neutrality in the whole affair. It was not as though the higher echelons of Egypt's military were dedicated revolutionaries; all of them had been handpicked by Mubarak, formed an essential component of his support base, and received more than their fair share of the state's largess. The top generals simply could not guarantee the loyalty of midlevel officers and the rank and file if an order to open fire had been given. On February 11, a mere eighteen days after the first demonstration, Mubarak agreed to leave office.

But other Arab autocrats proved more resilient. For every Ben Ali or Mubarak, who at some point would decide to put an end to confrontation, there were others, sadly many more, who seemingly had an infinite tolerance for killing their own people. Widespread popular eruptions akin to the ones in Tunisia and Egypt occurred in Bahrain, Libya, Syria, and Yemen; but, while there was no lack of resolve or capacity for sacrifice on the part of the insurgent masses, in no case were the swift and radical changes of Tunisia and Egypt replicated.

In the small Gulf state of Bahrain, demonstrations, consisting mainly of Shiites, broke out in mid-February. The Shiites, who form the majority of the population, demanded greater political rights and wider inclusion in the political power structure from

King Hamad bin Isa al-Khalifa, who along with the bulk of the political elite, belonged to the minority Sunni community. Initially, the king tried to buy himself out of trouble, a well-trodden path to success in the Gulf States, so he offered each Bahraini family a financial reward of 1,000 Bahraini dinars, about $2,650. When that did not dissuade the protestors, he ordered the release of a number of Shiite activists from prison, and proceeded to change a few cabinet portfolios. The effort at conciliation, however, was accompanied by strong-arm methods from the security forces, who beat up demonstrators and arrested them at will. This was bolstered by counterdemonstrations of support for the king by the Sunni population. But to no avail; the anti-government demonstrators increased, growing louder and more immoderate in their demands: a true constitutional monarchy, even the abolition of the al-Khalifa dynasty.

Calling the monarchy's legitimacy into question was a threat not just to Bahrain's king but to the Sunni population, which from the very beginning had looked at the upheavals as a Shiite sectarian project. The consistent demand of the demonstrators for freedom, for reform of the political system, and for strengthening of parliament would not assuage Sunni suspicion, indeed conviction, that the whole affair was being orchestrated by Shiite Iran from across the waterway. Even the assurances of Robert Gates, the U.S. secretary of defense, who publicly asserted that there was no evidence of Iranian instigation, would not hold sway. If anything, Gates's advice that the widespread popular demand for reform meant that the monarchy could no longer maintain the status quo[2] seemed to have convinced the king that the longer the demonstrations went on, the more lukewarm American support for his government would become. To the ruling elites of Bahrain, the time for concessions was over, and a resolute response was needed. But they also well knew that Bahrain's security forces on their own did not have the capacity to suppress the demonstrations.

On March 14, two days after Gates left the country, and a month after the eruption of the first demonstration, troops from neighboring Saudi Arabia and the United Arab Emirates entered Bahrain at the request of the king, and with unrestrained belligerence forcibly removed protestors from all public areas in the capital city of Manama and destroyed their encampments in the city center. Immediately martial law was instituted, to be followed by wholesale arrests and trials of "plotters against the regime," which included not just intellectuals and political figures but also doctors and nurses who had committed the seemingly inexcusable infraction of caring for injured protestors. One of the founders of the leading opposition paper, *al-Wasat*, was arrested and later died in police custody. Other editors and columnists who wrote for the paper were assaulted and charged with crimes against the state.[3] In the meantime, scores of Shiite mosques were destroyed. Shiite parliamentarians, who had thought of themselves as the bridge between the king and the protestors, became convinced that government resolve had turned into a vendetta against its Shiite population. By the middle of May, all had resigned, and two of them, having lost their parliamentary immunity, were promptly arrested. By now, King Hamad and his government, still aided by outside troops, had succeeded in erasing all remnants of the revolt that had erupted less than two months earlier. And when President Barack Obama made a public plea to the king for the jailed opposition members to be set free and for the government and opposition to engage in dialogue,[4] Bahraini authorities responded by mounting an attack on the home of a prominent human rights activist, and by not budging an inch on a death sentence imposed on two young Shiite activists, who had been convicted by a secret military court.

On June 1, convinced that the revolution had exhaled its final breath, the king and his Saudi backers ended the state of emergency and pulled the tanks and armed troop carriers from the center of Manama, signaling the return to normalcy. But the quiet that reigned was illusory, born out of naked force. As fear engulfed the Shiite community, they saw more of their youth arrested, more of their jobs taken away, and more, much more, of their dignity and self-esteem abused by Sunnis convinced of the Shiites' fickle loyalty to the state. Whatever religious and political bridges had been built in the past aimed at fusing the Sunnis and Shiites into a united and coherent Bahraini nation stood damaged, perhaps irreparably, by the events of the country's winter of violence.

In Yemen, President Ali Abdullah Saleh, at the helm of the ship of state since 1979, had his first taste of his people's discontent in late January 2011. Following the pattern already set in Tunisia and Egypt, young protestors flooded the main square of Sanaa, the capital city, demanding that Saleh step down. And again, following the example of Ben Ali and Mubarak, Saleh immediately flooded the streets of Sanaa with his security forces, while volunteering a few cosmetic reforms and promising not to run for reelection when his term finished, in 2013, or to pass the presidency on to his son, Ahmad. These promises would ring hollow. Fresh in people's minds were past promises that were made, then conveniently forgotten by the wily president. Prior to the last presidential elections in September 2006, Saleh had declared repeatedly that he would not be a candidate, yet in June 2006, he reversed himself, arguing that he was simply "acceding to the will of the people."[5] Five years on, mired in corruption, and with little appetite for change or reform, Saleh could hardly expect the people to take him at his word. Perhaps the barbiturate effect of imperious political control over three decades made Saleh believe that a few concessionary and conciliatory words backed up by pointed guns and tank turrets would make people desist from such tiresome behavior as demanding basic political and economic rights.

But the protests did not cease; indeed, they grew in size, with demonstrators continuing to demand the ouster of Saleh and his political order. Within less than a month, the uprising would spread to other cities in Yemen. Hundreds of thousands of opponents would rally in Taiz, Aden, and Hodeida. This prompted Saleh to announce plans for constitutional changes to take place by the end of the year that would devolve power from the president to parliament. None of this, however, would pacify the irate crowds, who wanted nothing less than to show Saleh the door—obviously not something that the president was contemplating.

That is when things began to get ugly. The security forces abandoned any restraint they might have had and started to attack demonstrators willfully and maliciously. The sound of live bullets would be heard with sickening regularity, and casualties began to multiply. In one day in the capital city of Sanaa, over 50 demonstrators were shot dead and more than 250 were injured when snipers fired at them from the rooftops of nearby buildings. By the end of March, as casualties mounted, a number of politicians, diplomats, and tribal chiefs, all key players in Saleh's political order, publicly supported the protestors; and more critically, over a dozen senior army commanders, including a key military figure, General Ali Mohsen al-Ahmar, defected, along with their troops, to the cause of the opposition.

But Saleh's predicted imminent demise would stretch for weeks, even months. The fragmentation of the army was a blow, yet one that he could survive. He had made sure to put his son and three nephews in charge of four key security and military units, including the pivotal Republican Guard and the Central Security Forces.

And the presidential palace was protected by thousands of loyal soldiers tied to the president through tribal roots. Indeed, years of exploiting Yemen's tribal structures had stood the president in good stead.

Saleh was a master at manipulating the country's complex societal mosaic. About three quarters of Yemen's population is rural, belonging to a variety of tribal confederations, and Saleh had worked hard at co-opting key tribal leaders into the state apparatus, increasing their wealth and cementing their status. Along with their tribes, these tribal chiefs became a critical base of support for the regime, and would come to its aid whenever they were needed. So, while the urban youth would come out in large numbers against the president, and some tribal chieftains would withdraw their support, Saleh still had enough support to withstand the pressure, or to drive a hard bargain if it became necessary to negotiate with the opposition.

By the end of May, there was a surreal feel to the Yemeni situation. Time after time, a huge anti-Saleh demonstration, protected by some elements of the army, would erupt in one part of Sanaa, while another equally large pro-Saleh demonstration, protected by other elements of the same army, would take place in another part of the city. And breaking the stalemate seemed beyond anyone's capacity; more than once, mediators from the Gulf Cooperation Council (GCC), worried about a spillover effect into their own countries, would announce a negotiated agreement, only to be reneged on a day or two later by the old-timer in the presidential palace.

Another old-timer, in fact of longer duration, was to be jolted out of the comfort of ruthless oppression into the horrid reality of revolutionary fervor. Colonel Muammar Qadhafi had ruled Libya since 1969 through a combination of state-perpetrated violence and clever manipulation of the country's tribal society. He, his many sons, carefully chosen tribal and clan members, and scores of associates, cronies, and hangers-on, had so successfully put the lid on any trace of dissent that they felt secure that the events of next-door Tunisia would not happen in their own country.

But happen they did. In mid-February, widespread protests erupted in many Libyan cities. Thousands took to the streets, shouting anti-Qadhafi slogans and demanding a return to the pre-Qadhafi constitution. As clashes with the police intensified, a number of buildings belonging to state security, the symbol of state oppression, were attacked and torched. And this would happen even in Tripoli, the country's capital and the colonel's seat of power. In the past—even the recent past—the state-controlled media, in a shameless orgy of cultural capitulation, would show huge demonstrations of popular support for Qadhafi, all organized by the colonel's mobilizational arm, the General People's committees. Now many in the crowds would wave pictures of the leader, distributed to them earlier in the good old days of political submission, except this time with a huge "X" adorning his face.

The greatest revolutionary intensity was felt in the eastern half of the country, which is the furthest from Qadhafi's tribal roots. Benghazi, the largest city in the east, and relatively neglected in comparison with western cities, particularly Tripoli and Sirte, the colonel's birthplace, quickly became the capital and administrative heart of the rebellion. In less than ten days, Benghazi and a bunch of eastern cities fell into the hands of the rebels, with a number of military units defecting to the anti-Qadhafi forces. A Transitional National Council (TNC), to be headquartered in Benghazi, was established, which would act as the political authority until Qadhafi's political order was finally overthrown. Imbued with revolutionary exuberance, the young protestors, armed with weapons that most of them did not know how to use, jumped into cars and trucks and headed west to the seat of Qadhafi's power.

But to assume that Qadhafi's regime would swiftly unravel at the sight of young men brandishing machine guns from the windows of speeding sedans was mere wishful thinking. The colonel might have been erratic and compulsive when handling economic and foreign policy issues, but he held a steady and unforgiving hand when it came to the business of oppression. This was not a man who would flinch at the sight of bullet-ridden citizens. He and his sons repeatedly insisted that they would "fight to the bitter end and martyr themselves" against the demonstrating "cockroaches," all of whom, according to the colonel, were "drug addicts and deviants."[6] Qadhafi's fighting words echoed his belief that the majority of army units, drawn from friendly tribes and favored regions in the west and south, would remain loyal. And he was right, even though by the first week of March the protestors had seized a number of cities and seemed to be marching resolutely toward Tripoli.

Having silenced any whiff of dissent in Tripoli with little regard for the niceties of individual and human rights, Qadhafi began his counteroffensive on March 6, and quickly retook some of the western cities in rebel hands. Exploiting his superior firepower, he would literally flatten the cities with rolling artillery barrages and airstrikes before his troops would enter and mop out any resistance left. By March 15, his troops were able to defeat the rebels in Ajdabiya, the last rebel-held city before Benghazi. They then proceeded to march toward Benghazi. The rebels, by now in dire straits, were clamoring for help from the international community. This came on March 17 when the United States, Britain, and France were able to secure a resolution from the United Nations Security Council to impose a no-fly zone in Libyan airspace in order to protect Libyan civilians.

The bulk of the military responsibility fell onto Britain and France, with logistical and intelligence support from the United States. Very soon it became clear that the concept of protecting Libyan civilians through the imposition of a no-fly zone was going to be interpreted liberally to mean aerial attacks against Qadhafi's forces as well as his command and control centers. The impact of this intervention was immediate. Qadhafi's troops, who had marched to within a few miles of Benghazi, and had actually begun a bombardment of the city, were now subjected to lethal air attacks by British and French aircraft, which had already neutralized the colonel's air force. Within less than forty-eight hours the attack on Benghazi was stymied, an event that was to become the turning point in the month-old civil war.

From then on, things began to go downhill for the dictator, and as winter turned into spring and early summer all signs pointed to a balance of forces that had shifted to the rebels. By May, the aerial attack against Qadhafi, now under the command of NATO, was taking a heavy toll on the dictator's forces and morale. Whatever command and control system he had possessed had been pulverized by the incessant barrage of deadly airstrikes. The rebels, taking advantage of the NATO-led intervention, and now fighting less chaotically, were able to finally expel his forces from Misrata, Libya's third largest city (strategically situated between Tripoli and Sirte), most of which had been turned into rubble by the colonel's forces. The TNC was beginning to deal with economic and security issues in a way that gave the impression of a viable government, and as a result was gaining international recognition.[7] And to add insult to injury, the prosecutor of the International Criminal Court at The Hague issued a warrant for Qadhafi, his son, and his brother-in-law to be tried for war crimes.

May had turned out to be a rotten month for the colonel, but he was not out for the count. Although his forces had been substantially degraded, and the rebels seemed to gain the upper hand, Qadhafi could still rely on considerable support. He retained the allegiance of tribal areas that spanned Sirte, the city of his birth in the north, through the center of the country, all the way south to the tribal lands on the border with Chad. By the end of May, a brittle stalemate seemed to characterize Libya's civil war, but a betting man would not put his money on the beleaguered, and increasingly erratic and incoherent, leader.

In Syria, support for President Bashar al-Asad that for months had kept a gathering uprising at bay came primarily from his own minority Alawite community. Numbering no more than 12 percent of the population, the Alawites had been poor and marginalized at the time of the country's independence in the 1940s. Seeing the military profession as their best chance for upward mobility, they flocked into the armed forces, so that by the 1960s they had come to dominate the military establishment. Military coups in the 1960s were led mostly by Alawite officers. In 1970, the Alawite minister of defense, Hafiz al-Asad, came to power by virtue of another coup. His rule was to last for thirty years, during which the Alawite community would attain political and economic prominence. He also made sure to make the most sensitive and pivotal positions in the military-security area the exclusive domain of Alawites, particularly the agencies and forces that were entrusted with defense of the regime. Whatever promises of change Bashar al-Asad made on inheriting the presidency from his father, these did not extend to reducing the Alawite domination of the country's institutions of violence.

Recognizing the immense power of the Asads and their clan, disgruntled Syrians had been cowed into political placidity. This, however, seemed to have been interpreted and was publicized by

Bashar al-Asad to indicate the people's happiness with the regime. In a January 31, 2011, interview with the *Wall Street Journal*, two weeks after the ouster of Ben Ali and eleven days before Mubarak would hit the deck as well, a confident, even brash Asad would scornfully dismiss the possibility of an uprising in Syria. After all, he would lecture the interviewers, the leadership in Syria was in tune "with the beliefs of the people," and that was why Syria "did not have the vacuum that created the disturbances" in Tunisia and Egypt.[8] But for the Arab despots, regardless of their true or manufactured confidence, the ghastly reality was that the events in Tunisia and Egypt were breaking down the pervasive walls of fear in many Arab lands, and Syria was no exception.

Large-scale protests erupted in the middle of March in a number of Syrian cities, with protestors demanding freedom and a greater say in the political affairs of their country. The largest and fiercest of demonstrations took place in the southern city of Daraa. In response, Asad promptly fired the district's governor. It is not clear whether the hapless governor was dismissed for not using enough force to quell the disturbances, or whether this was some kind of concession which Asad thought would blunt the crowd's anger. A few days later, over 20,000 people took to the streets, this time venting their anger specifically at Asad and his cousin, Rami Makhlouf, thought to be one of the richest and most corrupt men in Syria. The ruling elite responded by sending crack security forces made up mostly of Alawite men whose unrestrained brutality was meant to remind the crowd that this would be no Egypt or Tunisia.

The Syrian rulers also were being tutored by the Iranians, who had gained invaluable experience in the art and science of suppressing dissent. In the summer of 2009, the Iranian regime crushed a similar popular uprising, known as the "green revolution," and many of the tactics used then were passed on to the Syrians. The main lesson here was not to repeat the mistake of the Tunisian and Egyptian regimes in hesitating to stifle the transmission of information and knowledge. Instead, the Syrians imposed a ban on all foreign journalists, leaving the state media as the only conduit of news to the outside world. Simultaneously, the Iranians passed on a wealth of expertise gained from their 2009 experience in terms of intercepting or blocking Internet, mobile phones, and social media communications amongst the protestors themselves and between them and the outside world.[9] The purpose was to hermetically seal Syria, so that the Asad clan and their minions could coerce the population into submission, without worrying about meddling outsiders concerned with such annoying notions as the sanctity of human rights.

Still, Asad continued to make decorative concessions, thinking that somehow, the seething crowds would swallow these meaningless gestures and promptly return to the hitherto happy state of political servitude. He asked the cabinet to resign, but then appointed ministers with no record of reform, and in any case even the young illiterate kids who line the streets polishing shoes would know that the cabinet in Syria wielded little political influence. And then to pacify the Islamists, seen as active dissidents by the regime, Asad allowed female teachers to wear the full face veil called *al-niqab*, and he offered to consider the creation of an Islamic party and an Islamist satellite TV channel. To the 200,000 restless Kurds, he promised to make their New Year festival a national holiday.[10] But on the critical issue of "freedom," he would not budge.

In a much anticipated speech to the National Assembly, the country's parliament, scheduled for the end of March, the word had gone out that real reforms would be promised and the draconian state of emergency, in place for almost five decades, would be lifted. Yet when the president met with his parliamentarians, all of whom had been thoroughly vetted for their unquestioning loyalty to the regime, he skirted over the issue of reform, delivering a speech full of jaded clichés and banalities. He would declare, much as he had on an almost annual basis, that Syria was "the subject of a big conspiracy . . . from countries near and far." He made no mention of electoral reform, freedom for the media, or allowing political parties to be formed, and not a word about the emergency laws. All this apparently could not be a priority because his job first and foremost was to fix the stagnant economy. "We can sometimes postpone dealing with suffering that the emergency law may cause," he asserted to thunderous applause, "but we cannot postpone the suffering of a child whose father does not have enough money to treat him."[11]

Moving words indeed, but in the midst of an orgy of parliamentary adulation, no one seemed to wonder who exactly was responsible for the dysfunctional economy that the caring and concerned president was intent on fixing. After all, Bashar had been in charge for eleven years, and before him his father Hafiz had ruled for thirty years—more than ample time to fix the economy and treat the miseries of suffering children. Indeed, his heartwarming concern might have been believed had he, his family, and henchmen not been milking the very economy he supposedly was trying to mend. In a leaked confidential cable, sent in January 2008, the U.S. ambassador to Syria had detailed the extensive financial corruption that embroiled the president, his father-in-law, Fawaz al-Akhras, who lives in England, and his cousin and uncle, Rami and Muhammad Makhlouf. The cousin was referred to in the cable as "Syria's poster boy for corruption" and the uncle as "the brain" behind a vast business empire, created through shady nepotism and influence-peddling.[12] But in the parliamentary meeting, no questions about such practices were going to be asked. The Syrian parliamentarians, who owed their seats, and all the associated privileges, not to their constituents but to the president and the ruling clique, knew that under the stern and probing gaze of the state-controlled media they had one task to perform, and one task only—to act like doting cheerleaders.

The appearance in parliament was preceded by a well-orchestrated demonstration in which thousands filled the streets of the capital, Damascus, expressing their allegiance to the president. Asad of course could count on the loyalty of the Alawite community, as well as key members of the Sunni community, who had been appropriated into the political and economic edifice of the country through more than four decades of rule by the Asad family. And over the following weeks, ultra-loyal military units, better equipped and trained than the rest of the army, all commanded by Asad loyalists, would take on primary responsibility in confronting the demonstrators. Indeed, at the forefront of governmental forces ranged against the demonstrators were the Presidential Guard and the army's notorious Fourth Division. Commanded by Bashar's younger and more ferocious brother, Maher, these were the regime's praetorian guards, whose reputation for brutality was matched only by their fierce loyalty to the regime.

That the government was intent on using all means possible to crush the now two-month-old rebellion came through clearly in an interview with Rami Makhlouf, the reviled cousin of the president. He told the late Anthony Shadid of the *New York Times* that "the decision of the government now is that they decided to fight." Makhlouf's reference to "the government" was in fact an allusion to the extended Asad family. "Each one of us knows we cannot continue without staying united together," he continued; "we call it a fight until the end. [The protestors] should know when we (the ruling clan) suffer, we will not suffer alone."[13] The not so veiled menacing tone signaled the determination of the ruling family not to be deterred from inflicting the harshest punishment on those who dared to challenge its dominion.

By the end of May, over 1,000 people had been reported killed and some 10,000 arrested, many of whom were reportedly severely roughed up, then sent back home to show others the perils of dissent. Injured protestors were forcibly taken from hospitals and moved to military prisons, and in many cases, their family members were rounded up.[14] Amnesty International issued a statement accusing the security forces of implementing a "shoot to kill" policy.[15] The deployment of heavy armor, artillery, and snipers shooting directly at unarmed crowds had become the mantra of a regime determined to obliterate, with seeming sadistic pleasure, any manifestation of popular dissent.

The record of the winter of Arab discontent, the critical first six months of Arab uprisings against authoritarian regimes, brings to the fore a curious puzzle: why did the paths of revolutionary developments in Egypt and Tunisia differ so markedly from those undertaken in the other four countries? What factors allowed the rulers of Syria, Bahrain, Libya, and Yemen to avoid the rapid regime collapse that occurred in Egypt and Tunisia? First, unlike their colleagues, who had no compulsion about employing lethal force, it is clear that Mubarak and Ben Ali decided early on that wholesale killing of their populations was not going to be a policy option. Giving them the benefit of the doubt, it could be that this decision reflected a personal predilection—that neither had the stomach for mass murder. More to the point, they were well aware that they could not get the military to go along with this option. The generals in both countries had set boundaries to physical coercion that they were not prepared to trespass. Once these boundaries were reached, in both cases pretty quickly, the two rulers had little option but to bow to the demands of the insurrectionists.

Secondly, in contrast to the demographic homogeneity of Egypt and Tunisia, the other four countries have brittle societal structures. While communal fissures are usually considered a state's Achilles' heel, in fact in times of crisis they can be a valuable asset for those intending to maintain the status quo. Regimes aware of such demographic vulnerabilities tend to nourish and strengthen their own communities economically and militarily, creating from their ranks the necessary barricade against any potential assault by other groups demanding more seats at the table of political power. The late Saddam Hussein of Iraq had perfected this survival technique by filling political and security posts with members of his community—Sunnis from the area north of the capital, Baghdad. That arrangement kept him in power for thirty-five years, and would have continued to keep him in power for many years to come had he not been deposed by outside forces.

To varying degrees, the same can be said of Syria, Bahrain, Libya, and Yemen. President Bashar al-Asad of Syria originates from the minority Alawite community, and while he and his father had incorporated elements from the Sunni majority into the ranks of the military and into a widening network of financial and other business concerns, the regime depended ultimately for its survival on family and clan structures within the Alawite community. As we have seen, Alawites populated the most sensitive security and military units, particularly those charged with the defense of the regime, such as Presidential Guard units, the special forces, and a number of key armored units.

A similar strategy of political control was followed in Bahrain, but in a circumstance of reversed sectarian balance. In the tiny Gulf kingdom, the king and the minority Sunni population, numbering no more than 20 percent of the country's inhabitants, held sway over the majority Bahraini Shiites. Here again, one was hard put to find any Shiites in the country's security and military forces. In the domain of political power, their role in government, determined solely by the king, was limited by the less than weighty positions they were given. And when Sunni military and political power was stretched to a crisis point, the king could draw on the Gulf's monarchical fraternity, all brothers in the Sunni faith,[16] to help in the suppression of dissent by the majority.

Finally, in Yemen and Libya, demographic dislocations and allegiances fell along not sectarian but tribal and regional lines. In both cases, the men at the helm were able to maintain their paramount power for decades by relying on the loyalty of tribal and regional cohorts, who had been favored by state institutions. It was men from these tribes and areas, bound by primordial ties and cognizant of their privileged positions, who populated the key military units that were assigned to the defense and survival of the regime. Hence, in the face of mounting popular dissent and even military confrontation, Saleh and Qadhafi, very much like Asad and Hamad al-Khalifa, all rulers of divided societies, would be able to put up a more determined fight.

Another puzzle was the absence of revolutionary fervor in other Arab countries. After all, when commentators and analysts talked about the "Arab revolution" (and rather loosely about the "Arab Spring"), they were in fact referring to revolutionary activity in a mere one third of the Arab world. The rest of Arab lands experienced either no real convulsions to speak of or a few demonstrations that quickly petered out, and the question is what factors allowed these countries to be bypassed by the tumult of revolutionary trauma.

It is hardly coincidental that of the eight Arab countries in which the production of gas and petroleum constitutes the major domestic industry, responsible for the bulk of the national income, only one, Libya, experienced revolutionary upheavals in which freedom and political representation constituted essential demands. This would not come as a surprise to political scientists, especially specialists on the Middle East, who had labeled these countries as "rentier states," and had argued for some three decades that such states are probably the most resistant to either forcible or voluntary democratic changes. According to one of the idea's early exponents, three main characteristics define a rentier state. First, the state relies on *external rent* (e.g., the sale of petroleum) for much of its revenues. Second, the generation of this rent (the country's wealth) is controlled by a small fraction of the society, the majority being involved only in its distribution or utilization. Third, the government is the principal recipient of the external rent in the economy, and consequently plays a central role in distributing the wealth to the population.[17]

Given the abundance of revenue that is controlled by the government, these states levy few or no taxes on their citizens. Having to pay no taxes, the people do not feel entitled to demand governmental accountability.[18] The critical notion of "no taxation without representation" is therefore missing. The concentration of wealth in the public sector also inhibits the development of a vibrant and entrepreneurial middle class that is independent of the state, and that historically, for example in nineteenth-century Britain, has created the basis for democratic civil life.[19] Moreover, excess revenue allows the ruling and political elite to spend disproportionately more money not just on internal security, but also on the state-controlled media (television, radio, the printed press) whose main raison d'être is to lionize the country's rulers. These perpetrators of physical and cultural violence dampen and ultimately block people's democratic aspirations. Finally, the availability of ready cash allows the rulers to literally buy their populations' acquiescence, particularly in troubled times.

Even though it does not produce the desired results in every instance, throwing money around to subdue dissent has a good track record, and tends to be the default position of first choice for the oil producers. As the protests began to produce results in Tunisia and Egypt, King Abdullah of Saudi Arabia swiftly announced $37 billion worth of pay raises, unemployment checks, and other benefits to the citizens of the kingdom. Kuwait's sheikhs gave each of their citizens the equivalent of $4,000, and the Sultan of Oman raised the minimum wage to $520 a month and decreed that anyone without a job would be eligible for a monthly stipend of $375.[20] Later, a subvention of $1 billion to Bahrain accompanied the entry of Saudi troops in the Gulf kingdom, and at the same time the Saudis promised another $1 billion to Oman.

While the kingdoms of Morocco and Jordan did experience some protests and demonstrations, these had nowhere near the staying power of the popular convulsions in Tunisia and Egypt. Yet in those cases, it was not an abundance of money that allowed the two cash-strapped monarchies to escape popular upheavals. Neither country constitutes a model of Jeffersonian democracy, but both have allowed enough political liberties to distinguish them from the more rigid authoritarian Arab regimes. Fareed Zakaria pinpoints this distinction well. Writing before the invasion of Iraq, he argued that "despite the limited political choices they offer, countries such as Singapore, Malaysia, Jordan, and Morocco provide a better environment for the life, liberty and happiness of their citizens than do the dictatorships of Iraq, Libya, and the illiberal democracies of Venezuela, Russia and Ghana."[21] In both Morocco and Jordan, the institution of the monarchy had traditionally garnered broad-based popular support. This facilitated a degree of trust which, while not at the level found in true democracies, still allowed the two monarchies to escape the sustained upheavals going on elsewhere in the region.

Much in the spirit of what was happening in other Arab cities, Jordanians and Moroccans did take to the streets in the winter of 2011 demanding more freedoms and substantive political changes, but both monarchs responded with a few immediate gestures, coupled with promises for meaningful political reform. King Abdullah of Jordan dismissed the government, appointing a new cabinet that was tasked with making the electoral process less subject to governmental interference, and, in a conciliatory gesture to the opposition, redrawing electoral districts, which had been heavily skewed toward rural and tribal areas. King Muhammad VI was even more concrete in his response. He called for a drastic overhaul of the Moroccan constitution that among other proposals would enhance the independence of the legislative and judicial branches of government, would devolve power away from the center toward the regions, would strengthen the role of political parties and civil society organizations, and would allow the prime minister, previously appointed by the king, to emerge from the winning party in parliamentary elections.[22] The king then appointed a broad-based committee to come up with procedural recommendations by June, which would be put to a national referendum in September. He promised that once ratified, the reforms would be implemented.

By early summer, debates raged in both countries as to whether these reforms were simply decorative, mere promises to dampen down a potentially explosive revolutionary situation, or whether they would be actually enacted. If genuine, the reforms could lead to palpable political changes, which would amount to a peaceful political transformation. Still, in both cases, because of the higher level of trust between monarchy and populace, the concessions and promises of the Jordanian and Moroccan kings were able to put out the flames of revolution where similar efforts by other leaders had fallen short.

Iraq and Lebanon, with political leaders in office less than ten years, also avoided the turmoil in Arab countries that for many decades had been ruled by individuals, families, and father-son combos.[23] In post-2003 Iraq, Prime Minister Nuri al-Maliki came to office as the candidate of coalitions that won the elections of 2005 and 2010, both of which were deemed by international observers to have been free and fair. So the few demonstrations that occurred focused their anger primarily on the government's failure to provide basic services such as regular supply of electricity and a functioning sewage system. There were few if any political demands, and in any case the prime minister preempted them when he publicly announced that he had no intention of serving beyond his second term.

Lebanon too experienced very few eruptions in 2011, and these came to nothing as they lacked ideational direction and political purpose. Not to be confused with a mature democracy, Lebanon still is a country which, particularly since the forced departure of Syria's occupying forces in 2005, has conducted two elections, whose results were accepted by all competing parties. True, the "confessional system" that tries to balance the country's myriad ethnosectarian groups is at best cumbersome and at worst dysfunctional. The Shiite Hizbollah group, which occupies the opposition mantle against Christian and Sunni forces, and which is labeled a "terrorist group" by the American government, does exert inordinate and, more often than not, deleterious influence on the political process. But through all the chaos, standoffs, and the resultant political immobility, Lebanon would remain the least illiberal of

Arab systems—a country with a number of active political parties and groupings, boasting a vibrant civil society and an independent press, and generally acceding to the rules of an electoral democracy. When the results of the 2009 elections, which Hizbollah was expected to win, were announced showing that the militant group had come second to a Western-backed coalition, Sheikh Hassan Nasrallah, Hizbollah's leader of the militant group, appeared on television looking visibly shaken; yet he accepted the results gracefully and congratulated his opponents.

Notwithstanding the Arab countries which, for different reasons, did not experience major political convulsions, when the winter of Arab discontent morphed into the summer of 2011, more than half a year after the first revolutionary spark was ignited by Muhammad Bouazizi in Tunisia, revolutionary conditions varied substantially. The uprising in Bahrain had been resolutely and successfully suppressed, and Yemen, Libya, and Syria were in the volatile hands of the war gods. But in Tunisia and Egypt, preparations were afoot to do away with the old authoritarian structures, and finally, at least in these two countries, to make good on hopes for a better, more inclusive future.

There was universal agreement among the protestors and demonstrators that the better, more inclusive future would ensue with the institution of robust democratic institutions, and that the journey toward this outcome would begin by dismantling the existing Arab political orders. But it was hardly a foregone conclusion that the journey would inevitably end in the promised land of democracy—an observation validated by the Arabs' own historical experience. This, after all, was not the first time that Arabs had risen and changed the established political order.

Some sixty years before the 2011–12 winter of Arab discontent, revolutionary upheavals aiming at fashioning a new era of self-determination also swept the Arab world. The essence of the story was the same in both cases: firsthand experience of injustice and corruption, a decision to do something about it, and a course of action that would rewrite the chronicles of history. While the resulting narrative of the revolutionary movements of the 1950s and 1960s would speak of many laudatory achievements, it would make scant mention of democracy. Whatever thoughts of representative government had resided in the minds of the instigators of those revolutions, these were to quickly fade and be overtaken by the seemingly more immediate and critical goals of freedom from imperialism and restoration of nationalist pride. The man destined to lead this first Arab awakening was the Egyptian Gamal Abd al-Nasser.

PART ONE

THE FIRST ARAB AWAKENING

The 1950s and 1960s

Syrians welcoming the arrival of President Nasser on his first visit to Syria after the creation of the United Arab Republic in February 1958. *Associated Press*

Chapter Two

NATIONALIST
REVOLUTIONS

I n the early summer of 1948, Major Gamal Abd al-Nasser
joined some 10,000 Egyptian troops as they headed to
Palestine, in the hope that along with six other Arab states,
they would dismantle the newly announced Jewish state of Israel
and return the land to the Arab population. The Palestinian
experience turned out not to be a happy one for the thirty-
year-old Egyptian officer. Chaotic and ineptly led, the Egyptian
expedition scored a few early successes, but after a short truce,
suffered major reverses at a high human and material cost. The
Egyptians were frequently short of ammunition and spare parts,
yet they were persistently ordered to attack heavily fortified
Israeli positions. Nasser would soon realize that the poor military
performance resulted not only from the bungling of the military
high command but also from the endemic corruption in high
places in Cairo. Political leaders close to the Egyptian monarchy,
and their business associates, were making huge profits arming
Egyptian soldiers with defective field guns and grenades, and pre–
World War One rifles.[1] Nasser would quickly surmise that while

Egyptian soldiers were getting killed, someone back home was making a killing on the black market.

After a few months of fighting, Nasser found himself and his small unit besieged on all sides by Israeli forces. Yet a series of strong Israeli attacks, supported by heavy air and artillery bombardment, could not budge the Egyptian unit from its position, and all demands for surrender were rebuffed out of hand. Indeed, Nasser would mount a counterattack using all men under his disposal, about a hundred in total, including the cooks, which would relieve the immediate pressure on his line of defense. The young major would hold his position right up until the 1949 armistice agreements that ended the first Arab-Israeli war to the advantage of the Jewish state. While the Egyptians suffered a telling defeat, Nasser returned to Egypt as one of the war's heroes.

Later on, he would write that while he and his comrades were fighting in Palestine, their dreams were centered in Egypt, and their hearts "hovered over our distant country, which we had left to the care of the wolves." The siege he and his men endured in Palestine became for him a metaphor for what was happening in Egypt. What he had experienced in Palestine, he would recall, was "a picture in miniature of what [was] happening in Egypt . . . besieged by enemies and difficulties . . . her fate the toy of greed, conspiracy and lust, which had left her without weapons under fire." The dying words of a fallen comrade would stay with him: "the real battlefield is in Egypt."[2] To Nasser, his beloved country was sinking into an abyss, and he made it his mission to do something about it.

Three years after the Palestinian debacle, Nasser led a military coup that would usher in far-reaching revolutionary changes in Egypt as well as triggering similar revolutions in other parts of the Arab world. Initially, Nasser and the coup leaders concerned themselves exclusively with Egypt, vowing to reform the decaying political and economic order and to liberate the nation from the asphyxiating clutches of the foreigner. Their gaze hardly went beyond the borders of their beloved Egypt to other Arab lands. When Nasser fretted over the area's social and political ills, he thought essentially of Egypt. When he searched for ways of combating foreign interference, his concern was directed primarily at Egypt. If other Arabs came to mind, it was only in ways to help bring about Egypt's salvation. Apart from the customary flow of diplomatic relations with countries that shared the larger geographic milieu which Egypt inhabited, the policies of the fledgling revolutionaries in Cairo were centered on Egypt—eradicating domestic corruption, implementing more egalitarian social and economic policies and dealing with the British occupation of the Suez Canal, which they regarded as continued British colonialism.

But prevailing global circumstances, manifested in the escalating cold war, would force the new Egyptian rulers to recognize that limiting their ideational frontiers to Egypt's geographic borders was in fact detrimental to the well-being of Egypt. The shift from Egyptian to Arab revolution, from Egyptian to Arab nationalism, began with a visit to Cairo in May 1953 by John Foster Dulles, the American secretary of state. Dulles was on a tour of Arab capitals trying to muster support for a Western defense alliance against what he depicted as an imminent Communist threat. Faced with the formidable task of rejuvenating Egypt, the last thing Nasser wanted to do was to get embroiled in global conflict. And to the Egyptians, the whole scheme seemed incongruous: Egypt would be allied with Britain, the country that was occupying Egyptian land, against the Soviet Union, a power that had no colonial history in the area, and whose forces, Nasser pointedly emphasized, were 5,000 miles away.[3] Egypt's polite but firm response left no ambiguity in Dulles's mind that he should look elsewhere for support.

And this he did: in February 1955 he was able to persuade the leaders of Iraq, who presided over a country which was tradition-ally considered the main competition to Egypt for the leadership of the Arab world, and which, for Dulles, had impeccable credentials as steadfastly anti-Communist and pro-Western, to sign a secu-rity treaty with Turkey, a standing member of the North Atlantic Treaty Organization (NATO). The Baghdad Pact, as the treaty was called, was designed as a first step for a wider membership. Other Arab countries were immediately invited to join.

Nasser found himself truly cornered: either join a pact to which he was adamantly opposed, or have his country be regionally iso-lated—unless, that is, he went on the offensive, preempting any effort at pushing Egypt to the margins of regional Arab politics, and taking the fight to those Arab leaders who found their protec-tion in Western alliances. It was at this juncture that Nasser took the consequential decision to shift Egypt's gaze away from itself to the full expanse of Arab lands, which now Nasser would claim was Egypt's natural political domain. And in an audacious leap, he would appropriate for himself and his country the mantle of Arab leadership. Not that this was an egregious claim. By virtue of the size of its population, superior cultural output, and geographic position as the bridge between the Asian and African parts of the Arab world, Egypt was the political and cultural center of the Arab world, a fact recognized even by Nasser's nemeses. King Faisal of Saudi Arabia, who at various times had been the linchpin of the anti-Nasserist forces in the area, once confided that his father, King Abd al-Aziz, the founder of modern Saudi Arabia, had given his children one piece of advice: "He told us to pay attention to Egypt's role, for without Egypt, the Arabs throughout history would have been without value."[4] Such sentiments, held uniformly throughout the Arab world, made Egypt's shift to purposeful involvement in Arab politics that much easier.

Egypt's sudden self-discovery, indeed its reincarnation of itself, would be anointed by Nasser as a revolution aimed at bringing about other Arab revolutions. From now on, Egypt would not be constrained by state frontiers or diplomatic niceties, but would carry its message directly to Arab peoples everywhere. Muhammad Hasaneen Heikal, Nasser's confidant and the most influential Arab journalist of the period, articulated Egypt's new regional priorities:

> We should distinguish between two things: Egypt as a state and as a revolution. If as a state, Egypt recognizes boundaries in its dealings with governments, Egypt as a revolution should never hesitate to halt before these boundaries, but should carry its message beyond the borders [to the people] in order to initiate its revolutionary mission for a unitary Arab future."[5]

Revolutionary anti-Western Arab nationalism—the belief in the linguistic unity and historical continuity of all Arabs, and their resolve against all odds, particularly Western perfidy, to bring about organic Arab unity—now defined Egypt, its identity, its political doctrine, and its relationship with the other Arabs. And at the forefront of this revolutionary onslaught stood the charismatic Nasser.

A towering figure, with a magnetic personality, Nasser was an eloquent and passionate orator, a dazzling public speaker who mesmerized his listeners and kept them in rapt attention throughout his usually long speeches. Nasser and his message of revolutionary renewal would find ready ears among Arabs everywhere. He had a knack for creatively manipulating the Arabic language—a linguistic medium whose intrinsic poetic meters and rhythm were ideally suited to elicit the desired emotional response from his audience. He had great command of classical Arabic, but was not afraid to intersperse the colloquial to imprint into the consciousness of his listeners a "folksy" image of himself as the common man. If one word is associated in the minds of people with Nasser's oratory, a word that was repeated over and over again in his speeches, it was *karameh*, "dignity." For millions of Egyptians and Arabs who had suffered untold indignities at the hands of the colonizers, *karameh* would find a sure resonance in their hearts.

Economically disgruntled, feeling abandoned by corrupt and self-satisfied leaderships, and humiliated by the extent of indigenous political power ceded to foreigners, the Arab street was ready to follow in the footsteps of this new prophet promising them salvation and the restoration of their usurped dignity. Mainly urbanites, students and professionals, they soon would become the custodians of Nasser's radical nationalist ideas; his foot soldiers, ever ready to do his bidding, all in the service of revolutionary Arab nationalism. This unbridled devotion was put in poetic form, and very quickly was on the lips of the millions of Nasser's disciples and devotees throughout the Arab world:

Minal khalij al-tha'ir	From the rebellious Gulf
Ilal muhit al-hadir	To the roaring ocean
Labaika Abd al-Nasser	At your service, Abd al-Nasser

Arab leaders who dared to challenge Nasser and his revolutionary message would do so at their peril. No less a figure than King Hussein of Jordan gave a vivid account of the consequences of taking on Nasser. He describes what happened when a senior British officer visited Jordan in December 1955, a visit that was assailed by Nasser as a prequel to Jordan's joining the Baghdad Pact:

Without warning, the Egyptians launched a heavy barrage of propaganda against Jordan. Within a matter of hours, Amman was torn by riots as the people, their senses blurred by propaganda, turned to Nasser, the new *mystique* of the Arab world. . . . All hell [broke] loose. Riots such as we had never seen before . . . disrupted the entire country [and] bands of arsonists started burning government offices, private houses, foreign properties. I had no alternative but to call out the [army], who with tear gas and determination met force with force. I imposed a ten-day curfew on the country.[6]

And if the beleaguered Arab leaders thought they had seen the worst of it, the summer and fall of 1956 would put to rest any such wishful thinking. In July 1956, the West refused to finance the construction of a large dam on the Nile in Egypt's Aswan region which had been trumpeted by Nasser as the symbol of a new dynamic and industrialized Egypt. Infuriated, the Egyptian leader announced the nationalization of the Anglo-French Suez Canal Company. In an era of colonial retreat, Nasser might have hoped for a subdued response. But the British and French were in no mood to be upended by an upstart, whose policies they perceived as dangerously bellicose, reminding them of Germany's Hitler some two decades earlier. Not only were they adamant about not giving up sovereignty over the canal, but they saw this as a golden opportunity to remove the perfidious Egyptian from power, and in so doing, reestablish the authority and prestige of their tottering imperial dominions. Colluding with the Israelis, they jointly attacked Egypt in November 1956. They scored quick military successes, but could not maintain the momentum of the attack, particularly in the face of American displeasure with the whole affair, a chorus of global condemnation, and Soviet warnings of retaliation. The operation concluded in an ignominious evacuation of all Anglo-French troops, which to Egyptians and Arabs was nothing short of a miracle. What wondrous force, what *baraka*, the blessings of God, the Arab street would ask, did the Almighty endow their young leader with to allow him such extraordinary triumph over the mighty British and French? Rather than defeating Nasser and with him revolutionary Arab nationalism, the failed attack on Suez actually ended up contributing to a steep elevation not only of Nasser's stature in the Arab world but also of the revolutionary potential of the movement he was spearheading.

Less than fifteen months later, Syria, torn by political and ideological strife, was ready to implode. The military decided that the only salvation was a merger with Egypt under Nasser's leadership, and they knew that they would have the enthusiastic support of the Syrian population. So Syrian officers flew to Cairo and demanded the immediate unity of the two countries. When Nasser finally accepted, they went back to Syria's capital, Damascus, and told the political leadership of their negotiations with Nasser. A number of the politicians resisted, some of them incensed at not having been consulted. In an ominous move that would serve as a harbinger for things to come, the officers calmly told the politicians that there were two roads open to them, one leading to Cairo, the other to Syria's most notorious prison.[7] The politicians promptly chose the high road to Cairo. On February 1, 1958, the United Arab Republic (UAR) was born.

The people of Syria heard the news with stunned amazement, which quickly turned into uncontrollable euphoria.[8] Spontaneous celebrations erupted everywhere, and Damascus was invaded by hordes of people from Aleppo, Hama, Homs, Latikiya, and other Syrian cities and districts, filling every street and every square of their capital. Unable to contain their joy, they sang, listened to patri-

Nasser and the first United Arab Republic cabinet following the 1958 merger of Egypt and Syria. *SyrianHistory.com*

otic orations, danced the *dabka*, the famed folk dance, and made up instant verses and rhymes that were repeated by all. One that was sung repeatedly extolled the power of this new united entity:

Wahdat Misr wa Suriya	The unity of Egypt and Syria
Jisr al-wuhda al-arabiya	Is the bridge of Arab unity
Shawka bi ayn al-raj'iya	A thorn in the eye of reaction
Dhid al-ist'imar wa ahlafu	Against imperialism and its military
al-askariya	alliances

Having been told of the public delirium in Syria, Nasser arrived unannounced in Damascus and headed to the official guesthouse.

As news of his arrival spread, hundreds of thousands of Syrians converged onto the square in front of Nasser's temporary residence. Nasser and the Egyptian delegation stayed in the presidential guesthouse for a week, during which hundreds of speeches were made to the adoring multitude camped outside. Anwar al-Sadat, a member of Nasser's entourage, wrote in his autobiography:

> I really feel incapable of describing that week. It was like a constant delirium—a stream of [speeches] that flowed day and night. . . . The crowds couldn't get enough and seemed to grow increasingly frenzied. All that was said was hailed, applauded, and celebrated. People chanted and screamed and called for more. For a whole week the crowds besieged the Guesthouse. They camped outside in the wide square, eating, drinking, and sleeping in the open air.[9]

The manifestation of spontaneous joy was not confined to Syria. Celebrations erupted everywhere in the Arab world, and people congratulated one another in their homes, on the streets, and in their offices, as though something intensely personal had happened to each one of them. In those heady days, everyone believed that this momentous event, this crowning achievement, was but the first step in the path to the ultimate victory of revolutionary Arab nationalism over the forces of colonialism and imperialism.

A few months later, the nationalist generation would hammer another nail, more like a stake, into the heart of "Western imperialism." On July 14, 1958, Iraq's army executed a bloody coup that toppled the most pro-Western Arab government. In the following tense hours and days, a betting man's money would be placed on the same thing happening in Jordan and Lebanon. That it eventually did not was a testament not to the strength of these two governments or their domestic popularity, but to the immediate help extended by the governments of Britain and the United States. Cognizant of the seemingly unstoppable power of revolutionary Arab nationalism, London and Washington calculated that neither of the two pro-Western Arab countries could survive on its own in the wake of the momentous happenings in Baghdad. On July 15, one day after Iraq's revolution, the Americans landed troops in Beirut, Lebanon's capital, and two days later London followed suit by dispatching British troops to Amman to bolster the Jordanian king. The two great powers' swift reaction enabled both belea-guered governments to keep revolution at bay, allowing time for incendiary conditions to subside, and the political situation to gradually normalize.

Throughout the 1950s and 1960s, the first Arab awakening, steeped in nationalist revolutionary discourse and policies, was the domi-nant political force in the area, even though it did suffer a number of reverses. The first was the unwillingness of Iraq's revolutionary officers to act on what had been thought to be a foregone conclu-sion—joining the UAR. Indeed, within months of its revolution, Iraq, coming under the influence of Communists, would again become a virulent nemesis of Egypt and the nationalist Nasser. But the most heartbreaking event for the devoted believers in Arab unity was the dismantling of the UAR. Three years after the euphoric 1958 unity of Egypt and Syria, a group of Syrian army officers executed a military coup, and extracted Syria from the UAR. The follow-ing year, a military coup in Yemen against an archaic monarchy necessitated the dispatch of Egyptian forces to bolster the young revolutionary officers. What Nasser had anticipated as a swift and successful military venture turned out to be a long and debilitating involvement that lasted more than five years. The deposed king quickly rallied the conservative and warlike Yemeni tribes behind his cause, and waged a relentless and bloody war against the new government. Unable to survive on their own, the coup leaders continued to ask for more Egyptian help, so that Nasser's commitment would vault from a few hundred soldiers at the onset of the coup to more than 60,000 men four years later. The stalemated conflict did untold harm to the economy of Egypt, to the reputation of Nasser, and to the aspirations of the nationalist generation.

But all these setbacks were dwarfed by the costly and humiliating defeat of Egypt and the Arabs at the hands of the Israelis in June 1967. In six short days, Israel routed the Arab armies that were ranged against it. And in the process, it captured the Sinai Peninsula, including the Gaza strip, from the Egyptians, the Golan Heights from the Syrians, and the entire West Bank of the Jordan from the Jordanians. Most upsetting for the Arabs and Muslims generally was the loss of East Jerusalem.

Yet such was the strength of revolutionary Arab nationalism that in the face of all of these adversities, it remained throughout the 1960s the dominant political force in the area. By the end of the 1960s, eight of the fourteen sovereign Arab states, including the pivotal states of Egypt, Iraq, and Syria, would identify their political systems and policies as nationalist and revolutionary. Status quo states like Jordan, Morocco, and Saudi Arabia, whose governments did not share the vision of revolutionary Arab nationalism, were constantly on the defensive, reeling from its relentless assaults.

During the two decades of the first Arab awakening, a batch of young idealist leaders usurped power through military coups and revolutions. Following in Nasser's footsteps, these reform-minded young men would declare their fidelity to the nationalist ideals of independence from the outsider and radical social and economic reform. It is not that these leaders with their revolutionary agendas saw eye-to-eye on all things; there were many public disputes, a number of them acrimonious. But by adhering to the nationalist creed, they were indeed one fraternity, sharing in convictions and aspirations. And those of them who at times did not agree with Egypt knew well that they would not have been in their positions, and their countries would not have undergone their sociopolitical transformations, had it not been for the initial revolutionary spark that was lit by Nasser in the 1950s.

If one were to look back at the era and evaluate the performance of this thirty-something crowd, one is bound to conclude that there was much that was eventually achieved. New economic policies led to radical shifts in priorities that had a significant impact on society. It is not that the new policies, driven on the whole by socialist economic ideas, were singularly successful; in most cases they would lead to large deficits, diminishing reserves, weak currencies, and increased dependence on foreign aid. Economic weakness and stagnation also would hinder the efforts that were initially undertaken to diversify these economies; the result was that all remained, as they had been in the past, dependent on one or two commodities. So in terms of economic performance alone, there was little to distinguish the nationalist revolutionaries from the *ancien régimes*.

The palpable difference would occur in the distribution of economic resources. The purpose of the exercise begun by Nasser and followed universally by other reformist leaders was to bridge the vast divide between the abjectly poor majority and the obscenely rich minority. It is in this area that successes, some pretty impressive, were achieved. Landless peasants, living in squalid conditions, and at the mercy for their meager existence on absentee owners, were given small tracts of lands, allowing them the opportunity for the first time in centuries to control their own livelihood. In Egypt, for example, over half a million acres were expropriated by the government and then distributed to some 120,000 landless farmers,[10] and in Iraq, where some 3,000 individuals owned more than half of the country's cultivable land,[11] a large redistribution of landholdings was put in place in which eventually over 3 million acres were distributed to over 300,000 peasants. And for those peasants who had escaped the servitude of their landowning masters to settle in cities in appalling conditions, thousands of houses with electricity and running water were built and distributed free of charge.[12] Similar efforts at land reform were pursued with varying intensity and success in Syria, Libya, Sudan, and Algeria.

Along with the efforts to improve the economic lot of the disinherited in these societies came parallel improvements in the quality of life. Education is a case in point. In all countries, the new leaders put immense resources into broadening educational entitlement, increasing and improving facilities, and upgrading performance. Thus at one time in the second half of the 1950s, the revolutionary government in Egypt opened new schools at the rate of two every week, and between 1953 and 1967, the total number of students increased from under 2 million to over 5.5 million.[13] Similarly, in the two decades after the Iraqi revolution of 1958, student numbers in primary and secondary education increased from under half a million to 3.5 million.[14] Again, this improvement was not unique to Egypt and Iraq but occurred generally in other countries in this revolutionary era.

Perhaps more critical and more defining of the revolutionary era of Arab nationalism was the fundamental change that occurred in the Arabs' psychological landscape. Years of colonialism had taken their toll on the Arabs, leaving them with an overwhelming sense of inferiority toward Europe and the West. In the eyes of Arabs, the dazzling scientific and cultural achievements of the West elevated its people to the status of demigods, who during the long years of colonial and imperial subjugation seemed to walk the Arab streets with a sense of arrogant entitlement. And the military power of Western countries and empires implanted fear and submission in the hearts of ordinary Arabs, to whom the dominance of the West appeared unchallengeable, its position untouchable.

But that would dramatically and permanently change as the young revolutionary reformers challenged the mighty West, casting aside its dictates, and moving resolutely against its interests. Arabs would watch with amazement tinged with proud pleasure as their leaders hurled a multitude of denunciations and insults at the West, seemingly without any concern for possible consequences. For instance, when the Americans hinted that unfriendly Egyptian policies might affect a U.S. food shipment to Egypt, Nasser angrily responded in a major speech in front of thousands:

> I am telling those who do not approve of our behavior to go and drink the Mediterranean and if this is not enough, then they can try the Red Sea as well. . . . We shall cut the tongue of anyone who dares to insult us. . . . We do not tolerate pressure and we do not tolerate humiliation. We are people whose dignity cannot be sacrificed.[15]

To Western ears, the words might sound petty, even infantile. But to Arab ears, these were words of liberation, of national assertiveness—to challenge the mighty Americans, to insult them, symbolized the final delivery from imperialism's stranglehold over the Arab spirit.

This defiant attitude would be emulated in years to come by

Egyptians blanketing the streets of Cairo at the funeral of President Nasser, who died on September 28, 1970. *Associated Press / Eddie Adams*

other revolutionary leaders who, unlike Arab kings and presidents of years past, would not accede to Western interests, and would not cower to Western power. This was the nationalist generation determined to mold a new Arab people, who would emerge from the midst of the struggles against colonial rule and imperial dominion to become the masters of their own future. That they were able to achieve this must rank as the abiding accomplishment of the first Arab awakening.

But the triumphs and successes were short-lived, spanning the 1950s and 1960s, and the revolutions of the era, instigated by radical Arab nationalism, remained unfulfilled. They gave the Arabs political independence, enhanced their self-esteem, and improved the lot of the poor. But they did not create the political institutions that would inherit and become the custodians of the political legitimacy won by the young reformist leaders who led the revolutionary movement. That era gave the people many things, but it did not give them the institutions that would represent their interests and provide them a voice in the political process. It did not give them *freedom*.

Is freedom a necessary element or outcome of revolutions? The answer to this question depends on how the term "revolution" is defined. The study of revolutions is an academic industry. It has generated many books, scholarly articles, and doctoral dissertations. But to this day, Hannah Arendt's revisionist exposition of the American and French revolutions stands alone in its brilliance of argument and originality of thought. Arendt's magisterial analysis yields a definition, more like a conceptualization, of "revolution" that is at once intriguing and compelling.

To Arendt, the concept of revolution "is inextricably bound up with the notion that the course of history suddenly begins anew, that an entirely new story, a story never known or told before, is about to unfold. . . ." She goes on to emphasize that this story is one of "liberation" from oppressive rule or foreign dominion, but it is her absolute belief that the purpose of the story, what she terms the "plot," is the notion of "freedom." The two terms might sound the same, but they are not. "Liberation may be the condition of freedom, but by no means leads automatically to it."[16] Indeed, liberation may lead to the absolute opposite of freedom, and this may happen because the plot is either different, something else, not freedom, or as the story unfolds, somewhere along the line, the plot changes. Is this not what happened to the French Revolution? Nicolas de Condorcet, a leading figure in that Revolution, and secretary of the Legislative Assembly, would declare that "the word revolution can be applied only to revolutions whose aim is freedom."[17] Indeed, that is what the French Revolution promised its children; but soon, under Robespierre and the Jacobins, it would turn on those very children, unleashing a wave of terror that sent the idea of freedom to its doom. Robespierre would later lament, just before the Revolution devoured him as well, "We shall perish because . . . we missed the moment to found freedom."[18]

The distinction between liberation and freedom is important to the telling of this story, because if the focus is simply on liberation, the first Arab awakening, the revolutionary era of the 1950s and 1960s, can be characterized as a revolution that fulfilled its potential and mission. But employing Arendt's definition, the analysis is not complete until we explore the role that freedom played in that revolutionary era, as well as in the contemporary one that was ignited by the self-immolation of Muhammad Bouazizi in December 2010.

In deconstructing the revolutionary period of the first Arab awakening, one finds that freedom figured not at all in the brave new world that the nationalist generation was creating. The nationalism espoused by those young Arab revolutionaries of the 1950s and 1960s was at best oblivious, and at worst hostile, to the idea of freedom. They were influenced by a vision of politics that trivialized democratic institutions. Any suggestion about the role of democracy, the possibility of a freely elected parliament, prospects for the formation of political parties, or decoupling the media from governmental control, would be dismissed out of hand as irrelevant, even inappropriate to the needs and concerns of the times.

Such a cavalier disposition to the idea of democracy is not surprising. After all, revolutionary Arab nationalism reflected the ideas of nineteenth-century German cultural nationalism. Faced with over 2,000 German-speaking states at the end of the eighteenth century, German nationalist thinkers focused obsessively on unifying the German nation. This became a supreme goal and a sacred act, which necessitated subsuming individual needs and rights into the national will. Notions of liberty or freedom were distractions, and when they contradicted the national will, they had to be repressed. This was how the eminent German historian Heinrich von Treitschke would justify the annexation in 1871 of the German-speaking population of Alsace, the majority of whom wanted to remain politically within France. "We desire," Treitschke says in a chilling tone, "even against their will, to restore them to themselves."[19] This authoritarian and unapologetically coercive streak was reinforced in the wake of the Prussian defeat at the hands of Napoleon in 1806. The word "liberty" was indeed resurrected; only its goals and meaning were not to secure "individual" liberty but "to drive out a foreign ruler and secure national independence. . . . When Western peoples strove for regeneration, they were primarily concerned with individual liberty; in [Germany] the demand for regeneration often centered on the unity and power of the group."[20]

This was the intellectual legacy upon which the ideas of Arab nationalism were developed. Arab nationalists would advocate the forcible amalgamation of the Arab nation, and its defense against foreign and domestic enemies, but they would have little to say about individual liberty and personal freedom, except, that is, for their complete subordination to the national will. Sati al-Husri, who through his voluminous writings was considered to be the foremost theoretician of Arab nationalism, wrote that

> Freedom is not an end in itself but a means toward a higher life. . . . The national interest which could sometimes require a man to sacrifice his life, must by definition require him, in some cases, to sacrifice his freedom. . . . Because of this, I unhesitatingly say: patriotism and nationalism above all and before all . . . even above and before freedom.[21]

Revolutionary nationalism therefore operated in a sea of authoritarianism throughout its glory days not because of some unfortunate circumstance. Indeed, it was the way that Arab nationalism was defined and developed that was to blame, if not wholly then at least partially, for the absence of democracy.

Beyond the realm of theory, there was also a practical reason for discounting democracy. The revolutionaries of the 1950s and 1960s saw Arab nationalism as the vehicle by which a distinguished future would be built upon the foundation of a glorious past, in which Arabs were the custodians of a luminous civilization at a time when the West languished in the darkness of the medieval ages. But that was easier said than done. The task ahead was fraught with untold difficulties and obstacles. There was still a heavy presence of foreign powers in parts of the Arab world; the British were in control of the Gulf States and Aden, and the French were fighting a dirty war in Algeria. There were also the political divisions within the Arab world, artificially created by the outsiders, so nationalists believed, but gaining legitimacy with the passage of time. These dislocations were not just the usual fault lines that pitted the likes of conservative Saudi Arabia or Jordan against such revolutionary states as Egypt or Syria. More disheartening to the nationalists were the hostilities within the radical and revolutionary camp that were caused mainly by divergent national interests. On a number of occasions, states with impeccable revolutionary credentials would advance the interests of their countries at the expense of the welfare of the Arab nation, such as republican Iraq deciding against joining the UAR in 1958 and Syria extricating itself from the UAR in 1961. And then there were the many communal schisms that permeated the Arab world: the scourge of tribalism in broad swaths of Arab lands that was compounded by ethnosectarian divides—Muslims and Christians in Lebanon, Alawites and Sunnis in Syria, Shiites and Sunnis in Iraq and in the Gulf, Arabs and Africans in Sudan, and Arabs and Berbers in North Africa.

This was indeed a titanic struggle, and as the first Arab awakening was embarked upon, its foot soldiers, cognizant of these entrenched and grueling challenges, which they fervently believed to have been perpetuated by the perfidious imperialists, naturally had little patience for democracy and its cumbersome institutions. What need was there to listen to an opposing point of view, to argue a contrary perspective? Would it not be a distraction, a diversion from the course of the revolutionary struggle? Were not all Arabs united in their one sacred endeavor to achieve radical reforms of their societies, and to fight Western domination? How could there be a contrary position to that?

In the midst of this intellectual ferment emerged the towering and charismatic Nasser, who would vilify the West as the uncommonly treacherous "other," the undying nemesis of the Arabs, the determined obstacle to their progress. Nasser was never enamored of the Western-style multiparty system that had operated under Egypt's monarchy, which was racked by privilege, corruption, and institutional weakness. Liberal democracy had no place in Nasser's new order. He did not offer it; he disdained it. In a meeting in 1963 with Syrian and Iraqi leaders to discuss the possibility of some form of union among the three Arab countries, he ridiculed the notion of political pluralism, waving it off as a Western deception. "I consider the separation of powers as nothing more than a hoax," he said, "because in reality there is no such thing. . . ."[22] He insisted on a highly centralized and determinedly centralizing political leadership that would be in absolute control of the reins of power.

It is important to understand that Nasser was not out of step with the people on this issue. He did not need to coercively impose his ideas on the cheering and ecstatically supportive multitude. In those heady days of revolution, of deliverance, of confronting Western powers and rubbing their noses into the blistering Arab sand, the nationalist generation believed in the necessity of the centralization of power. The hundreds of thousands who flooded the streets of Arab capitals in support of Nasser demanded results—and quick results at that—and no one had much patience for democracy's tiresome fondness of debate, or taking the time to decide on things properly. So the people did not ask for democracy, let alone demand it.

What sealed the fate of democracy was that the popular antipathy to the West and its perceived imperial ambitions in the area translated into hostility not only to the policies of the West but also to its institutions. Prior to the revolutionary era, a number of pro-Western Arab countries had adopted parliamentary systems modeled on Britain and France. Admittedly, theirs fell far short of the standards of Western liberal democracies. But, when all was said and done, these systems were still more open and civil than those subsequently instituted by the revolutionary nationalists. Their Achilles' heel was their association with the West at a historical juncture when the West represented everything that was evil. In light of this instinctive emotional allergy, it is hardly surprising that the nationalist generation feared Western democratic institutions as instruments of maintaining Western hegemony.

In Western societies, competitive political parties are accepted as essential elements of functioning democracies. But this view was hardly shared by the nationalist generation of the first Arab awakening. It was not just that the revolutionary nationalists of the era would simply dismiss political parties as irrelevant; they were intent on delegitimizing the very concept itself. For instance, one of the favorite slogans shouted by rioters and demonstrators in celebrations of the demise of the pro-Western Iraqi monarchy in 1958 was al-qawmiya al-Arabiya tufny al-ahzab al-gharbiya ("Arab nationalism exterminates Western political parties"). Political parties were seen as pernicious; they would do the bidding of the imperialists, become a fifth column for greedy outside powers, and sow divisions in Arab ranks, undermining the revolutionary march. When asked by the editor of the daily Egyptian Gazette whether there were any plans for a multiparty system in Egypt, Nasser retorted that if political parties were allowed, there would be a party acting as an agent for the American CIA, another in the pay of MI6, the British intelligence service, and a third working for the Soviet KGB.[23] By the same token, Nasser argued that feudalists and crony capitalists would manipulate and exploit political parties and other institutions of democracy in the same way that they did during the reign of the *ancien régimes*. And the new revolutionary elites were determined that there would be no going back to the bad old days. Nasser expressed this widely held sentiment when in 1957 he told an Indian journalist:

> Can I ask you a question: what is democracy? We were supposed to have a democratic system during the period 1923 to 1953. But what good was this democracy to our people? I will tell you. Landowners . . . ruled our people. They used this kind of democracy as an easy tool for the benefits of a feudal system. The feudalists [would] gather the peasants together and drive them to the polling booths. There the peasants would cast their votes according to the instructions of their masters. I [on the other hand] want to liberate . . . the peasants and workers to be able to say "yes" and "no" without any of this affecting their livelihood or their daily bread. This in my view is the basis of freedom and democracy. [24]

The result was the elimination of the multiparty system, and its replacement with a succession of unitary political institutions. First in 1953 Nasser created the Liberation Rally, which was replaced by the National Union in 1956. The breakup of the United Arab Republic in 1961, which Nasser blamed on Syrian feudalists and capitalists, plus his increasing dependence on the Soviet Union, pushed him to create the Arab Socialist Union (ASU), which he modeled on the Communist Party of his patron. The party's function was purely to mobilize popular support for the political leadership. Nasser's close friend, the influential journalist Muhammad Hasaneen Heikal, confirmed, without any effort to obfuscate or camouflage, that the ASU had one purpose and one purpose only: to safeguard the republic from capitalist, feudalist, and foreign elements.[25] Leaders of other emerging Arab revolutionary states looked to the ASU when they were deciding on organizing their own political organizations. By 1970, a spate of ASU clones had been created in other Arab countries by young revolutionary leaders who burst onto the Arab political scene in the 1960s—the Arab Socialist Unions of Abd al-Salam Aref's Iraq and Muammar Qadhafi's Libya, the Sudanese Socialist Union of Jaafar Numeiry's Sudan, the National Liberation Fronts of Hourai Boumdienne's Algeria and Rubayi Ali's South Yemen, and the Baath parties of Hafiz al-Asad's Syria and Saddam Hussein's Iraq.

All these one-party systems, symbolizing the ideological disposition of the first Arab awakening, were supposed to eschew political dissentions, time-wasting political debates, and dysfunctional conflicts that are generated by considerations of self, rather than the national, interest. This blatant authoritarianism was necessary, the leaders argued, to achieve quickly and efficiently the sacred goals of the revolutionary era: defeat of the imperialists, catching up with the West, bringing about economic rejuvenation, and effecting social and cultural progress. And for the promise of achieving these goals, the new and young revolutionary leaders, with the acquiescence of the nationalist multitude, would sacrifice freedom.

In the front row from left to right: Tunisia's Zine al-Abidin Ben Ali, Yemen's Ali Saleh, Libya's Muammar Qadhafi, and Egypt's Hosni Mubarak at the Afro-Arab summit held in Libya in October 2010. *Associated Press / Amer Nabil*

Chapter Three

. . . AND THE DICTATORS THEY PRODUCED

Looking back at the nationalist era, one can easily imagine the derision with which Arab revolutionary leaders would dismiss Hannah Arendt's insistence that freedom constituted a critical element of a revolution. If nothing else, Arendt's claim would negate the revolutionary credentials of the leaders of the first Arab awakening. But beyond that, neither the leaders nor the people gave the time of day to considerations of the role of democratic ideas and structures. In the many philosophical treaties, intellectual debates, and deliberations over policies, "freedom" claimed little if any space in Arab public discourse, and was not considered to be a component, let alone a vital ingredient, of the concept of revolution. Leaders and people alike believed that they had other far more pressing goals to think about, tackle, and achieve.

Yet postponing the introduction of democratic institutions until some supposedly higher revolutionary purpose was achieved, even if genuinely believed in, carried the risk of institutionalizing authoritarian practices and attitudes. And indeed that was what ultimately happened. The dedicated and visionary young leaders of the past, and their inheritors, grew into self-obsessed and self-aggrandized fat cats, caring little about political reform, and less, much less, about the welfare and political rights of their citizens. Much as they would promise a new brand of leadership, committed to no other concern but the general good, they in fact would end up falling prey to the moral corruption of power and the myriad of material privileges that come with it. They would neither relinquish power, nor even share it. What started as an ideological allergy to democracy, borne out of genuine belief and conviction, became with the passage of time simply an excuse to cling for as long as one could to the many intoxicating seductions that came with the exercise of absolute power.

Without such democratic institutions as opposition parties and elections, leaders would hold on to power making the same stale promises year after year which on the whole they could not deliver. The restoration of Palestinian rights, or the attainment of palpable economic progress, or achieving a semblance of Western living standards, or indeed even liberalizing the political order—all these were goals that were supposed to be just around the corner. Yet that corner, like a Potemkin village, resided more in the illusions and purposeful mendaciousness of the leaders than in reality.

Today, according to the World Bank, if the small petroleum-producing sheikhdoms of the Gulf are excluded, Arab countries have some of the lowest gross domestic product per capita in the world. Transparency International endows the Arab region with the unenviable distinction of having a number of the most corrupt regimes in the world. And according to Freedom House's survey of freedom in the world in 2010, fourteen of the seventeen core Arab states were considered not free, the other three being only partly free. As a region, the Arab world fared worse than any other world region in terms of political rights and civil liberties. Prior to the spate of revolutionary eruptions in 2010–11, the contemporary Arab world was universally looked at with dismay, disdain, and a sad shake of the head. The much vilified imperialist domination of the area had been replaced by the totalitarian tyranny of predatory indigenous regimes and their leaders.

Determined to be the sole arbiters of power, those regimes and leaders designed constitutions, and wrote electoral laws, aimed at keeping them in office unchallenged, and their ideas and policies uncontested. To that end, they stuffed ballot boxes to prevent the opposition from mounting even the most insignificant of challenges to their authority. They gagged the media, making it an instrument of political control, and they made the judiciary an arm of the regime. From an idealistic beginning, with time they created some of the most corrupt orders in the world.[1] Perhaps the most damning transgression of all was the institutionalization of one-party systems, which originally were touted as unifying agents in the fight against common enemies. Instead, they became a tool for mobilizing the population, treating citizens like sheep, herding them from one end of the ideological spectrum to the other in accordance with the will and whim of the omnipresent leader. And when all else failed, the man in charge would unleash the unforgiving fury of his security apparatus against the unsuspecting citizens.

The first Arab awakening, which began so full of promise, with so much popular support and goodwill, was eventually choked to death by the willful action of rulers and elites determined to sabotage any effort to build representative institutions that might encroach on their limitless hold on power.

At the forefront were Iraq under Saddam Hussein and Syria under Hafiz and Bashar al-Asad, all card-carrying members of the Baath Party. The Baath was created in the 1930s by Michel Aflaq and Salah Bitar, two young Syrians who formed a strong friendship while studying in Paris. Influenced by the Fascist ideologies prevalent at the time, Aflaq and Bitar advocated a radical program of uniting all Arabs in one national state. The party's founders were aware that to dismantle existing states was no easy matter, so a pivotal element of the party's ideology was the sanctioning of violence as a legitimate method for achieving its mission. Hence, the party's ascension to power in Iraq and Syria in the 1960s occurred not through the ballot box but through military coups. Throughout its tenure in power, the party never lost its appetite for violence, and its adherents never flinched at the prospect of inflicting pain.

Barbarity was indeed the hallmark of Iraq's procrustean authoritarianism under Saddam Hussein.[2] The eventual murderer of hundreds of thousands first came to political prominence in the wake of the July 1968 military coup that usurped power in the name of the Baath party. Initially a committed member of the party, Hussein, while less than lukewarm about individual rights, nevertheless was to put in place substantial socioeconomic reforms and improvements. Embarking on a series of ambitious development plans in the 1970s, Hussein would preside over a breathtaking increase in the country's GDP per capita from $382 in 1972 to $2,726 by 1979. These plans were undertaken with an eye toward reducing the gap between rich and poor. He introduced a variety of governmental initiatives aimed at the poor classes, including a substantial building program of modern dwellings for the poor, an expansion of free health services, and free education. Indeed, the number of secondary and university students doubled in a period of less than ten years.

That Iraq was able to achieve so much in such a short time was attributed in no small measure to the absolute control of the all-powerful man at the helm. Hussein's unforgiving displeasure with corruption and incompetence made Iraq in the 1970s a model of economic development and a haven of prosperity. By the end of the decade, many Iraqis believed that these successes would not have materialized with such speed and efficiency had Iraq possessed a democratic system in which every policy is scrutinized and debated minutely, sometimes ad infinitum.

But if Iraqis had begun to feel comfortable with the many offerings of authoritarian rule, they soon would be jolted out of their comfort zone. The contented and unsuspecting citizens of Iraq would shortly find themselves and their country on a disastrous downward slide. And that eventuality could have been averted had public discussion and debate been allowed, had Saddam Hussein been willing to listen to an opposing point of view.

The decade of success came to a screeching halt in September 1980, when Hussein decided to invade Iran. What Hussein had predicted to be a few weeks' venture dragged on for eight years of debilitating stalemated war. And by the time of the conflict's messy conclusion, Iraq had suffered more than half a million casualties. Its economy was left in tatters: when the war began, Iraq had over $35 billion in foreign reserves; by 1988, it had accumulated foreign debts of over a $100 billion. Then, barely two years later, Hussein embarked on an even greater military misadventure, this time invading Kuwait. Iraq's stunning defeat by an international coalition, followed by severe United Nations economic sanctions, was the second stop on the country's path to eventual ruin.

Along with these national mishaps, Hussein would radically change the structure and means of domestic political control. During the 1980s, as the war took its toll on Iraq's middle class, which provided the bulk of Baath Party membership, Hussein would elbow the party out of any meaningful position in the power structure, building instead a coercive and predatory political edifice that devolved onto members of his family and clan, supported by military units drawn from tribal elements loyal to him personally, and cemented around the manufacture and purposeful marketing of a personality cult intended to inhabit the consciousness of all Iraqis. A deluge of books and articles, underwritten by the Ministry of Culture and Information, raved about Hussein's unparalleled wisdom and genius. Films extolled his revolutionary exploits, and his valor in the face of adversity. He gazed down on people from huge street billboards, and was serenaded in song and poetry. It was essential that Hussein be perceived as the sole arbiter of power, the lone dispenser of justice, the unitary figurehead to whom the loyalty of all true citizens would be directed.

At the very basis of Hussein's system was the institution of a reign of terror. Intelligence services proliferated, the numbers of secret police and spies multiplied, and armed militia roamed the streets. The slightest divergence from state policy would result in years of dreadful incarceration and unspeakable atrocities. People would be picked up from their homes, imprisoned and tortured for no reason other than appearing amused by an innocuous joke about the regime. Schoolteachers were in a state of constant panic lest they said something in class that might contradict a passing utterance by Hussein. And when the reckless few attempted a move against the untouchable leader, the sadistic wrath of the state descended not just on the perpetrators but on their families, clans, and villages as well. In the late 1980s, Hussein waged a genocidal assault against Iraq's Kurdish population, a horrific atrocity that he would repeat with carefree abandon after Iraq's defeat in the Kuwaiti war in 1991, this time taking in the country's Shiite community as well.

Simultaneously, state agencies in charge of cultural production focused their attention exclusively on the glorification and aggrandizement of Saddam Hussein. Books and articles sponsored by the state lauded Hussein's leadership prowess. And beyond the written word, Hussein's cronies began to draw a continuous cultural and political line, starting from the glittering civilizations of ancient Mesopotamia, running through the famed Baghdad-based Islamic empires, and ending with contemporary Iraq. By the 1980s and 1990s, the two most disastrous decades in Iraq's twentieth-century history, it had become commonplace to see Hussein mentioned not just as one of the luminaries of Mesopotamian and Islamic history but decidedly as the overachiever among them.

By the beginning of the twenty-first century, Saddam Hussein and his family ruled over a country with a decaying economy and a fragile social structure, which had been terrorized into submis-

Saddam testifies on September 18, 2006, during his trial for genocide against the Kurds. To Saddam's right in the back row sits his cousin Ali Hassan Abd al-Majid, known as "Chemical Ali" for ordering the use of chemical weapons against the Kurds. Both were found guilty and were hanged later.
Associated Press / Erik De Castro

sion. With no hopes and no prospects, and under harsh international sanctions, the majority of the people must have watched with concealed resentment, learned through years of oppressive rule, as hundreds of thousands of Iraqi children died from disease and malnutrition while Hussein nonchalantly built one grandiose palace after another. Thirty-five years in power, for the most part uncontested, ended up leaving a legacy that had no redeeming features. Few would remember that in his early years Hussein had achieved a lot; for when he was ousted in 2003, the abiding memory was of the cruelty and callousness of his reign, a testament to a monster of a man who had been an enthusiastic admirer of Stalin and his methods of political control.[3]

If Hussein was Baathism's Stalin, then Hafiz al-Asad of Syria was its Brezhnev—dour, closed to the outside world, without Hussein's brazen excesses, yet cruel and predatory when the occasion demanded it. Asad was a member of Syria's minority Alawite sect, which constituted no more than 12 percent of the population. In socioeconomic terms, the Alawites were decidedly second class, and in religious terms, they were perceived by the majority Sunni community as heretical. During the 1940s and 1950s, Alawites had found in the army their best and quickest path to upward mobility. Trying to overcome their sectarian identity that tended to separate them from the majority Syrian population, they flocked to the Baath Party, pledging undivided fidelity to its Arab nationalist mission. Now, they could stand on equal footing with the rest, identified not by their Alawite roots but by their shared Arab identity. By the early 1960s, after the collapse of the United Arab Republic, young Alawite officers, many of them Baathist, occupied a number of sensitive military posts, and before long they would become active and central participants in a spate of military coups during the 1960s. A lifelong member of the Baath Party, Asad was the defense minister in a Baathist regime in 1970. Not content with his status, and unhappy about the regime's drift to ultra-leftist politics, he led a successful military coup in November, officially called the Corrective Movement, which launched his absolutist rule for the following thirty years until his death in 2000.

Asad's first concern upon taking power was to write a constitution for the country that would legalize the dominance of the presidency over all other institutions, including a toothless elected assembly that was to become a cheering, rubber-stamping forum for the president. In addition to the presidency, Asad took the office of secretary general of the Baath Party, thus appropriating for himself the two most powerful political institutions in the country. With his hold on the political process and power levers now established, he used the Baath Party, which like an organizational octopus had its tentacles spread throughout all levels of Syria's society, as his primary mobilizing instrument. His political dominance meant that within a few years, Baath Party leaders who initially had considered themselves Asad's colleagues, participating fully in the policy-making process, would come to accept him as the undisputed leader and pivotal decision maker. And their role and status gradually would be downgraded to that of enthusiastic devotees ever ready to support his utterances and sing his praises. After the Sixth Baath Party Congress in April 1975, the following official statement was trumpeted repeatedly in the country's official media and over the airwaves:

> The Congress declares its adherence to the Corrective Movement under the leadership of Comrade Hafiz al-Asad. . . . As regards Arab and international policy, the Congress

confirms the soundness of the policy under the leadership of
Comrade Hafiz al-Asad. . . . The Congress placed on record
Comrade Hafiz al-Asad's responsible and courageous attitude
to the Palestine question . . . and it greeted the masses of our
people, rallying round our party and the leader of their march,
Comrade Hafiz al-Asad.[4]

The deference to Asad was no doubt cemented by his decision,
together with Egypt's Anwar Sadat, to attack Israel in October
1973. Though the brief war ended with a military victory for the
Jewish state, it nevertheless earned Asad considerable kudos for
having the grit to take on the Israelis, whom Arabs were beginning to perceive as invincible in the wake of the June 1967 war.
Asad would build on the Syrians' belief that their country was at
the heart of the Arab nationalist project, and that it was, as portrayed in billboards across the country, *qalb al-uruba al-nabidh*,
the "throbbing heart of Arabism." The feeling of pride in Syria's
centrality in the Arab world, vigorously constructed by Asad, was
heartily cherished by the Syrian population, and credited of course
to their president.

There were also economic and social achievements. Endeavoring
to create a synergetic balance between the public and private sectors, Asad presided over a palpable economic boom in the 1970s. He
managed his Arab nationalist foreign policy in a way that would
not be perceived as threatening by the conservative oil-rich states
of the Gulf, which brought his country substantial foreign aid. A
number of social gains followed: modern irrigation systems were
introduced into Syria's vast agricultural domain; new roads were
built and existing ones widened; medical and educational services
were extended to the countryside, which traditionally had woefully lagged behind the major urban centers like Damascus and

Aleppo; and extensive credit was provided to peasants. The expansion of education was a hallmark of Asad's first decade. His government embarked on an ambitious program of building schools, graduating teachers, and actively encouraging parents to seek education for their children. In Asad's first decade, the secondary school population in Syria more than doubled, from under 215,000 to over 550,000.[5] Teachers were dispatched to the countryside to try to eradicate illiteracy, which stood at about 60 percent. These efforts yielded some improvements, the high annual birth rate of 3.7 percent militating against spectacular successes; still, within ten years, the illiteracy rate had dropped to under 50 percent. All in all, Asad's achievements outstripped the setbacks, as testified to by an Israeli scholar who argued that in the early part of Asad's rule, Syria had become "the most stable regime in the Arab world [and] had made more impressive progress in the socioeconomic revolution than Egypt."[6] By no stretch of the imagination could Asad's first decade be called a failure.

Ultimately, however, the purposeful centralization of power, aiming as always to eliminate people's oversight over the political process, would undermine these foreign policy and socioeconomic gains. Coming from the ranks of the military, Asad did not need to be told of the importance of the army in cementing his authoritarian political structure. Having been a military conspirator himself, he was determined to ensure the loyalty of the armed forces. So he retreated into his sectarian roots. He promoted Alawite officers to the most sensitive commands of the army and other security agencies, and lavished them with privileges that tied their well-being to the health of the regime. Beyond that, he put members of his own family and clan in charge of special forces that operated in parallel to the regular armed forces. The primary responsibility of these troops, the most notable of which was the Defense Companies, commanded by Rifaat al-Asad, the president's younger brother, was defending Asad's political order.

And when defense of the regime was needed, his loyal troops would respond ferociously. In February 1982, an insurrection in the conservative Sunni city of Hama, engineered by Islamists, spread so quickly that most of the city fell under their control. In the process, a number of Syrian soldiers and Baathists were killed. Asad responded by sending over 12,000 of his most loyal troops, mainly Alawites, but with some committed party cadres, to the city with orders to extinguish the rebellion at all cost. What follows is best described by Patrick Seale, the noted British writer and journalist, in his generally sympathetic biography of Hafiz al-Asad:

> As the tide turned slowly in the government's favor, the guerrillas fell back on the [city's] old quarters. [Here] the common people living deeper in the maze of streets were the main victims, as . . . they were all too often buried in the ruins of their homes. After heavy shelling, [government] commandos and party irregulars supported by tanks moved in to subdue the acres of mud-and-wattle houses whose interconnecting rooftops and courtyards were the guerrillas' habitat. Many civilians were slaughtered in the prolonged mopping up, whole districts razed, and numerous acts of savagery reported, many of them after the government had regained control of the town. Entire families were taken from their homes and shot. . . . In nearly a month of fighting about a third of the historic inner city was demolished.[7]

In situations such as this, when people challenged the authority of the regime, Asad's military and tribal roots, combined with the violent ideology of the Baath Party, made for a potent, vengeful brew. On one occasion, the party's founder, Michel Aflaq, had extolled the virtue of cruelty. "When we are cruel [to others]," Aflaq would nonchalantly explain, "we know that our cruelty is meant to bring them back to their true selves, of which they are ignorant."[8] The party therefore was useful to Asad in providing an ideational platform that would legitimize the use of coercion, as well as being an effective agent for mobilizing support among the population for the regime. So while Asad depended mainly on his family and clan within the Alawite community for survival, he continued to consult with, and shower privileges on, members of the party's hierarchy. For their part, party leaders hoped that the greater their success in engendering conformity and unquestioned fidelity to the president and his government, the closer they would get to the center of power and its beneficence.

In such an environment of total political control, where privilege is defined solely in terms of proximity to the political center, corruption was bound to flourish. All the political rhetoric about Syria's many advances and achievements, heavily marketed by the state-controlled media, could not mask the increasing web of corruption practiced by government officials, party aficionados, and high military officers, and the biggest transgressors seemed to be members of Asad's own family and clan. Not that dissimilar from the condition of the Soviet Union on the eve of Brezhnev's death in 1982, Syria in 2000, the year of Asad's death, was a country that had lost its purpose and direction, found itself no longer imbued by the revolutionary enthusiasm of years past, and had had its creative energy snuffed out of it by years of suffocating authoritarian political order.

Hafiz al-Asad was to die in June 2000, but the old man had worked hard to ensure a smooth succession. His eldest son, Bashar, had been groomed to take over in a move that left many observers wondering whether Syria was a republic or a monarchy. There was a hitch, however, in fact a major hitch. Syria's constitution stated that the president of the republic had to be at least forty years of age, and young Bashar was thirty-four when his father died. As it turned out, this was not much of an obstacle after all. It took the discerning members of the People's Assembly no time at all to amend the constitution and bring down the legal age limit to accommodate Bashar. And after fifteen years of dormancy, the Baath Party convened a congress that promptly elected Bashar to the party leadership. Within a month of his father's death, Bashar al-Asad became the country's president after a referendum in which his candidacy (he was the only candidate) won 97.2 percent of the vote. In 2007, another referendum extended his presidency for a further seven years, this time improving on his earlier numbers by garnering 97.7 percent of the vote. Such percentages should not raise any eyebrows, for as tyrants go, Bashar's numbers are par for the course.

In fact, in his first year in office Bashar was greeted with much goodwill. An ophthalmologist with a training stint in London under his belt, able to speak English and French, he projected a modern, forward-looking demeanor that promised a welcome break for the Syrians from his father's insular orthodoxy. Hopes were even raised further when he soon married a highly educated and professional British-born woman of Syrian parentage. Articulate and highly photogenic, she with her husband represented the onset of a new and more liberal age.

A few months into his presidency the new president would address his population's aspirations by embarking on a program of political liberalization. This soon would be called the "Damascus Spring," akin to the 1968 Prague Spring which liberalized communism's hold on Czechoslovakia's political institutions. Asad talked of the need for greater transparency and freedom; he began by

Official ceremony on June 10, 2001, marking the first anniversary of the death of Hafiz al-Asad. The first row is occupied by the two sons Bashar and Maher along with Lebanese president Lahoud and Iranian vice president Habibi.
Associated Press / Bassem Tellawi

releasing many political prisoners, and encouraging citizen debates in open forums, promising no interference from the ubiquitous security forces. When people were finally convinced that the new environment of liberalism was genuine, and not a trap for identifying possible dissidents, droves of intellectuals, professionals, and ordinary folk participated, voicing their many concerns and submitting petitions and blueprints for a more open society. Those who were outside the political power circle, non-Baathists who had no opportunity for political participation, founded new political parties, published independent newspapers, and formed civil society organizations. Syria's most notorious prison was closed, and in the economic sector, the government legalized private banks, and reduced restrictions on trade and foreign investment. In those heady days of reform and promise, many Syrians came to believe that under their new young president their country was finally on the verge of a truly momentous and welcome change.

But the Damascus Spring was to suffer the same fate as its earlier namesake in Czechoslovakia. While it was Russians who snuffed the life out of the 1968 Prague Spring, in Damascus it was the indigenous Syrian ruling elites who were responsible for the death of the reform movement in its infancy. Whether it was Bashar al-Asad himself who began to fear the consequences of reform, or the old guard ruling elites who made sure that he quickly came to his senses, or the Alawite community fearing for its privileges, even safety, the era of reform would last but a few months. Then the state flexed its muscles and closed down all the discussion forums, putting an end to any fanciful ideas about political parties outside the Baath, and arresting those who had felt safe enough to talk about democracy and ask for an open society. By the fall of 2001, Syria, young president and all, had fully and with gusto returned to the closed society that Hafiz al-Asad had passed on to his son.

The decade of Bashar's rule that preceded the eruption of wide-spread riots and demonstrations in March 2011 was characterized by the kind of predatory authoritarianism that is typically associated with the practices of an out-and-out police state. Bashar's Syria was forced into fearful silence through a web of security agencies that in times of crises cooperated with elite military units commanded by ultra-loyal Alawite officers, with immediate family members at the helm. Even though Asad occasionally would repeat his promise for political openness, his rule was distinguished by its thorough disregard for human and political rights. On this score, a 35-page report released in July 2010 by Human Rights Watch was a damning indictment of Bashar's first decade in power. Contrary to governmental claims, "Syria's security agencies," the report maintained, "continue to detain people without arrest warrants, frequently refuse to disclose their whereabouts for weeks and sometimes months, and regularly engage in torture."[9] While the president (and at times the first lady) continued to promise reform, the reality was that over eleven years of rule, the harsh and oppressive legacy of his father lived on and prospered.

In Libya, the rule of Colonel Muammar Qadhafi was no less cruel or repressive, but it tended to be somewhat camouflaged by Qadhafi's eccentric personality and in many instances erratic policies. During his more than forty years in power, he was literally the loose cannon among the fraternity of Arab despots, and as such he was frequently referred to in other Arab countries as *al-majnun*, "the crazy one." Still, until 2011, there were very few challenges to his rule, because in addition to the pervasive and menacing presence of the state's coercive agencies, Qadhafi adroitly exploited the tribal and regional divisions of his country by creating tribal and clan allegiances drawn from friendly regions. In return, he favored these regions with privileges and largess, and in doing so he ensured the persistence of their loyalty.

Growing up idolizing Nasser, Qadhafi followed faithfully in the footsteps of his hero after he came to power. He demanded the evacuation of the American and British bases on Libyan soil and their return to Libyan sovereignty. He confiscated foreign-owned businesses, leaving their owners little choice but to leave Libya. He assaulted the private sector, nationalizing almost everything in sight, built schools and clinics across the country, and created a one-party political system meant to harness the country's energy into a purposeful pursuit of economic and social development. Education was a particular beneficiary, so that, for example, the number of high schools rose from 203 in 1971 to 1,135 by 1980.[10] A decade after coming to power, Qadhafi could show off a per capita income that had grown fivefold.[11] And in terms of the recognition factor, there can be little doubt that in that first decade of Qadhafi's rule, he was able to move a country that had resided very much on the periphery of the Arab world to the center and mainstream of Arab politics.

But autocrats generally tend to follow similar patterns of behavior. They become intoxicated with their successes, and at some point they eventually come to believe in their faultlessness. In Qadhafi's case, this began pretty early in his journey toward megalomania, sometime in the mid-1970s. At some point, the colonel began to favor himself as an original thinker, and he set out to produce a theoretical body of work designed not only to inform and regulate the conduct of life in Libya but in the world as a whole. The result was his "Green Book," consisting of three treatises on the political, economic, and social bases of his pronounced "Third Universal Theory," which was supposed to supplant the Western model of democracy and capitalism, and the Communist ideas of one-party rule and socialism. Fabled for its modest, at times infantile, philosophical logic, which depicts constitutions, parliaments, and political parties as treacherous instruments of dictatorship, it contained such memorable gems as "women are female and men are male. According to gynecologists, women, unlike men, menstruate each month."[12]

Fortified by the political and internationalist prescriptions of his Third Universal Theory, Qadhafi would plunge Libya into a series of baffling ideational initiatives and botched foreign policy adventures, and the end result was that every political institution found itself held hostage to the restless soul of the country's sole leader. When Qadhafi became frustrated with the Arab Socialist

Union, Libya's only political party, modeled after Nasser's original brand, particularly its seeming inability to "educate and mobilize the masses," he promptly abolished it. To fill the institutional void, he decreed the creation of a plethora of popular committees. Presented as the core institutional idea of Qadhafi's new democracy, the committees would supervise and make policies for localities and send delegates to the annual meeting of a new organization, the General People's Congress, which would deliberate national policy. Qadhafi then raised eyebrows when he himself relinquished all formal positions, a step, according to him, more in tune with the persona of a revolutionary comrade.

The new Qadhafi brand was advertised as an effort by the consummate revolutionary to ensure that the revolution he created would not be subverted by reactionary tendencies that apparently still persisted in the country. So, for good measure, he pledged to oppose anyone who was not sold on practicing "popular power." To that end, he styled himself as the "leader of the opposition" in what essentially was his own political system, and this opposition was encapsulated in an array of revolutionary committees who were tasked to bring about "the era of the masses."[13] What this turned out to mean in actuality was giving these committees carte blanche to use at will a variety of more or less unsavory methods, including liquidating the real opposition, considered "enemies of the revolution." In the meantime, the colonel formed an elite guard for his personal protection made up entirely of women. These were called *al-rahibat al-thawriyat*—the Revolutionary Nuns. They were handpicked by Qadhafi, trained in firearms and martial arts, and had to take an oath of chastity.

Apart from the predatory and indulgent aspects of Qadhafi's institutional changes and innovations, which on the whole did serve the purpose of keeping him in power, his reorganizations, which would frequently change as the mood took him, produced political confusion and administrative chaos. Political oppression and the draconian imposition of incoherent socialist edicts meant that by 1988 the gross domestic product per capita had fallen almost 42 percent from five years earlier. And while these failures of the revolution generally would be blamed on the shortcomings of the committees' revolutionary credentials, they were in effect entirely Qadhafi's doing, since for all his trumpeted commitment to the rule of the masses, the colonel never surrendered his monopoly of political power.

Qadhafi's erratic domestic policy was equaled, even outdone, by the volatility of his foreign policy. Looking back at his many adventures abroad, some of them truly disastrous, the only discernible motivation was the preservation of Qadhafi's supposedly revolutionary reputation. He would finance and logistically support a motley group of killers, rapists, and cutthroats masquerading as revolutionaries from Uganda and Sierra Leone to Chad and Darfur. In the words of one analyst, Qadhafi "supported whoever was willing to pay homage to his leadership [and] came to see himself as the CEO of the liberation camp in Africa." When some years ago Ugandans debated term limits on the presidency, the colonel inserted himself into the national debate, pronouncing: "Revolutionaries do not retire."[14] And apparently nor do aggressors, as evidenced by Qadhafi's catastrophic adventurism in Chad, his southern neighbor.

When Qadhafi assumed power, a civil war in Chad was raging. Within a year, Qadhafi entered the fray, supporting one side and annexing a swath of northern Chad. Determined to place a client government in Chad, Qadhafi persisted and with the passage of time increased his intervention. In December 1979, thousands of Libyan forces, spearheaded by scores of Soviet-made tanks, entered the Chadian capital, N'Djamena, an event that Qadhafi trumpeted to cement his reputation in the Arab, African, and Third worlds. But this flagrant intervention, and the human cost it extracted, alarmed other African countries, particularly those with strong French connections in West Africa, which eventually induced Qadhafi to withdraw his forces. Disdainful of international norms (after all, according to him, he was no longer a head of state but a freewheeling revolutionary leader), and subject to whims of fancy, Qadhafi did not rest on his laurels and soon entered the Chadian melee again, this time with humiliating results. In a series of engagements with Chadian irregulars, the much better equipped Libyan forces, supposedly imbued with the revolutionary spirit of Qadhafi's Third Universal Theory, suffered crushing defeats that eventually pushed them out of all of Chad.

If the international community had hoped that the more than a decade of meaningless war costing many lives would dissuade Qadhafi from further adventures, their optimism soon proved to be very wide of the mark. Qadhafi sponsored a series of terror-ist attacks in Europe and against American interests worldwide, which eventually resulted in an American air attack on Qadhafi's headquarters in 1986 in Tripoli, the Libyan capital. The colonel was naturally enraged by the American operation, but more so by the response of the Libyan people, which at best was nonchalant. He obviously could not let this go. In 1988, his agents blew up Pan Am's Flight 103 over Lockerbie in Scotland. A similar fate befell a French airliner the following year, France having supported Chad in its war against Qadhafi. The two terrorist operations would result in heavy UN sanctions, which by the mid-1990s were having a discernibly deleterious impact on an economy already suffering from Qadhafi's arbitrary and erratic policies. So, by the dawn of the twenty-first century, Libya's economy was growing by under

1 percent a year, its gross domestic product was falling, its trade was crippled, and it suffered "a heightening sense of national disgrace and isolation, even from Arab neighbors."[15]

Yet Qadhafi was not worried. As a seasoned dictator, he knew how to remain in office unchallenged. He would use his control over the country's treasury to build strategic support by conferring privileges to selective segments of society, drawn from favored regions. He also would manipulate the command and control of his army to minimize the possibility of rebellion, and additionally he would create special military units, commanded by family members, whose exclusive responsibility would be the defense of the regime. And when in early 2011 revolution toppled the dictatorship of Tunisia, Libya's next-door neighbor, Qadhafi reacted as though it was just another day at the office, taking refuge in tired old clichés about Western perfidy. He was "pained" by the overthrow of Tunisia's president, his heartache directed at the Tunisian nation "whose sons [were] dying each day." He warned Tunisians not to be tricked by Wikileaks, which published "information written by lying ambassadors in order to create chaos."[16] Qadhafi might have felt Tunisia's pain, but he considered the misadventures of its citizens not to be much of a contaminant. His main preoccupation was not with revolution but with regime succession—deciding which of his many sons would inherit the levers of power. But then the winter of Arab discontent would engulf Qadhafi and his country in a revolution that he had not foreseen, and for which he was not prepared.

Even more ill-prepared was Tunisia's Zine al-Abidin Ben Ali, who lasted only a few weeks after the eruption of demonstrations before fleeing to Saudi Arabia. On a scale of sheer beastliness, Ben Ali does not compare with the likes of Iraq's Hussein, Syria's Asad, or Libya's Qadhafi, and perhaps that was why he did not stand up to the revolutionaries in his country the way Asad or Qadhafi did, or Hussein would have done had he not been booted out in 2003. This is not to say that Ben Ali's rule was anything but authoritarian; it is simply that when it came to the business of the indiscriminate shedding of blood, he possessed neither the historical legacy and institutional experience, nor the carefree attitude, of his brother dictators in Syria and Libya.

Ben Ali came to power in a bloodless coup in 1987, when he ousted Habib Bourguiba, who had ruled Tunisia since it gained independence in 1956. Bourguiba, who had made himself "president for life," ruled the country through the usual one-party system, which he controlled. A modernizer, with a strong pro-Western disposition, Bourguiba introduced a number of progressive socioeconomic reforms. This was especially true of gender issues. Tunisia's personal status law was enacted as early as 1956, abolishing polygamy, setting a minimum marriage age for women, and making divorce a right for both sexes. He also gave women the right to vote and made education at all levels available to them. Indeed, by the time he was ousted from power, Tunisia was considered one of the most socially advanced countries in the Arab world.

Ben Ali was Bourguiba's protégé, having been promoted through the ranks to become the minister of the interior, the man in charge of the police, and later prime minister. Ben Ali made his move in 1987, charging that Bourguiba at eighty-four was beginning to suffer from senility and as such was unable to run the country effectively. With his connection to the security forces, there was hardly any opposition to the takeover from the public. Tunisians were not particularly eager to challenge the security forces, and in any case after over thirty years of unitary rule, where they had heard no other voice but that of the ruler, they had come to accept the directives that came their way from the man in charge.

While Ben Ali initially made a few "democratic" gestures, such as abolishing the title of "president for life," setting a two-term limit for the presidency, and promising a multiparty system, almost twenty-five years on the main feature of his political system would continue to be characterized by tight presidential control of politics. Although a number of political parties were licensed and did participate in various elections, the president's party, the Constitutional Democratic Rally (RCD), never relinquished control of parliament. In the country's last, pre-revolution parliamentary elections in 2009, the RCD commanded 152 seats in the 189-seat legislative institution. And while Ben Ali had set a two five-year terms limit to his presidential tenure, an endeavor played to huge public fanfare, he in fact ended up winning five elections by simply getting parliament to keep modifying eligibility requirements in the constitution. And he would win these elections by margins of 90–99 percent, average figures among Arab despots, forever determined to show the world and each other how much their people love them.

Ben Ali did not control only the parliament but also the constitutionally sanctioned independent judiciary. Judges were expected to do the bidding of the president and his cronies, even those with no official standing. A word from the well-connected would signify the position of the politically powerful on the issue, and the courts were expected to take the hint. Like other institutions— political parties, civil society institutions, and most regrettably, the media—the judiciary operated on the whole as another arm of the regime. And when the reckless few raised a dissenting voice, they would find themselves on the streets, regardless of their seniority or status. In 2001, a senior judge wrote an open letter to the president complaining about consistent state interference, in which judges were forced "to deliver verdicts which are dictated to them by the political authorities."[17] In no time, this man would find himself the center of a smear campaign that led to the loss of his judgeship.

If there was one abiding characteristic of Ben Ali's regime during the first decade of the twenty-first century, it was its unremittingly rancid corruption. In a country where one in three Tunisians in their twenties was unemployed, fabulous riches were concentrated in a handful of people connected mainly by familial ties to the president and his wife. Businessmen familiar with regime practices would paint a picture of a kleptocratic administration intent on expropriating the wealth of the country for personal use. They would estimate that about fifty people in total were responsible for about 60 percent of the country's economic activity. If corruption on this scale sounds egregious, almost implausible, a close scrutiny of a secret cable to Washington written in the summer of 2008 by the American ambassador to Tunisia at the time, Robert Godec, might dispel any lingering doubts.

The ambassador begins his devastating indictment of Ben Ali, his wife Leila Trabelsi, and their relations by referring to them as a "quasi mafia," who had no compulsion about using "strong arm tactics and flagrant abuse of the system" to amass their wealth. For example, Leila's brother, Belhassan Trabelsi, by using predatory and corrupt schemes, ended up with extensive holdings which the ambassador details: "an airline, several hotels, one of Tunisia's two private radio stations, car assembly plants, Ford distribution, a real estate development company, and the list goes on." Apparently, lax oversight made "the banking sector an excellent target of opportunity with multiple stories of 'First Family' schemes." One of these involved a son-in-law of Ben Ali who acquired a controlling interest in a state bank immediately prior to the bank's privatization, then promptly sold it at a huge profit. And when a brother of the first lady was asked by the governor of one of Tunisia's twenty-four governorates to abide by laws requiring insurance coverage for his amusement park, the man charged into the governor's office in a rage, knocking an elderly office clerk to the ground. True to form, punishment for the obviously impertinent governor was not long in coming—he was swiftly removed from his post. The cable goes on through a number of pages listing many other transgressions committed by members of "the family" and their minions, who acted with brazen disregard for the law because they knew they were above the law.[18] Ben Ali's quasi-mafioso family, friend of the West and all, could not find a single Western country to take them in once they decided to escape the retribution of the people; they ended up, Westernized, secular, and moneyed, in the severe puritanical milieu of Saudi Arabia.

The ouster of an Arab dictator was soon to be replicated in Egypt, which held greater significance for the region. It was after all in Egypt, the traditional leader of the Arab world, marching under the charismatic leadership of Gamal Abd al-Nasser, that the first incendiary seed was planted that sparked the revolutionary eruptions of the first Arab awakening. But Nasser's revolution was in a sense half done—precipitating no doubt many achievements, yet purposely keeping democratic ideas and institutions at bay, creating a one-party system that was to be emulated in other Arab revolutions. On his death in October 1970, Nasser had bequeathed to his successor in Egypt an unyielding authoritarian system.

Anwar Sadat, Nasser's successor, was no democrat, but he needed to please his American patrons. He had tried to gradually shepherd Egypt away from socialism and the Soviet Union toward a more free market–based economy and the United States. With Egypt depending more on American credit and military hardware, Sadat needed to make political concessions more in tune with the proclivities of his new benefactors. So he played up to American sensitivities by dismantling Nasser's Arab Socialist Union, creating his own party, the National Democratic Party (NDP), and allowing other parties to enter the political fray. But his was hardly an initiative borne out of a deep commitment to the democratic ideal. To ensure that among the crop of new parties there would be no troublemakers, he formed a committee made up mostly of members of the NDP to vet applications for new parties, and once licensed, to supervise and regulate the activities of these parties. Opposition parties would not be allowed to indulge in destructive political behavior—"destructive" basically meaning critical of the regime. But even this paltry effort at political liberalization went against Sadat's authoritarian instinct. After he signed a peace treaty with Israel in 1979, thereby tying the hands of American policy makers, his rule would become even more arbitrary. In October 1981, a month after his security forces swooped down on more than 1,500 political figures and activists and slung them into prison, Sadat was assassinated.

Muhammad Hosni Mubarak, Sadat's vice president at the time, became the new president of Egypt and the chairman of the NDP. Upon assuming power he promised democratic reforms that would be gradual yet real, and very soon he would release most of the politicians, activists, and intellectuals held in Sadat's prisons. The excesses of the censors were curtailed, and journalists and reporters found they could criticize political figures without having to entertain the prospect of losing their jobs, to say nothing of the fear of staring at the walls of prison cells. Non-governmental

associations, including active and vociferous professional syndi-
cates, grew exponentially, and the president showed a welcome
allergy to the use of force against citizens. Even when the NDP's
share of assembly seats fell sharply in the 1987 elections, Mubarak
seemed to take the reverse in stride.

But this would soon change. The longer Mubarak remained
at the helm, the harder it was to relinquish power and the many
seductive things that came with it. And it was not as though falling behind on the autocracy index was something that would win
him brownie points among his fellow Arab dictators. After the
1987 election until his ouster in 2011, Mubarak would doggedly
pursue one paramount goal: to continue to hold on to the reins of
absolute power.

To stay in power, however, could only come at the expense of
the few liberties Mubarak had bestowed on the Egyptian people.
The 1990s saw Mubarak embark on a swift and determined process
of "deliberalization." Using executive decrees and military courts,
and relying more and more on the feared and much detested security forces, Mubarak would tread the same path of unremitting
coercion already populated by other more established members
of the Arab dictatorial fraternity. He would resort with vigor and
purpose to Egypt's long-standing emergency law to arrest opposition activists without the slightest concern for due process.
Elections now would be rigged openly, and opposition supporters
bullied and abused. The press would be literally choked of whatever modest breath of freedom he had given it in the early days
of his rule, and civil society institutions, which by definition are
supposed to operate independently of the state, would come under
governmental control. When in the early and mid-1990s Islamists
won leadership elections in various unions and professional syndi-
cates, representing lawyers, doctors, engineers, and pharmacists,

the regime quickly brought these organizations under the management of government-appointed judicial committees.

Mubarak's tenure, 1981–2011, qualified him as the longest serving Egyptian president. He and his party, the NDP, won every election and referendum with large (and in Mubarak's case, gigantic) majorities. Until 2005, Egypt had a two-tier system for choosing a president: the People's Assembly, the country's parliament, nominated a candidate, and a national referendum followed. Mubarak would be nominated by large assembly majorities, and he would then go on to garner between 94 and 99 percent of the referenda votes. In the one open election, in 2005, running against a candidate who for his impudence was later imprisoned, Mubarak received what must have been for him an infuriatingly low 89 percent of the vote. The same eye-popping percentages were beyond the reach of the NDP; still, the party's performance in the various elections between 1981 and 2010 was more than stellar, the crucial point being that the NDP needed to be above the two-thirds majority required to rubber-stamp presidential decisions. And it succeeded in this objective in every parliamentary election during Mubarak's thirty-year presidency.

By now of course it would be understood that these heartwarming figures were hardly an affirmation of the people's devotion to their leader and his party, but an open expression of the contempt with which Mubarak and his cronies held the democratic rules of the game. Every election was severely manipulated; Mubarak's much detested security services, backed by a variety of thugs and heavies, would resort to threats, beatings, and arbitrary arrests on trumped-up charges of opposition figures and their supporters. Then, to have absolute peace of mind, they would produce already stuffed ballot boxes at the tallying centers. On the rare occasion when this system was deemed less than 100 percent reliable, Mubarak's state institutions would move in to correct the glitch. Because the 2005 election produced the lowest NDP representation of all elections thus far (only 68 percent), and allowed the entry of eighty-eight candidates with known Islamist sympathies into the People's Assembly (still a mere 19 percent), Mubarak and the NDP deemed the results a significant and disturbing setback, blaming it on the fact that the election was supervised by the judiciary, who apparently interfered with the state's self-assigned right to intervene in the electoral process. So, in 2007, control over ballot boxes was taken away from the judiciary and placed in the hands of local government employees, and an NDP-dominated commission was given the ultimate responsibility for ensuring the integrity of the elections.[19] No wonder that in the 2010 elections, the NDP achieved its best results, winning a whopping 81 percent of the seats.

Even with thirty years of the presidency under his belt, Mubarak was looking forward to the 2011 scheduled elections for another six-year term.[20] His resolve to stay in power ad infinitum became the subject of many jokes told on the streets of Cairo. One of them tells of an aide asking Mubarak whether it was time for him to deliver a farewell speech to the Egyptian people. Mubarak, looking confused, asks: "Why, where are they going?"[21] After all, echoing the same refrain used by other members of the Arab club of despots, Mubarak would present himself to the Egyptian people as "the father of the nation," a father who had the power to reward good deeds, as he would define them, and to punish (severely when the occasion merited it) wicked behavior, characterized essentially as opposition to the regime. By the end of 2010, not in his wildest dreams would Mubarak think that his ungrateful children might rise and discard the repressive shackles of patriarchy he had imposed on them.

———

Mubarak's rule was a microcosm of the despotism that plagued the Arab world prior to the eruption of popular uprisings instigated by the self-immolation of Muhammad Bouazizi. The sorry state of authoritarian rule by corrupt and inefficient regimes, built around the hegemonic presence of one man, brooking no restraint on his power—all of this was in fact the offspring of the Arab revolutions of the 1950s and 1960s.

The transformation from the initial high hopes of the first Arab awakening to the paralysis of the authoritarian Arab political order of the twenty-first century occurred over time and in some cases spanned a number of regimes and personalities. But the seeds of failure were sowed early on when Nasser, in his determined mission to achieve independence and socioeconomic justice, eschewed the political ideal of freedom. The tragedy for the Arabs was that the charismatic Nasser would be followed by a motley crew of undistinguished military men who lacked Nasser's innate concern for social justice and personal dignity, yet proved themselves more than proficient at refining his authoritarian prescriptions into violent and repressive rule, in which the support of the people was neither required nor sought.

The promise of the first Arab awakening, so ebullient in its early years, had withered by the end of the 1960s. The decline began when Nasser decided to sacrifice democracy at the altar of other purportedly more immediate and critical political goals. And it is at that historical juncture when "freedom" disappeared from Arab political vocabulary that, in Hannah Arendt's eloquent words, the story of the revolution lost its basic plot.[22]

The less than sterling fate of the first Arab revolutions—the way they allowed for the emergence of despotic rule—would provide a salutary lesson to those who instigated and carried through the second Arab awakening. It was hardly accidental that the uprisings and revolts that characterized the winter of 2011 posited as their primary goals the elimination of the established political orders and the institution of democracy. The men and women who poured onto the streets and squares of Arab cities had learned from the experience of the first Arab awakening; they understood that their revolutions would not be fulfilled without the establishment of democratic institutions. And indeed, in the summer of 2011 and later, the narrative accompanying the revolts was shifting. During the Arab winter of discontent, the primary focus of the revolutionaries was on driving out the despots. By the summer, they had broadened the discussion, in some countries more keenly than others, to include the mechanisms best suited to an effective democratic transition. Even countries that did not experience revolutionary upheavals, but whose leaders could see the writing on the wall, took up the challenge of democratic reforms. Not all arguments were informed, and not all actors were genuine democrats, and there were opposing forces that were still formidable. But the debate over democracy (writing constitutions, forming political parties, designing appropriate electoral systems, etc.) continued to spread and intensify. And the two countries that were leading the way in deliberating the elements of this brave new world were Tunisia and Egypt.

PART TWO

THE SECOND ARAB AWAKENING

December 2010–

Voters standing in line, sometimes for hours, to vote in the elections of Egypt (above) and Tunisia (below). *Mona Sosh; Andrea Calabretta*

Chapter Four

HITTING THE DEMOCRATIC ROAD RUNNING?

Tunisia and Egypt

T here was a compelling unity of purpose and method that epitomized the mass Arab discontent of the winter of 2011. Young men and women arose in almost spontaneous mass eruptions demanding nothing less than an end to the pervasive and stifling authoritarianism that had become the distinguishing feature and political hallmark of their region. Those in power, who by then had very little, if any, legitimacy but possessed an abundance of firepower, responded with varying degrees of violence. As days went on and the cycle of fear, implanted in the hearts of citizens by ubiquitous state security systems, was eroded, others joined in and the protests expanded not just numerically but also across age, religion, and gender. And in all this, the method and purpose of the rebellions changed little: it was the ordinary citizens who went onto the streets and public squares of their cities day after day, defying the state and its coercive institutions, and demanding the dismantling of the authoritarian regime and the initiation of meaningful democratic changes.

While the genesis of the Arab revolutions showed purposeful uniformity across the region, their development over the following months varied substantially. By the time the winter of Arab discontent had extended into the summer and fall of 2011, the fate of the revolts, particularly in terms of democratic attainment, spanned a broad spectrum of possible outcomes: from one pole where free and fair elections were embarked upon, as was the case for Tunisia and Egypt, to the other pole where, as in the case of Bahrain, the rebellion was successfully suppressed. In between, an armed insurrection, supported vigorously by European and American airpower, struggled for months to dislodge the malevolent Muammar Qadhafi and his family from power, not succeeding until well into October. And in Syria and Yemen, civil wars continued beyond 2011. In other countries where indigenous eruptions did not occur, some leaders, most notably in Morocco and to a lesser extent Jordan, promised and acted on political reforms; others such as those in Iraq, promised much and delivered little.

In terms of Hannah Arendt's insistence that a true revolution can only be measured by the democratic changes it brings about, the second half of 2011 and beyond bore witness to only two countries that could be said to have gone some way toward satisfying Arendt's requirement. Tunisia and Egypt were the first two countries to go through the convulsions of mass protests, the first two countries to discard their respective despots, and the first two countries to carve a path toward free and fair elections. Of course, there is more to democracy than just elections—civil liberties, guaranteeing of human rights, including minority rights, primacy of the law, freedoms of expression and association are all constituent elements of democratic life. But holding fair and free elections was indeed a pivotal and transformative event in a region where for many decades the term "electoral transparency" was an object of derision among contemptuous despots.

In Tunisia, once Ben Ali's political order was torn asunder, and the thrill of empowerment began to subside, a national debate ensued that centered on which should come first, presidential or parliamentary elections. But it was quickly resolved that the last thing the country needed, particularly a country like Tunisia whose modern history had been dominated by powerful presidents, was to elect a president before other democratic institutions were put in place. The various political forces also agreed that the writing of a new constitutional document in which the rights of citizens would be enshrined was the country's first priority. But to ensure that the constitution would be written by democrats, an election was needed. An interim government, made up of respected independent and opposition figures, immediately scheduled an election, to be held on July 24, 2011, for a constituent assembly which would be tasked to write a constitution for the post–Ben Ali Tunisia, and to form a government that would govern until general elections were held one year later. To prepare for the elections, the interim government passed a law creating an independent electoral commission. And in a move that won wide support, it nullified a Ben Ali ban on Tunisia's main Islamist party, *Ennahdha* (the Renaissance).

Initially, the electoral commission, made up of fourteen jurists and activists, made optimistic noises about getting the country ready for a July 24 poll. But very quickly the enormity of preparing for fair and free elections in a country that had not had real elections for over half a century began to overwhelm the members of the commission. In May, the head of the commission admitted the impossibility of the task, and asked for the election date to be postponed till late October, explaining that a massive number of identity cards still had to be renewed, as many addresses had to be checked, and an accurate register of eligible voters had to be certified. The commission was also far behind in its preparation of electoral lists because of the profusion of political parties and independent candidates. After heated discussions among members of the interim government and initial opposition from the Ennahdha Party, it was agreed that the elections would be postponed till October 23.

Once the date was set, preparations for the elections began in earnest. The country was divided into twenty-seven electoral districts, plus six districts for Tunisians living abroad. Each district received seats in accordance with its population density, and the total produced 217 seats for the envisaged National Assembly. Seats were allocated using an electoral system called closed party list proportional representation (PLPR), where voters vote for parties rather than individuals, and parties receive seats in proportion to their votes in each district. This system is specifically designed to prevent a single party winning an absolute majority and thereby monopolizing power. Indeed, the system almost always yields coalition governments, ensuring the broadest possible representation. PLPR is also meant to favor small and minority parties. To ensure an equitable representation of women in the assembly, each party was required to have male and female candidates alternating on its list. A campaign to register voters was launched, using 4,000 unemployed university graduates who were dispatched to all twenty-seven districts.[1] By the first week of August, more than half of the estimated 8 million voters had been registered.

The surprise of the pre-election period was the large number of political parties that registered to contest the elections. The electorate was given the over-generous choice of over 110 parties, spanning the entire ideological spectrum from the Communists to the Islamists, with a wide range of political orientations in between. Most of these parties were inconsequential, centered

A Tunisian citizen stands in front of a bewildering number of electoral posters.
Sarah Trister

on one man with a small regional following, and only a few were able to squeeze through with a seat in the October elections. But one party that was not going to have any representation in the new assembly was Ben Ali's Constitutional Democratic Rally (RCD), which had ruled Tunisia throughout the entire period of Ben Ali's dictatorship. A decree not long after the demise of the *ancien régime* barred the RCD, and all individuals associated with it, from political life.

Once it was legalized by the interim government, the Islamist Ennahdha Party immediately assumed the mantle of the front-runner. Banned by Ben Ali, it had operated underground, building a broad network of support across the country, but particularly in impoverished and rural areas. Its clandestine organizational structure, doggedly built in the Ben Ali days, would stand it in good stead as the electoral campaign began. Sure of its support among the poor classes, it concentrated much of its effort trying to lure the secular and liberal middle class. It unveiled a party manifesto that projected a moderate, even modernist, orienta-tion, with goals that hardly anyone could object to—individual freedoms, the rule of law, good governance, and combating cor-ruption[2]—no fear here of radical Islam. But unguarded remarks by some of its members, particularly about rights important to women, such as the personal status law and the issue of polygamy, left many women uneasy, wondering how genuine the party's commitment to liberalism was.[3] Cognizant of possible negative repercussions, the party hierarchy acted quickly and decisively to quash any lingering doubts. During the electoral campaign, Ennahdha's longtime leader, Rachid Ghannouchi, went out of his way to allay the suspicions of secularists and women that Tunisia's progressive laws on marriage, divorce, and inheritance would come under attack with an Ennahdha victory at the polls.[4] To further emphasize the moderation of his party, Ghannouchi would reiterate again and again that he had little admiration for Iran's clerical regime; that the model Ennahdha would want to emulate was that of Turkey's Islamist, yet modernist, ruling party, the Justice and Development Party.

Ghannouchi's assurances would fall on deaf ears when it came to the leaders of the Progressive Democratic Party (PDP), which in the run-up to the elections was considered to be Ennahdha's main secular rival. Running a slick Western-style campaign in its deft use of the media, it utilized its legacy as a vigorous opposi-tion party to the Ben Ali regime and its uncontested progressive credentials to present itself as the most viable secular alternative to the Islamist party. Of all the other parties, the PDP was the one that did not shirk from launching virulent verbal swipes at

Ennahdha. At the forefront of these attacks was Maya Jribi, the secretary general of the party and the first female party head in the country. She would depict Ghannouchi as an Islamist radical cloaking himself in modernist garb to win votes. And for good measure, another leader of the party would promise that once elected, the PDP "would not be lenient" with Ennahdha.[5] The PDP's seeming obsession with the Islamist party would dominate its campaign and in the process overshadow its other concerns. Increasingly during the campaign, the electorate would perceive the PDP as a one-issue party.

Other secularists distanced themselves from PDP's forceful anti-Islamist stand. The Congress for the Republic (CPR), a left-of-center party, declared from the beginning that it had no qualms about entering into a coalition with Ennahdha. Led by a well-known and highly respected human rights advocate, Moncef Marzouki, the party was seen as the main competitor with PDP for the secular, middle-class vote. Preservation of civil liberties was the party's main platform. Marzouki advocated the establishment of legislation that would place Tunisia's laws squarely within the prescriptions of the Universal Declaration of Human Rights. That these goals were articulated and promised by a figure of Marzouki's stature gave the party credence among Tunisia's voters.

Another secular party, which also refrained from attacking the Islamist character of Ennahdha, was *Attakatol* (the Forum), also known as the Democratic Forum for Labor and Freedoms. Yet another left-of-center party whose platform had pronounced pro-labor leanings, it was led by Mustapha Bin Jaafar, a doctor and a veteran opposition figure during the Ben Ali era. The party traditionally had attracted intellectuals and educated urban youth, hence its lively social media platforms, which focused on anti-corruption goals. And to emphasize that this was not just a campaign gimmick, the party leadership displayed their commitment to transparency by publicly disclosing the party's budget, as well as information about its members. In a country reeling from the corruptions of Ben Ali's family and cronies, the Attakatol's message would find great resonance among Tunisia's voters, allowing the party to gain a host of adherents in the weeks before the elections.

One party that was not taken seriously until very late in the campaign was *al-Aridha* (Petition), a synonym for the longer title, Popular Petition for Freedom, Justice and Development. The party was the creation of a Tunisian billionaire, Muhammad Hamdi, who for over twenty-five years had lived in exile in London. Not setting foot in Tunisia, he conducted his entire campaign via his own satellite television station, *al-Mustaqilla* (the Independent). Considered an oddity by the other party leaders, and viewed with suspicion for alleged ties with the Ben Ali regime, Hamdi had one striking advantage: he could point to his roots in the country's impoverished hinterland, whose rough dialect he spoke, thus setting himself apart from the political intelligentsia of the coastal areas from which the leaders of the other parties emanated. He also projected a populist persona combining Islamist values with European social democratic ideals. He promised universal health care, unemployment benefits for each jobless citizen, free transportation for everyone over the age of sixty-five, and "charity boxes" (inspired by the Quran and the teaching of the Prophet Muhammad) for those treated unjustly. To finance this wideranging program he would tax the rich, and for good measure he promised to inject 2 billion dinars (about 1 billion euros) of his own money into the state budget.[6] The other parties derided Hamdi's proposals, insisting that the numbers simply did not add up; but as electoral results would later show, Hamdi's message of social justice resonated with many of Tunisia's poor and unemployed, regardless of the questionable efficacy and lack of precision of its details.

The electoral commission had scheduled an electoral campaign of three weeks beginning on October 1 and ending on October 21, 2011, two days before the elections. The Tunisian electorate had to contend with some 11,000 candidates, distributed among 1,428 lists, 787 of them party lists, 587 independent lists, and 54 alliance lists. Long lines of voters formed early on, some stretching for hundreds of yards, but there was hardly a murmur of protest. On the contrary, there was a sense of wonderment, almost disbelief, among the voters at the activity they were undertaking. So overjoyed was one female voter that she was literally "shaking when marking her ballot." Another male voter was equally jubilant; he compared the elections to the other much-yearned-for aspiration of many young Tunisians. "I cannot describe my joy today," he said. "It's as if I just . . . obtained a visa for Europe." Then, demonstrating his political savvy, he added: "I am pleased with the large number of parties because this prevents one party from monopolizing power in the future."[7] This festive atmosphere was attested to not only by the thousands of independent local monitors but also by foreign observers from a host of democracy and human rights groups, who spread throughout the country to ensure the impartiality and transparency of the elections. One American monitor said that the process showed that "an Arab country can administer an election that's well run, that gives people an opportunity to choose their own destiny. [The election] was an enormous victory for the Tunisian people."[8] By the end of the day, over 4 million citizens had turned up to vote, some 90 percent of registered voters, but only about 52 percent of eligible voters. And these voters would produce results that had not been predicted by pundits or by polls taken during the campaign.

While Ennahdha's victory was predicted, for, after all, it had assumed the status of odds-on favorite from the very beginning, what surprised many analysts was the magnitude of the victory. In the pre-election survey polls, the Islamist party was expected to get around a quarter of the total votes, putting it ahead of its nearest rival, the PDP, by 8 to 9 percentage points. But when it came down to the one poll that really mattered, almost 35 percent of voters opted for Ennahdha, giving it 89 of the 217 assembly seats. Indeed, it received more votes than the combined votes of all the other parties who won assembly seats. The other party that received surprisingly good news was al-Aridha. Dismissed by other parties as an oddity, it garnered the third largest vote, giving it twenty-six assembly seats. In many ways, al-Aridha's impressive performance showed the power of television, as the party's leader, Muhammad Hamdi, had not even bothered to be physically present in Tunisia; instead, he campaigned exclusively from London via his satellite television channel, making sure to be interviewed by sympathetic questioners, and in the process making outrageous promises to the poor and unemployed of Tunisia's hinterland. The third surprise was the abysmal showing of the leading liberal party, the Progressive Democratic Party, which had been predicted to place second with about 16 percent of the vote. It ended up with some 2.5 percent of the total votes cast. It is not clear why it did so badly: it may have been punished for its vigorous and incessant attacks on Ennahdha; it may have been the main victim of the country's move away from liberal secularism, and if that was the case, the PDP hardly could have been helped by having a woman at its helm, and a politically hard-hitting one at that.

The PDP's dismal performance at the polls, in addition to its publicly antagonistic stance toward al-Ennahdha, meant that it would take no part in the formation of government after the conclusion of the elections. Rather than be an insignificant member of a coalition government, the PDP could in fact revive its political fortunes by putting up a strong opposition platform within the assembly, and so PDP leaders put their energy into creating and leading a viable opposition within the assembly. Invoking the memory of Tunisia's first assembly, which was dominated by Habib Bourguiba's Neo-Destour Party, a PDP leader commented, "We want to avoid the 1956 scenario when the constituent assembly had no opposition. It excluded political pluralism and promoted a unilateral system, and thus led to dictatorship."[9] Indeed, three months after the elections, the PDP announced that it was merging with other parties to create one unified party that would present a more coherent opposition in the assembly. Party leaders also expressed the hope that this new incarnation would be "strong enough to win the upcoming electoral battle."[10] By the end of March 2012, three secular parties had merged under the umbrella of the PDP, while another three formed their own coalition, calling it the Social Democratic Party. Although they talked enthusiastically of their prospects for the next election, in reality they would have a long way to go, given their unexceptional performance in the October 2011 election.

At the other end of the spectrum, the victorious parties went about the business of preparing for governance. Immediately after the elections, leaders in Ennahdha embarked on talks with the Congress for the Republic (CPR) and Attakatol, the two secular parties who between them had mustered forty-nine assembly seats, and who during the campaign had refrained from the kind of unbridled attacks on Ennahdha which PDP had waged. The negotiations went smoothly until Ennahdha's designated prime minister, Hamadi Jebali, seemingly riding an Islamist high, promised in a speech to the party faithful that, "God willing," the party now would seize the chance to "institute the sixth caliphate"[11]—an unfortunate choice of words, no doubt delivered in a moment of exuberance, that evoked the pristine seventh-century idea of an Islamic state. But the storm soon passed with appropriate Ennahdha assurances, and agreement among the leaders of the three parties was reached that confirmed Ennahdha's Jebali as prime minister, Moncef Marzouki, head of CPR, as president, and Mustapha Bin Jaafar, the leader of Attakatol, as speaker of the assembly. On December 23, 2011, the People's Assembly approved a forty-one-member cabinet, with the key ministerial posts going to Ennahdha, including the portfolio of Foreign Affairs, which went to Ghannouchi's son-in-law.

Women did not fare particularly well in the distribution of governmental portfolios. Only three of the cabinet positions were occupied by women, those of women's affairs and the environment at the ministerial level, and at the deputy minister level, that of investment and international cooperation. Given that forty-nine women were elected to the People's Assembly, constituting about 23 percent of assembly seats, women would have expected a fairer gender balance in the cabinet. Indeed, even the female representation in the assembly came as something of a disappointment. Party lists by law had to alternate between men and women, ideally ensuring equal representation in the assembly. But because most of the party lists were headed by a male, and there were a number of parties that ended up with one seat, or received an odd number of seats, the figure for women in the assembly shrunk to forty-nine. Still, given that in the United States, one of the world's oldest and most distinguished democracies, women occupy a mere 17 percent of congressional House and Senate seats, the perceptibly higher percentage in Tunisia's first democratically elected assembly is not an altogether inauspicious political beginning for women.

If one factor characterized the new era in Tunisia, it was the heavy political presence of Ennahdha. The party would have to contest another election, this time a general election, in 2013. To fare as well as, or to improve on, its performance in October 2011, it was expected to use the intervening period to confront a myriad of thorny challenges: bring stability to the country, manage a disparate coalition, supervise the writing of a constitution that would satisfy the polar ideological proclivities of secularists and Islamists, make a perceptible dent in the corruption malaise that had been culturally embedded through decades of Ben Ali rule, steer away from Islamic radicalism while keeping true to its Islamist identity, and fulfill its economic campaign promises.

None of this would be an easy task. Party leaders suggested that their victory in October 2011 owed less to religion than to people's belief that the party would be a pragmatic and scrupulous manager of the economy.[12] In their first few months in power, Ennahdha's parliamentarians advocated shifting the balance of economic resources from the privileged coastal areas, to the country's neglected heartland. They proposed an 80–20 distribution in favor of the non-coastal areas which constituted an exact reversal of the distribution balance that had existed under Ben Ali.[13] Still, for a country lacking in resources, the economy would be a herculean challenge for the Islamist party. In its election manifesto, Ennahdha promised to create jobs, reduce inflation, increase investment, and push annual economic growth from its anemic 0.2 percent in 2011 to 7 percent within five years[14]—an ambitious plan whose promises would not go unheeded by the hordes of the unemployed and dispossessed.

Another significant challenge to Ennahdha would come from its own ideological backyard—from Islamist radicals, increasingly headed by the fundamentalist Salafists, who would test the limit of Ennahdha's publicly articulated moderate brand of Islam. Very soon after the elections, Salafists organized demonstrations in a number of university campuses demanding segregated classes and the right of women to wear the *niqab* (full face veil), with academic deans even receiving death threats if they did not comply with the group's demands. Thousands of Salafists led protest marches against the screening of *Persepolis*, an Oscar-nominated Iranian movie. The animated motion picture contained a scene showing a character representing God, which to Muslim puritans is considered a sacrilege. When in May 2012 the government approved the formation of a Salafist party called the Reform Front, it was hoped that Salafist concerns and demands would be channeled through the party and not the street. But a month later the Salafists, protesting against an art exhibit that they deemed to be insulting to Islam, led widespread riots that left one dead and over a hundred people injured.

In essence, the protests were an attack on symbols of secularism in Tunisia. Ennahdha's response to this initial probing by the radicals in its midst was measured, cautioning that suppressed groups needed time to learn to set boundaries regarding personal freedoms.[15] Indeed, Ghannouchi defended the Salafists' right in a democracy to dress and behave as they pleased. Such utterances, while in no way anti-democratic, would simply intensify the secularists' suspicion that deep down Ennahdha and the Salafists are one and the same. And those reservations would percolate to Ennahdha's own coalition partners. Muhammad Bennour, an official from the Attakatol Party, confided to an American journalist that the governing coalition was "a marriage of necessity," which had enjoyed "no honeymoon," and added that he had refused a request from Ghannouchi to make a joint public appearance. "No," he had told the Islamist leader, "you defend the niqab and I defend the mini-skirt."[16] Increasingly, Ennahdha found itself in an untenable position, being pulled on the right by the radical co-religionists and on the left by its secular coalition partners.

In no other issue was this ideational tug-of-war more manifest than the question of what role al-Sharia, Islam's holy law, would play in shaping the country's new constitution. Islamist voices, not just from the Salafists but also from Ennahdha's rank and file, demanded that the Constituent Assembly in its writing of the constitution should make al-Sharia the main source of legislation. Secularists on the other hand wanted no mention of the Islamic law in the constitution. Three months into the assembly's deliberations, the issue was still not resolved, and was delaying work on other constitutional articles. Finally, on March 25, 2012, Ennahdha took the issue of al-Sharia off the table. It agreed to keep the first article of the country's 1959 constitution, which stated that the country's "religion is Islam, its language is Arabic and its regime is a republic." An Ennahdha spokesman explained that the party decided not to insist on an issue which so obviously divided Tunisians. It was enough to "recognize Tunisia as an Arab-Muslim state."[17] The first lesson of democracy, the pragmatic willingness to compromise even on issues of belief for the sake of moving the political process forward, seemed to have been learned by the first Islamist party to assume the reins of power in an Arab state.

The distinction of being first would always remain with Ennahdha. But in the summer and fall of 2011, Egyptian Islamists were also strong and favored to do well in the coming elections later in the year. There was, however, one glaring difference between the Tunisian and Egyptian cases. Unlike the Tunisian experience, the Egyptian Islamic parties had to deal with a powerful defense establishment that, in the wake of Mubarak's ouster, had appropriated for itself all presidential powers.

The military had won the support of the thousands of demonstrators in Cairo's Tahrir Square by refusing to use violence to suppress the uprising, which was a pivotal factor in Mubarak's speedy exit. With Mubarak's fall, the military, supported by the young men and women who had led the revolt, stepped in to fill the political void. Promising to lead Egypt through a peaceful and orderly transition to democracy, the army's top brass formed themselves into a twenty-four-member committee which they named the Supreme Council of the Armed Forces (SCAF), under the chairmanship of Field Marshal Muhammad Husayn Tantawi, who for over two decades had occupied the critical position of defense minister under Mubarak.

It would take less than three months for relations between SCAF and the youthful revolutionaries to sour. After a short period when Tahrir Square had been abandoned after the fall of Mubarak, people started to pour back in again as SCAF, in the name of maintaining stability, began to behave in a fashion not that dissimilar from the days of the ousted dictator. And even though it had appointed a civilian government, SCAF more often than not acted arbitrarily, betraying an entrenched authoritarian impulse.

Street violence began in the early summer of 2011, as SCAF seemed to drag its feet in bringing to trial members of the security forces responsible for the death of some 850 demonstrators during the February revolution. When demonstrators went onto the streets demanding that the killers be prosecuted, SCAF responded with the kind of high-handed ruthlessness reminiscent of the Mubarak days. By July, over 7,000 civilians had been arrested and quickly tried in military courts, put in prison, then subjected to coercive and humiliating treatment, including virginity tests for female demonstrators—all this while the hoodlums in the pay of the Mubarak regime, who were responsible for beating up, and in a number of cases killing, demonstrators before the fall of the regime, were generally left untouched. Indeed, the term *baltajiyya*, which was used to describe these goons, was now utilized by SCAF to characterize the young demonstrators. Using the same terminology, so pervasive in the Mubarak era, SCAF began to refer to the protestors as "subversives" and "foreign infiltrators," who were not the same revolutionaries who led the uprising against Mubarak. Yet an assortment of thugs who were unleashed by SCAF's security forces to attack peaceful protestors were portrayed by SCAF as patriotic elements trying to defend Egypt's stability. These hoodlums would be characterized by no less a figure than the head of SCAF, Field Marshal Tantawi, as representing "the people of Egypt." By the end of the summer, to the young protestors, the rule of the military felt no different from Mubarak's rule, prompting one human rights activist to declare, very much in Hannah Arendt's formulation, that the revolution was not over. Rather than ushering in democracy, the uprising seemed to have brought another dictatorship. In fact, by the end of September, less than two months before the elections, the number of civilians in detentions and prisons had swelled to more than 12,000, and the much hated emergency law, in place for over three decades, had yet to be revoked.

Another reason for the displeasure of the protestors was the way SCAF dealt with the issue of a new constitution for Egypt.

Initially, the protestors actively supported the military's decision to suspend the constitution that had legitimized some of the most egregious excesses of the Mubarak regime. SCAF then appointed a committee of jurists, whose task was to focus on amending constitutional articles that had made a mockery of the electoral process. Working with some dispatch, the judges came up with a new constitutional document that included eight amended articles. These amendments were put to a referendum in March 2011 and passed overwhelmingly. Yet, not long after, SCAF decided to simply shelve the amended document, and instead came up with its own "interim constitution," which included, in addition to the referendum-approved amendments, fifty-five other articles that were never put to a vote. It is not clear what exactly prompted the military leaders to exhibit such seemingly carefree indifference to the will of the Egyptian people, but specialists who examined the new document found that the mechanisms for limiting presidential powers had been watered down.[18] This was hardly accidental, given that SCAF had appropriated for itself the powers of the presidency.

And this was not the end of SCAF's cavalier attitude to constitutional matters or to people's publicly expressed preferences. One of the amendments voted on in the referendum stipulated that after the general elections, the new parliament would select a hundred-member committee from within its ranks to write a new permanent constitution and put it to a vote. This was a position strongly supported by SCAF at the time of the referendum in March 2011. By early November, perhaps because of increasing fears of an electoral victory for the Islamists later in the month, SCAF changed its tune. The generals suddenly advocated the introduction of a set of supraconstitutional principles designed to constrain future drafters. Included in these principles were provisos shielding the budget of Egypt's defense establishment from parliamentary oversight and giving the military hierarchy veto power over any legislation affecting the country's armed forces.[19] The proposals also suggested that the generals might pick eighty of the one hundred members of the envisaged "parliamentary" committee tasked with writing the new constitution.[20] A high-ranking member of SCAF explained that a free and fair election might not end up "representing all sectors of society."[21] Needless to say, the Islamists—the group at which SCAF's statement was obviously directed—quickly came up with a response that was strong in its condemnation, but also tried to assure the military and the Egyptian people in general that in the eventuality of their winning the election, they would be inclusive in their policies:

> No entity has the right to expropriate the will of the people and its legislative assembly by promulgating laws that will continue to be enforced after the new parliament is sitting. The constitution is the highest law of the land and it will not only affect this generation but generations to come. This constitution, therefore, must be drawn up by a body elected by parliament, on the condition that it represents all sectors of society so that the constitution it produces is consensual.[22]

It was not only the Islamists but broad sectors of society who condemned SCAF's proposal as an arbitrary and unconstitutional gambit by the military. Harsh denunciations came from secular and liberal groups, who, while fearful of potential Islamist dominance of the political process, saw this maneuver by the army as simply a ploy to ensure its continued control of political power. The intense admiration for the army and trust in its leaders that pervaded the ranks of the youthful demonstrators in the heady days of the February 2011 revolution had all but evaporated by the end of the year. Tahrir Square would be filled, yet again, by angry young demonstrators, this time demanding an end to the suffocating dominance by the army generals over the political process.

People were further infuriated when the military announced an electoral timeline which pushed the presidential elections to the end of 2012 or even to 2013, and then declared that not until then would SCAF hand over power to civilian rule. The statement triggered immediate protests and a new occupation of Tahrir Square, with the unifying demand that Tantawi and SCAF immediately pack their bags and leave the political theater. In the following weeks, intermittent clashes between security forces and protestors failed to dislodge the occupiers from the square. But as parliamentary elections, scheduled for November 28, loomed, SCAF resolved to make a decisive move. On November 19, military and riot police attacked the demonstrators with deadly intent, at times shooting into the crowd. As casualties mounted, tens of thousands of Egyptians descended onto the square in numbers reminiscent of Mubarak's last days. News of the murderous clashes spread throughout Egypt and angry protests erupted in a number of other Egyptian cities. Over three days of bloody confrontation, some 40 protestors were killed and no less than 3,500 were injured.[23] With international pressure mounting and stinging condemnations coming from Egypt's erstwhile supporters, including the United States, the civilian government that was put in place by the military resigned en masse, leaving SCAF with no mechanisms for the implementation of policies. With his options dwindling rapidly, Marshal Tantawi moved quickly to put the lid on the gathering crisis. On November 22, six days before the parliamentary elections, he made a televised speech to the country in which he expressed his condolences for those who died in the security crackdown, and in a pointed effort to address the demands of the protestors, he set June 2012 as the final deadline for holding presidential elections. While disturbances and demonstrations continued well into December and January, the setting of a clear deadline for the election of a civilian president— at least six months earlier than SCAF's original intention—did take the edge off the incendiary situation, allowing for popular fury to subside enough for parliamentary elections to be held on November 28 in a surprisingly orderly and peaceful fashion.

While the turmoil did wring concessions from SCAF, it led to a split within the ranks of the movement that had brought down Mubarak in February. The young activists who began and essentially led the anti-Mubarak forces were not fully satisfied with Tantawi's concessions, and wanted the protest to continue and expand. But the Islamists who, with their numbers and organizational skills, had solidified the revolution when they joined the uprising against Mubarak, becoming a pivotal element in its eventual success, were lukewarm toward the anti-SCAF protestors. This hardly endeared the Islamists to the revolutionaries, who had not forgotten the belated appearance of the Islamists on the revolutionary scene back in February.

The Islamists, with their eyes on a potential electoral victory, suspected that the secular youth movement, lacking any country- wide organizational structure, wanted to keep the protests going in order to delay the parliamentary elections. One Islamist put it bluntly: "Secular forces have been protesting in order to take power without the need for elections, their main goal being to exclude the Islamists."[24] Accordingly, Islamist groups declined to join the occupation of Tahrir Square. This was not a political ploy, they insisted, but a moral position. Putting the issue of morality aside, however, there can be little doubt that while the young and secular leaders of the anti-Mubarak revolution went on demonstrating and protesting and in the process extracting meaningful concessions from the generals, the Islamist parties were quietly building on decades of countrywide organizational expertise and long-standing networks of personal connections and relationships, with only one goal in mind: winning the elections.

The preparations for the elections began early on in the transition process when a Higher Electoral Commission was formed to come up with proposals for an electoral system that would be fair, yet workable. The process took months and more often than not lacked transparency, mainly because of SCAF's penchant for absolute control. Leaks and rumors proliferated and cries of foul filled the political space in late spring and early summer. Finally, in July, SCAF announced that half the parliamentary seats would be decided via a party list proportional representation (PLPR), which was the system that had been adopted by Tunisia, and the other half by individual candidacy. A howl of protest met this announcement. Many felt that individual candidacy would work against the new political forces, who individually were still relatively unknown to the wider public. On the other hand, politicians from the past, whose faces were familiar to people, would benefit. Indeed, even if the National Democratic Party (NDP), Mubarak's party, were to be banned from participating in the elections (debate over the party's fate was raging at that time in Egypt), NDP members with an established presence in rural areas would still be able to get into parliament through the back door of individual candidacy. A month of fierce argument ensued until, on August 18, the system was modified with two thirds of the seats decided by PLPR and the remaining third by individual candidacy.

The electoral system would apply to parliament's two chambers: the lower house, the People's Assembly, and the much less significant upper house, the Shura (consultative) Council. The People's Assembly would consist of 508 members, of which 498 seats would be decided by votes and 10 occupied by appointees. The Shura Council would have 270 members, with two thirds elected and one third appointed. Given the large number of eligible voters (about 50 million), and the limited resources available to the electoral commission, it was decided to have the elections staggered through three stages for the People's Assembly and two for the Shura Council. Voting for the People's Assembly spanned the period, November 28–January 11, and for the Shura Council, January 29–February 15.

Around fifty parties were licensed between May and September 2011, and some of them formed coalitions; others entered into alliances.[25] From the very beginning, the party to beat was the Freedom and Justice Party (FJP), the political wing of the mainstream Muslim Brotherhood organization, which for over eighty years had been a major political and social force in Egypt, even though it had been constantly harassed and outlawed by successive Egyptian governments. It was a foregone conclusion that its platform would be closely scrutinized not just within Egypt but also abroad. Cognizant of this, and in order to allay the fears of secularists, liberals, and democrats, the FJP campaigned on a variety of moderate, middle-of-the-road issues. The party emphasized its commitment to the concept of a "civil state," with al-Sharia (religious law) being simply a platform for guidance. In fact, in its exposition of Egypt's form of government, the FJP platform differed little from those of secular parties. And while it advocated social justice issues, it placed these within an economic framework that was quintessentially capitalist. It clearly supported private ownership and the free market economy. Indeed, it had no qualms about the principles of the liberal economic policies pursued in the Mubarak era, just about their implementation, which had been marred by corruption and nepotism. But FJP's position on women was not so clear-cut. Although it supported the right of women to participate in public life and to voice their opinions, it was rather mum on women's role in leadership positions—not surprising for a party that had no female leaders. Still, taken as a whole, the FJP's campaign platform was in many aspects not very far from that of Tunisia's Ennahdha Party.

One glaring difference between Egypt and Tunisia was the existence in Egypt of Islamist parties belonging to the radical Salafist creed. The party with the largest following was *al-Nour* (the Light) Party, which was established a few months after the ouster of Mubarak, receiving its license in June 2011. The formation of the party was the object of much controversy, as the Salafists had originally decreed that elections and Western democracy were forbidden by Islamic strictures. But after Mubarak's ouster, the Salafists proved more than adept at allowing political opportunities to trump seemingly unyielding moral beliefs. Changing their tune, they now argued that they had to enter the political fray to make sure that Egypt's Islamic identity would not be compromised. Indeed, their platform did betray a greater religious content than the FJP. They advocated the implementation of al-Sharia law, albeit slowly and gradually. Being literalists, the Salafists time and time again betrayed in their pronouncements the inflexible nature of religious dogma. Thus, they would consider art in any form, whether painting, sculpture, music, or dance, as sinful. That created problems for al-Nour leaders during the electoral campaign. "The tourists want to see statues, and that generates revenue for the country," admitted an al-Nour spokesman, then lamented, "but the statues are forbidden in

Islam." So how would he resolve this thorny problem? "I would suggest covering them with wax masks," was the triumphant answer.[26] And while supporting tourism (since it is responsible for about 30 percent of Egypt's national budget), another spokesman for al-Nour seemed uncertain what to do about bikini-clad tourists on Egyptian beaches. Flustered by a question in a television interview, a representative of the hard-line Islamist party declared, "The bikini issue is no big deal. The tourism industry in Egypt needs drastic changes that we should be more concerned about. It's like manufacturing a vehicle; you work on the important things, then you go to the minor details, like the brakes."[27] Obviously, imposing a strict dress code on female tourists was as trivial a matter as the brakes on a car! The dissonance regarding women's dress was natural, given that Salafists enjoin women to wear the forbidding *niqab*—with its narrow slit in front of the eyes, allowed presumably to help the women avoid crashing into potholes. All in all, the Salafists, who seemed to believe that the persistent chanting of *al-Islam huwal hal* ("Islam is the solution") was the remedy for solving all of the world's problems, were not thought of as major contenders.

Ranged against the Islamists were a large number of secular and liberal parties, a few of them of long standing, but the majority had sprung up after the ouster of Mubarak. Some of these parties decided to go it alone, while others entered into loose coalitions. But in stark contrast to the Islamist parties, almost all of the secular parties did not have established networks for organizing and mobilizing public support. The exception here was the Wafd Party. Established in the 1920s, the Wafd is still remembered as the party that wrested independence for Egypt from the British. That pedigree alone would allow it to survive even after President Nasser dismantled it and denigrated it as the party of privilege. In recent times, the Wafd had been wracked by internal dissentions, lack of clear purpose, and a penchant for political opportunism. And that would be reflected in its 2011 campaign platform, which tried to be all things to all people: it advocated strengthening the free market economy and it promised to enhance the state-controlled public sector; it extolled Egyptian nationalism and championed the cause of Arab unity; it declared the party's commitment to secularism, yet entered an alliance with the Islamists (from which it later withdrew). In spite of all this, the Wafd remained the secular party with the largest support base.

Other smaller parties recognized early on that only through coalition building would they stand a chance of winning parliamentary seats. As a rule, these coalitions were hastily built around the one overriding purpose of halting the Islamist march, and that rationale, at least temporarily, seemed able to override glaring differences in political beliefs. One such entity was the Egyptian Bloc, which was formed out of more than twenty anti-Islamist parties, with varying ideologies and political programs, but with a shared commitment to defending Egypt's secularist status. For a while that goal seemed to hold the disparate groups together, but defections would occur throughout the pre-election period, primarily by leftist parties that found it impossible to coexist with the fiercely free market party of billionaire Neguib Sawiris. More defections would occur after allegations surfaced that the bloc's leadership put the names of a number of ex-NDP members on the coalition's electoral list. By the time of the November vote, the bloc would consist of three parties only: two parties of social democratic proclivities and Sawiris's party. Making sense of this somewhat uncomfortable coexistence, the bloc advocated strong liberal economic and democratic policies tinged with elements of social justice aimed at bridging the chasm between rich and poor.[28] The bloc became the party of choice for the Christian Coptic community, which makes up about 10 percent of Egypt's population. Sawiris, a Copt himself, spent much time and energy expounding on the myriad of activities that allegedly would be banned by dour Islamists bent on banishing all of life's pleasures. "I am quite fanatic about my scotch in the evening, so I don't like anybody telling me that I can't drink,"[29] Sawiris told a television reporter, who, along with the viewers, must have wondered about the man's political priorities.

A number of those parties which defected from the Egyptian Bloc founded the Revolution Continues Alliance (RCA). The most interesting feature of the alliance is that its list contained over a hundred young Islamists who had defected from the FJP. This new alliance also featured a number of the thirty-something crowd that were at the forefront of the anti-Mubarak revolution. Other members of the RCA were older men and women with no unified political orientation. In its campaign, the RCA acknowledged this smorgasbord of liberal, socialist, and Islamist mix, but presented it as a strength, since according to its leaders the group would not be limited to a narrow ideological position, but would be open to a broader range of ideas and policies.

The RCA was the only serious entity contesting the elections that had even a whiff of youthful representation, and many pundits awaited its performance in the elections to gauge the popularity and political influence of the young leaders of the revolution. The truth, however, was that overall the elections were distinguished for the surprising invisibility of those who led the uprising. The revolutionaries seemed to prefer to stick to the sites of their greatest triumph—the streets, the public squares, and the television studios. Over time this would create in the minds of the public an image of the revolutionaries as an elitist group that had neither connections with ordinary people nor a strategy for moving beyond protests and demonstrations. And when they at last decided in late September to contest the elections, it was a case of too little too late. As one commentator put it, "the youth groups [did] not have the money or the organizational ability or the keys to electoral constituencies that would allow them to reach [the electoral success] that truly reflects the major role they played in Egypt's revolution."[30] The young leaders finally recognized that the street was not the only path toward achieving the goals of the revolution, but too late to challenge the Islamist parties, who for months had been organizing and planning for an electoral victory.

One of the major controversies that dominated the run-up to the elections was the apparent ability of former NDP members to register as parliamentary candidates by forming new parties or running as independents. The youth movement that spearheaded the revolution, backed vociferously by the Islamist parties, insistently demanded a legal ban on NDP members, and the civilian government that had been appointed by the generals kept promising that a law was being prepared. When that did not materialize, the opposition suspected the dark machinations of the military, who after all had worked hand-in-hand with the NDP for many years under Mubarak. In the meantime, former NDP members swarmed the first week of registration as independents, and others formed no less than six new parties to contest the upcoming elections. They pinned their hopes particularly on the agricultural areas of the Nile Delta and Upper Egypt, where they had years of institutional presence. Less than three weeks before the elections, however, a lower court in the Delta city of Mansoura issued a ruling that banned former NDP members from contesting the elections. The ruling set off a string of lawsuits from NDP members and from the opposition. A few days later, the matter was finally settled when Egypt's Higher Administrative Court decided in favor of the former NDP members, declaring that "depriving anyone of taking up their political rights is an attack on the rights that are protected and guaranteed in the constitution."[31] The ruling was met with great jubilation among members of the *ancien régime*, who believed that years of influence in rural Egypt, among a less politically savvy electorate, would net them considerable electoral gains. But like everyone else, they underestimated the power of the Islamists, who had just as long standing a presence in these areas, but one that was more socially activist and untainted by association with Mubarak.

During the campaign month of November, Cairo was a city of two tales. The first was of the continued daily demonstrations in Tahrir Square against the military, which on a number of occasions erupted in ferocious confrontations and gratuitous violence. The other narrative, to be found in other parts of the city and around the country, was one of festive, almost celebratory political campaigning. Colorful placards plastered the walls of buildings, thousands of volunteers and supporters distributed pamphlets, and candidates rode on top of cars and pickups that incessantly honked their horns. Images of candidates told their own stories—the Muslim Brothers' dark spot on the forehead which comes from years of prostrating during prayer, the long and bushy beards of the Salafists, the carefree Western look of representatives of the youth movement, and the total absence of pictures of women in the Salafist campaign posters.

Because of widespread illiteracy, the election authorities assigned each party and candidate a pictorial symbol, which given the large number of candidates made November a bumper month for resourceful, at times bizarre, branding—a chair, a blender, basketball hoops, tobacco pipe, high-speed train, a tank, even an intercontinental ballistic missile. As the BBC correspondent wryly commented, "you wonder what plans the candidate represented by a screwdriver has for the electorate."[32] In the end, violence in Tahrir Square would have no impact on the timing or conduct of the November 28 elections. The first of the three-stage electoral process, the elections in Cairo and eight other governorates, would go by peacefully, and so would the others. When the third and last stage was finished on January 11, 2012, local civil society monitors and international observers attested to the fairness of the process and the competence of those in charge of it.

Twenty-seven million of the 50 million or so eligible voters ended up casting their votes. They named the party of their choice from a large array of political parties and alliances in the party list proportional representation segment of the elections, which determined two thirds of the assembly seats. They then voted for the remaining one third of the seats in the first past the post (FPTP) individual candidacy part of the elections. The combined results of the three stages confirmed the supremacy of the alliance that was led by the FJP: it received 37.5 percent of the vote and a total of 235 of the 498 electoral seats. Of those, 213 seats went to the FJP. Coming second were the Salafists, who were supported by 28 percent of the electorate, which netted them 123 parliamentary seats, of which 107 went to al-Nour Party. This indeed was an earthquake of a political event, not only because of the weight and status of Egypt in the Arab world but also because of the magnitude of the Islamist victory. Pundits and observers who had been more than a little surprised by Ennahdha's impressive garnering of 35 percent of the vote in Tunisia were now left speechless by the Islamist performance in Egypt.

The real surprise of the elections was the performance of the Salafists. Consistently disregarded as lacking in sophistication and carrying an agenda that was too extreme for the easygoing Egyptians, their percentage of the vote was expected not to exceed 10 points. The other surprise was the shellacking dealt to representatives of the youth movement. The Revolution Continues Alliance, under whose umbrella most of the young leaders of the revolution ran, ended up with less than 3 percent of the vote and a correspondingly measly eight parliamentary seats. Along with the few who did not join an alliance, the final tally of parliamentarians who belonged to the youth movement remained in the single digits. Field Marshal Tantawi, the head of SCAF, appointed the ten remaining members of the assembly, a list that included five Copts and three women.

A month later, the results of the elections for the Shura Council, parliament's consultative upper house, a body with far fewer powers than the People's Assembly, produced an even more emphatic confirmation of the Islamists' political dominance. The FJP ended up with 37.5 percent of the vote, followed by the Salafists' 25 percent, and a bunch of secular parties and groups received the remaining 17 percent. The turnout was abysmally low; only 6.5 million of the 50 million or so eligible voters—a mere 12 percent—bothered to go to the polls, which probably was a reflection of people's estimation of the institution. Still, only one stark conclusion could be derived from both elections: the breadth and depth of support for the Islamists among Egypt's population.

The historic results of the elections ushered in a new political landscape, wonderful yet precarious, for Egyptians to ponder. If the victorious FJP was expected to tread the unchartered territory gingerly, the first few days after the results were announced would show that urgency and activism rather than caution would define the mood of the Muslim Brothers, who had waited for many decades for this moment to arrive, probably never believing that it would. On the day of the assembly's inauguration, FJP spokesmen told reporters that the party already had "a thick legislative agenda." Waiting to be submitted were no less than fifty-one draft bills, which included reform of the internal security apparatus, instituting a maximum and minimum wage, eliminating monopolies, redistributing public subsidies, and easing restrictions on civil society institutions.[33] Seemingly eager to get on with the job, and confident of its dominance in the assembly, the FJP officially nominated its secretary general, Muhammad Saad al-Katatni, for the pivotal position of assembly speaker. A day earlier, Katatni had resigned his party position to emphasize his intended neutrality as speaker of the assembly. He was duly elected to the position by 399 out of 503 votes. And by the time the inaugural session met, two days after the final results were announced, the newly appointed head of the FJP's parliamentary bloc, Hussein Muhammad Ibrahim, announced that his party had already negotiated with other blocs and parties the nominations for the various committees in parliament. Not surprisingly, the chairmanships of a number of important committees, including foreign affairs, national security, budget, and industry, were claimed by FJP; the nominated chairman of the critical constitutional committee was technically not a member of FJP, but he had been a member of the Muslim Brotherhood, and the FJP did back him heavily as an independent candidate in the elections. The Salafists claimed the chairmanships of three committees, including the important education committee.

But these early days also showed signs of possible future

stresses and strains, particularly in the assembly's relations with outside groups and constituencies. Women's rights groups, for instance, were mightily dismayed by the rules of the elections and its results. The new electoral rules eliminated the sixty-four-seat quota for women, which had been introduced by the Mubarak regime in 2010. Instead, each party in the 2011–12 elections was required to include at least one woman in its list of candidates for each constituency. Putting women at the bottom of their lists became the modus operandi for most of the parties, particularly the Islamist ones, with the result that only eight women ended up being elected, giving them a paltry 1.6 percent representation. Even with the appointment of three more women by SCAF, female representation went up to just over 2 percent—a preposterously low figure, particularly when compared with the forty-nine seats won by women in Tunisia, which accounted for 23 percent of the total. A splendid cartoon by Ibtisam Barakat in the online magazine *Jadaliyya* summed up the dismal state of affairs: In front of a road sign that declared: "Welcome to the New Egyptian ParliaMENt," stands a young woman carrying a placard that says: "should be called ParLAMENT."[34]

And the victory of Islamists in the elections would hardly comfort women activists. This is not a general statement on Islamist movements. After all, forty-three of the forty-nine Tunisian female parliamentarians belonged to the Islamist Ennahdha Party. In the Moroccan elections that took place in November 2011, an Islamist party that garnered the largest share of the vote supported an electoral gender quota that allowed sixty women to enter parliament. But Egyptian Islamists were obviously cut from a different cloth. They strongly advocated eliminating the sixty-four-seat gender quota requirements; they made a number of statements that betrayed a strong preference for women's traditional roles, and the Salafists would not even countenance putting the pictures of women candidates on their ad campaigns. It seems that even the female members of FJP were not particularly concerned with the lack of women represented in parliament. Manal Abu al-Hassan, FJP's spokesperson for women's affairs, argued that since her male colleagues in the assembly were avowedly committed to issues of social justice, women should not worry about their lack of representation. These views hardly raised eyebrows as they came from the same person who in a television interview seemed indifferent to police brutality against female demonstrators, putting the blame instead on the women themselves. Women should have stayed at home and protected their honor, she declared, adding that their fathers, brothers, and husbands should be entrusted with marching and protesting on their behalf.[35] Another female parliamentarian belonging to the FJP, Azza al-Garf, attacked the law criminalizing female genital mutilation. She tweeted a number of messages defending such mutilation as sanctioned by Islam.[36] These attitudes could not have come as much of a comfort to those concerned with safeguarding, to say nothing of improving, the political rights of women.

A more immediate concern for the new assembly was its relationship with SCAF, particularly on critical constitutional issues. The assembly expected that with the conclusion of the electoral process, SCAF would cede all legislative powers to the new assembly. But the constitution was ambiguous on this issue. Since SCAF appropriated presidential powers to itself, it maintained its right to veto bills. The question was whether the assembly had the constitutional authority to overturn such vetoes. Opinions differed sharply. FJP members argued that since parliament represented the will of the people, SCAF should no longer interfere in the legislative process. Those close to the military maintained that SCAF had the constitutional right to veto bills of which it did not approve, and that the assembly could not override these vetoes. The question pondered by observers in the early days of the People's Assembly was whether these constitutional ambiguities would lead to confrontations and crises that might result in political immobility at a time when the country could least afford it.

Right on cue the first political crisis occurred very soon after parliament convened. But the crisis was precipitated not by SCAF but by the parliamentarians themselves, when they deadlocked over their most important early assignment—forming a hundred-member Constituent Assembly tasked with writing Egypt's constitution. It was hardly a surprise when the Islamist-dominated parliament produced an assembly with a clear Islamist majority. Within days, some twenty-five liberal and secular members resigned, protesting the dominance of Islamists, and arguing that constitutions should not simply reflect the opinions of the majority but should provide principles that embody national consensus. The stalemate continued as neither group showed much willingness to compromise. Indeed, a number of lawsuits from NGOs and liberal groups were filed with Cairo's Administrative Court asking for the suspension of the assembly on the grounds that it did not represent the diversity of Egypt's society. And in mid-April 2012 the court complied with the request, arguing that minorities, women, and young people were underrepresented. In the meantime, while parliamentarians bickered over the constitution, such other pressing issues as a deteriorating security environment and plummeting economy were simply shelved. Egyptians, even Islamist supporters, were becoming frustrated with the performance of their representatives.

In the midst of this political immobility, however, at least one contentious issue was resolved. Expanding on their earlier decision to hold the presidential elections no later than the end of June 2012, SCAF announced that the elections would be held on May 23–24, and if no absolute winner emerged, a runoff round, involving the top two vote-getters, would be held on June 16–17.

On April 26, Egypt's Supreme Presidential Elections Committee issued a list of thirteen candidates, five of whom quickly established themselves as the front-runners. On the secularist flank were Amr Moussa, former secretary general of the Arab League and longtime Mubarak foreign minister; Hamdeen Sabahi, a disciple of President Nasser with strong socialist inclinations; and Ahmad Shafiq, a retired air force general who, for some thirty days, had served as Mubarak's last prime minister. The other two were Islamists: Abd al-Muneim Abul-Fotouh, an independent moderate Islamist; and Muhammad Mursi, the dour and uncharismatic leader of the FJP. Mursi was a last-minute substitute for the party's first choice, who had been disqualified from running on money-laundering charges.

The three weeks of campaigning saw walls plastered with placards, the candidates crisscrossing the country making speeches, appearing on radio and television talk shows, and even in one instance, involving Moussa and Abul-Fotouh, having a prime-time public debate on television. With the country's mounting economic problems, all of the candidates expended much time and energy promising solutions to Egypt's declining gross domestic product, its increasing debt and diminishing reserves, and its high unemployment rate. While little in the realm of detail was offered, the voters could at least be comforted in knowing that their future president was aware of their economic plight, and would work toward alleviating it.

Similarly, there was consensus among the candidates that a new, more assertive stance toward Israel was needed. Echoing the deep anti-Israeli sentiment of the public at large, the three candidates who had not been associated with Mubarak were shrill in their denunciations of the Jewish state. Sabahi vowed to support whoever resisted Israel; Abul-Fotouh could not bring himself to even mention Israel by name, consistently referring to it as the "Zionist entity"; and Mursi described Israeli citizens as "killers and vampires." Moussa and Shafiq were more restrained, but needing not to be out of step with the public pledged to be always diligent and firm with the Jewish state, which Moussa identified as an "adversary."[37]

Mirroring the parliamentary elections, the real divide separating the three secularist candidates from the two Islamists centered on the issue of religious intrusion into politics. Adding to the intensity of the debate was the Islamists' control of parliament, and thus the likelihood of their dominating the executive as well as the legislative branches of government. For secularists, this was not simply a matter of ideology; they worried about what it would do to Egypt's economically pivotal tourist industry and foreign aid and investment. Needless to say, such an Islamist dominion over government was a particularly alarming prospect for the 8–10 million Christian Copts. The problem for the secularists was that their two leading candidates, Moussa and Shafiq, were remnants of the Mubarak political order. The only non-Islamist candidate, with no ties to Mubarak, was Hamdeen Sabahi, a man with little name recognition compared to the other four.

The two-day election in May was by all accounts free and fair. Mursi ended up with the highest number of votes—24.4 percent of all votes cast, and Mubarak's last premier, Shafiq, came a close second, with 23.3 percent. The result set the scene, etched with irony, for a runoff battle for the presidency between an Islamist and a member of the supposedly defunct Mubarak order.

The battle lines of the campaigns were immediately drawn. Both candidates well knew that they had residual negatives that needed to be addressed and overcome in the three-week campaign period. Mursi needed to allay fears of an Islamist domination of Egypt's politics. He promised to consult and work with the youth movement, women, and Christian Copts. He said he would form a coalition government that would be drawn from all sectors of society, with a non-Islamist prime minister. He even hinted that his vice president might be a Copt, and in any case, Copts would be offered major positions on his presidential staff. He reassured women that no dress code would be imposed on them, and that they had the right to perform any job they wanted.[38] Aware of his most obvious vulnerability, he set out to emphasize an all-inclusive persona.

Shafiq's weakness was his association with the *ancien régime*, having served as Mubarak's last prime minister. But instead of apologizing for this seeming transgression, he in fact would vigorously endorse it, reiterating more than once his admiration for the departed president. Shafiq had sensed a gathering disillusionment among Egyptians with the results of the revolution thus far—political paralysis and parliamentary deadlock with hardly any policies to speak of. Egyptians were becoming less enamored of revolutionaries taking to the streets and clashing with police every time there was something not to their liking. Labeling Egypt's political environment as thoroughly chaotic, Shafiq predicted even greater turmoil under an Islamist president. And he darkly warned that if this came to pass, it would invite a takeover by violent religious extremists. Throughout the three weeks of campaigning he stressed his military background, portraying himself as the strong leader that Egypt needed to impose law and order and to tackle its myriad of economic and political problems.

Following electoral rules, the two candidates stopped campaigning on June 14, two days before the opening of the polls. But these two days of prescribed calm turned out to be anything but. A series of political bombshells would create immense uncertainty about the political process, indeed, even about the fate of democracy in post-Mubarak Egypt. On June 14, the Higher Constitutional Court declared the electoral law unconstitutional, since in the election for the National Assembly, party members had been allowed to contest seats (one third of the total) that were reserved for individual, non-affiliated candidates. SCAF, itching to neutralize the Islamists, jumped on the opportunity and dissolved the entire assembly rather than calling for a partial re-election. Next, SCAF unilaterally issued a constitutional addendum that appropriated for itself all of the assembly's legislative functions, including budget oversight. The Islamists, supported this time by many of those who had triggered Egypt's revolution, cried foul, and thousands descended onto Tahrir Square, venting their anger at the generals.

Against this background of heightened political turbulence, the presidential elections were held as planned on June 16–17. When the announcement of the results was delayed, the country became rife with tales of conspiracies and all kinds of evil doings. Much of the rumor mill centered on the army's preferred candidate, Ahmad Shafiq, stealing the elections. In the end, Muhammad Mursi was declared the winner with a less than impressive 52 percent of the vote, but celebrations did erupt in Tahrir Square, filled as it was with anti-Shafiq Islamists and revolutionaries. But with all the powers that SCAF had appropriated for itself, it was not immediately clear how much power the new president would be able to exercise. The inevitable standoff over the constitutional addendum between the army on the one hand and the people and their freely elected representatives on the other hand symbolized the continuing struggle over the fate of democracy in Egypt's revolution.

The army's muscular intrusion in politics undoubtedly undermined the democratic experiment in post-Mubarak revolutionary Egypt. To their credit, the generals did not interfere in parliamentary or presidential elections, a welcome departure from the Mubarak days. But democracy is a far larger undertaking than mere elections. In their cavalier handling of constitutional prerogatives and in their unilateral pocketing of power, the generals sullied the ideas of freedom and democracy. Like all fair-weather democrats, the generals would accept the people's choice only if it corresponded with the generals' preferences, and as it so happened, the Islamists were not the preferred choice of the men in uniform. This certainly was not the kind of democratic freedom that Hannah Arendt had so passionately defended.

But even setting aside the army's interference in the democratic process, the election of Islamist parties in both Egypt and Tunisia produced widespread concerns among liberal and civil society groups who doubted the Islamists' adherence to the democratic ideal. Thus, the most intriguing aspect of the victory of the Freedom and Justice and al-Nour parties in Egypt, as well as that of Ennahdha in Tunisia, was to see how well, or otherwise, would the Islamists be able or willing to keep burning the torch of democracy that brought them to power—how, if at all, would some of their creed's more rigid beliefs and edicts be reconciled with the requirements of civil, democratic society; how well would they perform in regard to such issues as inclusiveness in terms of religion, gender, and ethnicity, toleration of contrary political views, and respect for the freedom of speech and behavior. Still, with all these uncertainties, it has to be said that the assumption of political power by Islamist parties, which was achieved legally through the ballot box, was without doubt a pivotal event in modern Arab history.

King Hamad is represented as the bullet fired from a Saudi gun that sheds the blood of Bahrainis. *Carlos Latuff*

Chapter Five

POTHOLES (AND SOME CRATERS) ON THE DEMOCRATIC ROAD

Libya, Yemen, and Bahrain

B y the early summer of 2011, the revolutionary upheavals of the winter of Arab discontent had quieted down in Tunisia and Egypt. Mass demonstrations were hardly a thing of the past, yet on the whole they had lost their earlier potency, not least because the quick exit of the countries' dictators had poured cold water on much of the burning passion that fueled the initial revolutionary drive.

But in Libya, the third North African country to experience a mass uprising, there would be no such quick exit. The Libyan despot, Colonel Muammar Qadhafi, was made of sterner stuff. He would not give in to a bunch of rabble-rousers whom he characterized as rats and cockroaches, deserving no other fate than extermination. Unlike Egypt and Tunisia, Libya's tribal society and regional divisions meant that the colonel could back his belligerent words with enough guns and mortar to keep the pests at bay. And the performance of the armed rebels themselves in the winter and spring of 2011 made hardly a dent in Qadhafi's seemingly steely confidence. Disorganized, impetuous, and lacking a command structure, they were easy prey to Qadhafi's more disciplined and infinitely better equipped army. Had NATO not embarked on a regular bombing of Qadhafi's forces, the uprising surely would have failed. By the summer of 2011, the conflict had turned into a bloody stalemate.

Day after day the same scenario repeated itself. The rebels, mounting pickups and driving sedans, armed with machine guns and assault weapons, fortified by revolutionary enthusiasm, and given to repeated shouts of *Allahu Akbar* ("God is great"), would advance onto a village or town in haphazard fashion with no central command or direction. More often than not, they would succeed in pushing government forces back a mile or so, and would sound their horns and delightedly wave their AK-47s in the air with one hand while displaying the victory sign with the other, to more shouts of *Allahu Akbar*. A few hours, or a day or two, later, Qadhafi's forces would initiate a counteroffensive with tanks, artillery, and other heavy weaponry, and the rebels would put up a desperate but losing fight and start retreating, in their flotilla of pickups and sedans, all driving at breakneck speed down the road whence they came, no longer smiling or waving, yet still shouting the praises of the Almighty. Western television cameras, accompanied by bemused reporters, would show this pattern over and over again throughout June and into most of July.

At least the confusion was not replicated on the political level. From early on in the uprising, the revolutionaries established political institutions to parallel the military effort. Shortly after the eastern city of Benghazi erupted in protests and demonstrations signaling the birth of the Libyan revolution in February 2011, a group of disaffected politicians, specialists, and technocrats, some of them teaching and working in the West, got together and created the Transitional National Council (TNC), which for the following months acted as a government-in-waiting, and which by August had been recognized by about thirty countries, including Britain, France, and the United States, as the legitimate Libyan government. The TNC did a commendable job selling the revolution to the outside world, garnering not just political but economic support from key world and Arab governments, lobbying the United Nations Security Council to move against Qadhafi, and trying to maintain a semblance of political and economic normalcy at a time when fighting was raging, casualties were mounting, and cities were being leveled, mainly by Qadhafi's army.

By the end of July, a new pattern to the fighting was emerging. As time went on, government forces were relying more and more on defensive postures, content with merely pushing back the rebels, and embarking less and less on opening new fronts or capturing new territory. It was also evident that their effectiveness was being degraded, with clear signs of incapacity and fatigue; their response was getting slower, more cumbersome and less direct. Their shelling, which at one time was purposeful and disciplined, had become indiscriminate and consequently less efficient. Much as the rebels would tell eager and generally sympathetic reporters that this was their doing, in fact, the beginnings of this seeming reversal of fortunes occurred primarily because of NATO airpower.

By early June, Britain and France, the two main NATO protagonists, had already established uncontested air superiority over Libya, and their bombers and fighter planes were conducting regular sorties against Qadhafi's command and control centers, as well as communications and economic targets, thereby slowly diminishing his strategic capacity to wage an effective and coordinated war effort. An important feature of NATO's strategy was to deny Qadhafi's war machine access to fuel. With his ability to control roads linking Libyan oil fields and refineries to Tripoli, Sirte, and other cities still loyal to him increasingly curtailed by the civil war, Qadhafi needed outside oil. In early June, however, the European Union imposed sanctions on six Libyan ports still held by Colonel Qadhafi. From then on, NATO warships would prevent tankers from unloading fuel to government forces.[1] Moreover, European economic sanctions made it almost impossible for Colonel Qadhafi to sell whatever exportable Libyan oil he could muster, thus denying him badly needed foreign capital to finance his war effort.

On the tactical level, the British and French would begin an extensive use of attack helicopters in their air war against Qadhafi. Jet fighters were effective in hitting strategic targets, but what the rebels desperately needed was a palpable degrading of the weaponry that his army used in local battles with the rebels around the country. In early June, British Apache and French Gazelle helicopters began to target Qadhafi's tanks, rocket launchers, troop carriers, artillery pieces, antiaircraft encampments, and sniper positions. By the middle of July, NATO attacks were extracting a heavy toll on the increasingly beleaguered government forces. Sensing the colonel's vulnerability, the British and French intensified their military operations, flying at times more than seventy sorties a day against targets in the capital, Tripoli, particularly Qadhafi's fortresslike headquarters in Bab al-Azizia; at government positions in the contested and strategically vital city of Misrata to the east of Tripoli; and in the Nafusa Mountains, southwest of the capital, home to non-Arab Berber tribes, who had been politically oppressed and culturally disparaged by Qadhafi. And then, as though Qadhafi's mounting troubles were not enough, the International Criminal Court issued arrest warrants for crimes against humanity to Qadhafi and his equally homicidal son, Seif al-Islam, holder of a doctorate from the prestigious London School of Economics.

The NATO effort not only weakened Qadhafi but gave the rebels breathing space to improve their tactics and operational performance. By the end of July, greater coordination among the groups that were fighting Qadhafi in various parts of the country, and between these groups and NATO, was evident. By now, the talk in Western governmental circles and in the media was no longer "if," but "when" the colonel would be overthrown. This became all the more evident when in a scratchy-sounding telephone recording, broadcast on August 15, a hysterical Qadhafi pleaded with his fast-dwindling supporters to "move forward, challenge, pick up weapons, go to fight and liberate Libya inch by inch from the traitors and NATO."[2] By now, more than forty privately organized, privately funded militias had taken up the fight against Qadhafi.[3] For them, the light at the end of the tunnel could now be seen, and it became brighter when fighters from Misrata and the Nafusa Mountains, closely supported from the air by NATO warplanes, captured two strategic towns to the east and west of Tripoli.

This significant success created the opportunity for a final advance on the capital from opposite directions. In anticipation of the rebel advance anti-Qadhafi elements in Tripoli, who for weeks had been clandestinely receiving weapons mainly from Gulf countries, rose in a citywide uprising on August 20. They quickly engaged government forces in fierce fighting in all parts of Tripoli, and it was around this time that the hitherto invincible "Brother-Leader" fled Tripoli to the city of Sirte, his birthplace and home to the tribe to which he belonged.

The Tripoli uprising did not have to confront Qadhafi forces on its own for long. Within less than forty-eight hours, thousands of rebel fighters from the east and the west had converged on the city with little if any resistance from government forces. And on August 23, they celebrated their complete control of the city when they seized Qadhafi's fortress compound at Bab al-Azizia. In contrast to the widespread looting and destruction that followed the forcible eviction of Saddam Hussein from Baghdad, neither the victorious fighters nor the city's residents indulged in wholesale anarchic behavior. Repeated appeals for discipline and calm from religious figures and political leaders certainly helped; but unlike Iraqis, who did not participate in the removal of their dictator, Libyans were heavily invested in the ousting of Qadhafi, and finishing the job properly and with dignity became a matter of pride and obligation.

As the revolution expanded and other cities in the middle and west of the country were liberated, the earlier consensus and cohesion within the TNC were severely tested as regional, ethnic, and ideological loyalties proliferated. Groups that hailed from Tripoli and the western part of Libya complained of heavy Benghazi representation in the organization. Islamists, inside and outside the TNC, felt that the liberal and secular members of the council were out of touch with the country's conservative roots. The man who received the lion's share of the criticisms against the TNC was Mahmoud Jibril, a onetime University of Pittsburgh political scientist, who had defected from the Qadhafi regime at the beginning of the uprising to become the council's designated prime minister. His critics faulted him for spending most of the time during the revolt outside Libya. The fact that Jibril had used that time abroad to bring the world to the side of the rebels was not considered relevant. The truth was that to the conservative and Islamist groups, his staunch liberal views, to say nothing of his Western ways, put him irredeemably in the "not to be trusted" column. By the fall, the pressure on Jibril was such that he had little option but to resign.

The dissentions within the TNC and the increasing conflict between the council and the militias, who after all were fighting

and winning the civil war, diminished much of its earlier authority. This became evident in the days after the liberation of Tripoli,
as various militias converged from all sides and established their
own fiefdoms in separate parts of the city. When a number of these
militias agreed on a commander of an Islamist group, a man by the
name of Abd al-Hakim Belhaj, to become the head of the newly
formed Tripoli Military Council, they did this without consulting,
indeed without even a reference to, the TNC.

The fall of Tripoli did not end the civil war. It was not until
two months later, on October 20, that the city of Sirte, to which
the "Brother-Leader" had escaped, would fall. A day later, news
surfaced of the capture and killing of the colonel. The precise circumstances of his capture remained unclear, but it seemed that
NATO airplanes attacked a convoy of cars leaving Sirte at high
speed, after which anti-Qadhafi fighters would find the man who
had held unchallenged dominion over them for over forty years
hiding in a rubbish-filled drainage pipe by the road. Shortly after,
he was summarily executed by his captors.

With the final demise of the Qadhafi political order, thoughts
turned to the future. Given the proliferation of militia groups,
divided as they were by region, tribe, and ethnicity—and given the
powerful presence of radical Islamists in Tripoli and Benghazi—
prospects for a peaceful and orderly transition seemed a bit uncertain. Each of these groups could legitimately claim to have played a
crucial role in the gradual and piecemeal liberation of the country.
Their reluctance to surrender their newfound power was evident
when TNC appeals to the various groups to give up their arms
and join a national army were met with less than the hoped for
exuberant enthusiasm. But the TNC did have an advantage: unlike
the militias, it was a national institution, in fact the only national
institution, purporting to speak on behalf of all Libyans. And it

behooved the members of the TNC to act and behave in a way that would reinforce this perception.

The TNC began this process on October 31, 2011, when it elected Abd al-Rahim al-Keeb to the position of prime minister. Al-Keeb, who for more than a decade and a half had been professor of electrical engineering at the University of Alabama, received the support of twenty-six of the fifty-one TNC members. Less than a month later, he picked a transitional cabinet, in which, al-Keeb assured the country, "all of Libya [was] represented."[4] The two security portfolios, Defense and Interior, were given to powerful militia leaders, while diplomats and technocrats took control of the Foreign Affairs, Finance, Oil, and Trade ministries. Two women were named to head the ministries of Health and Social Affairs. It was interesting that one disappointed candidate for the Defense portfolio, the powerful Islamist militia leader Abd al-Hakim Belhaj, pledged to support the new government, but shied away from pledging to disband his heavily armed 25,000-man force, using the proverbial "we will . . . but not yet."[5] Nevertheless, al-Keeb and his cabinet were doing all they could to bolster their legitimacy. The cabinet met regularly, and the minutes of the meetings were made public. The ministers appeared often on television, speaking openly about governmental policies and taking questions by telephone.[6] This effort at transparency came through also in the way the TNC announced the electoral law for a constituent assembly in early February 2012.

Two earlier drafts of the law had been floated, but each had met with resistance to a number of its articles. The electoral commission, which was appointed by the TNC, used the social media to review thousands of comments and criticisms sent by e-mail and through Facebook from civil society groups and the public at large. The final law announced by the government for the election of a 200-member assembly contained a parallel voting system in which 120 representatives would be elected individually through a simple majority system, and the remaining 80 members would get their seats through party list proportional representation. In this last segment of the elections, political party lists had to alternate according to gender, with the expectation that women would end up constituting between 15 and 20 percent of the institution. Shortly after the announcement of the electoral law, the commission recommended, and the TNC approved, the number of assembly representatives for each of Libya's regions. There would be 102 representatives from Tripoli and the western region, 60 from Benghazi and the eastern region, 29 from the south, and nine from the middle of the country, including the city of Sirte. The election was set to take place on June 19, 2012, later postponed to July 7. Once elected, the assembly, called the Public National Conference, would appoint a cabinet and prime minister, write a constitution, and put it to a national referendum.

The need for a new government, fortified by the legitimacy of free and fair elections, was becoming more urgent by the summer of 2012 as the TNC faced nationwide dysfunctions that painted less than a bright future for the country. One of the most pressing problems was the economic devastation wreaked upon the country by nine months of bloody civil war. Cities lay in ruin, basic services were sporadic at best and in some places nonexistent, and unemployment soared. Ever larger numbers of families simply could not make ends meet, and this was translated into mounting frustration with the revolution. Like Egypt and Tunisia, demonstrations were organized against the TNC, demanding swift improvements to the deteriorating socioeconomic conditions.

Unlike Egypt and Tunisia, however, two economies that lacked natural resources and were due to grow only slowly, Libya's economy was expected to expand rapidly and substantially in 2012.

Its growth rate during the year was predicted by the Economist Intelligence Unit to reach a stunning 22 percent, higher than any other country in the world.[7] None of the country's main oil wells was badly damaged in the civil war, and oil production, which had fallen to little more than 50,000 barrels per day during the war, more than quadrupled by the end of October 2011, and by the spring of 2012 had reached near prewar level production rate of 1.6 million barrels per day.[8] Both parties to the conflict well recognized the centrality of oil production and marketing not only to the war effort but also to the post-conflict reconstruction period, and as such seem to have exercised due restraint when it came to the oil installations. Moreover, Libya had more than $170 billion worth of foreign assets. Part of that was a $65 billion sovereign wealth fund, about half of which was in ready cash that the Libyan government could use for reconstruction projects or financial aid.[9] In February 2012, when unemployed former fighters demonstrated and threatened to become violent, al-Keeb was able to announce an outright grant of 2,000 Libyan dinars (about $1,650) to Libyan families, with a total cost to the treasury of around $2 billion[10]—a handy thing to be able to do to keep the lid on popular frustrations.

But the TNC and al-Keeb government would encounter other, seemingly more intractable problems. Security, the natural domain of the state, was contested by rival militias who were still roaming the streets of major cities. These former revolutionaries, most of whom had simply refused to relinquish their arms, engaged in regular armed skirmishes with each other, and continuously challenged the government and its fledgling army and police force.[11] By the summer of 2012, on the eve of Libya's July election, it was clear that building an effective national security force, capable of subduing the militias would be a primary objective of any new government.

Meanwhile, increasing demands for regional decentralization

threatened to divide the country. Unlike the cohesive societies of Tunisia and Egypt, Libyan society is fragmented regionally and tribally. Jealousies and mistrust set the western part of the country, which had been favored by Qadhafi, against the east, where the revolution began. In March 2012, a large gathering of tribal leaders and militia commanders in Benghazi demanded an autonomous region with its own parliament and military council. Two months later, candidates and voters in local elections, expressed disdain for the idea of a unitary state based in Tripoli. And one week before the July national elections, protestors and militiamen in Benghazi and other cities in the east stormed the headquarters of the election commission and burned voting slips. Their anger was directed at the TNC for refusing to give the east an equal share of seats in the assembly. In the city of Misrata, an elected city council regularly disregarded the authority of the TNC and the al-Keeb government. By the summer other Libyan cities would follow suit and demand greater political powers to local and regional councils.

It was in this inauspicious political and security environment that elections were held on July 7, 2012. But on the day, Libyans went out in huge numbers, and stood in long lines under a scorching sun waiting to cast their votes. The expectation was that the Islamists would replicate the victories of their cohorts in Tunisia, Egypt, and Morocco. But when the results were announced, the National Forces Alliance, a non-Islamist coalition under the leadership of Mahmoud Jibril, the ex-prime minister in the transitional government, won thirty-nine of the eighty seats allocated to parties. Trailing in second place was the Islamist Justice and Construction Party (JCP), which garnered what had to be a disappointing tally of seventeen seats. A plethora of parties followed, each winning one to three seats. The real shock was the performance of the *al-Watan* (Homeland) Party, led by Abd al-Hakim

Belhaj, an Islamist who had fought with al-Qaeda, and whose militia was credited with liberating Tripoli. Running a glitzy and well-financed campaign, with billboards dominating most streets and squares of Tripoli, his party was expected to be the main challenger to the JCP. In the end, it won only one seat, with Belhaj himself losing in his Tripoli constituency.

So why did the Islamists' electoral performance fall below expectations? First, unlike Egypt, Tunisia, and Morocco, the Islamist /secularist divide in Libya's electoral campaign was purposely blurred by Jibril, who adamantly rejected the "secularist" label, pronouncing himself a devout and practicing Muslim, and declaring time and time again that his coalition adhered to Sharia law as one of its main principles. Secondly, Qadhafi's penchant for absolute political and social control denied the Islamists in Libya any space to create social connections with the population. By way of contrast, in Egypt, the Muslim Brotherhood was allowed to engage in nationwide charitable work and social welfare. Thirdly, there was widespread suspicion that before the revolution, a number of Islamists had been talking to Qadhafi's son, Seif al-Islam, about a possible political role when power eventually transferred from father to son.[12] Finally, people were wary about the Islamists' cozy relations with foreign governments, particularly Belhaj and his *al-Watan* Party, whose chief sponsor was the Gulf sheikhdom of Qatar. It did not help that the maroon-and-white colors of *al-Watan*'s posters matched those of the flag of Qatar.[13]

While a number of the elected independents had Islamist sympathies, and would swell the ranks of the Islamists in the assembly, this would not camouflage the fact that in Libya those fighting the elections on an I slamist ticket fell far short of their cohorts' electoral achievements in Egypt, Tunisia, and Morocco. Still, regardless of the results of the elections, Libyans would not have been able to create a new political order, one that held the promise of transition to some form of democracy, without Qadhafi's ouster. And that lesson was not lost on the thousands of protestors who jammed the streets and cities of Yemen almost on a daily basis demanding an end to the thirty-three-year rule of President Ali Saleh.

During the summer and fall of 2011, a betting man would have put his money on Saleh's imminent demise. After all, the al-Ahmar family, leaders of the powerful Hashid tribe, and for long the backbone of Saleh's political order, had withdrawn their support as early as March. No less devastating for the regime was the defection around the same time of the First Armored Division under the command of General Ali Mohsen, who until then had been a pivotal ally of the president. The fact that Saleh would survive, and on many occasions carry the fight to his enemies (with little regard for loss of life), was a testimony to the complex tribal networks that he had been able to put together for the purpose of regime survival.

Even more remarkable was that in addition to the powerful forces ranged against him in Yemen, he had few friends abroad. His neighbors in the Arabian Peninsula, the kings and emirs of the Gulf Cooperation Council (GCC), had decided that Yemen could not return to normalcy with Saleh continuing at the helm, a position echoed by the United States which previously had tolerated Saleh as an ally against al-Qaeda. With the active endorsement, even prodding, of the United States, the GCC came up with a plan that would bring government loyalists and opposition forces into a political settlement that would also provide Saleh with a gentle and dignified exit. During the spring and early summer of 2011, Saleh agreed to the tenets of the GCC document no fewer than three times, only to renege on it a few days later. By early June, even the Gulf Council seemed to have had enough of the unpredictable Yemeni leader, giving the impression that the initiative was dead, and would be revived only if Saleh showed real commitment to the suggested process.

There was no sign that a change of heart would occur on the part of the Yemeni president until one crucial (and bloody) event ushered in a gradual process that led to the implementation of the GCC plan. On Friday, June 3, 2011, two bombs exploded in a mosque while Saleh was attending Friday prayers. Saleh was severely wounded, with second-degree burns on almost half of his body, as well as shrapnel wounds to his chest and abdomen. Such was the seriousness of his condition that he was quickly transferred to the more sophisticated medical facilities in Saudi Arabia. While there, his loyal and compliant vice president, Abd Rabbo Mansour al-Hadi, took over as acting president.

It remains a wonder how the country functioned at all during the summer. Thousands of protestors filled the streets of Yemeni cities on an almost daily basis, demanding Saleh's ouster, and in the process throwing economic life into chaos. The capital Sanaa no longer had any geographic unity, divided as it was into areas controlled by the forces of the central government, by General Ali Mohsen's First Armored Division, and by armed men from the Hashid tribal confederation. Clashes and firefights occurred regularly, and proved particularly deadly when protestors were caught in the middle of the gunfire. In the north of the country, an insurgency by al-Houthi tribes was gathering pace. Belonging to the Shiite Zaydi sect, the Houthis had long complained of being discriminated against by Yemen's Sunni political order. A rebellion had fought the Yemeni army since 2004; but the events of 2011, and the mounting fragmentation of the armed forces, allowed the Houthis to spread their military and political control in the north of

Yemen demands Saleh's resignation. *Carlos Latuff*

the country, particularly in the governorates of Saada and al-Jawf. The central government was also facing rebellions in the southern provinces, particularly those of Abyan and Shabwa, where militant Islamists took control after the army withdrew from the main cities as the uprising against Saleh continued. Masked and heavily bearded, Jihadists imposed a Taliban-like political order on the towns and provinces in which they had established a presence. During July and August, the Islamists fought pitched battles with tribes and government forces, attempting to evict them from the areas under their control. Nor was this the only conflict in the south of the country; indeed, the entire southern region, with Aden as its capital, was getting restless, with mounting demands for secession and a return to the independent and sovereign status the region had possessed until 1990 as the People's Democratic Republic of Yemen.

As the country teetered between protests and fragmentation,

with the United Nations beginning to warn of a looming humanitarian disaster,[14] Saleh's Saudi hosts, who were being nudged by the American administration, tried to revive their patient's interest in the GCC plan. Saleh began to hint at the possibility of accepting the plan, but placed a number of conditions, including having himself supervise the transition period, which he thought would last many months.[15] In any case, given his record, which was checkered at best, there was little jubilation among those who had been clamoring for his exit. But suddenly in late September, after bloody clashes in the capital of Sanaa that cost upward of a hundred lives, Saleh returned to Yemen, and in a speech shortly thereafter he yet again promised to adhere to the GCC plan. Three weeks later, the UN Security Council voted unanimously for an end to violence against Yemeni civilians, and for Saleh to transfer power immediately.

After stalling for months, Saleh seemed to realize that the Council vote had ushered in a new resolve amongst global powers that left him with little choice but to finally bow to their demands, and save himself and members of his family further global actions, including the possibility of being referred to the International Criminal Court. On November 22, 2011, Saleh boarded a plane to Saudi Arabia, and put his signature to the latest version of the GCC's peace plan. Knowing his tendency to renege on such agreements at the last minute, the Saudis made sure to bring to the signing ceremony ambassadors of the five permanent members of the Security Council, as well as delegations from Saleh's ruling party and from the Yemeni opposition.

Finally, Yemen's autocrat for over three decades would relinquish power. Brutal as Qadhafi, never allowing impulses of humanity to restrain him from killing civilian demonstrators, Saleh nevertheless did not end his career in a ditch next to a garbage heap. He was able to secure an immunity agreement that protected him from future prosecution. And in truth the world was happy with that meager result, given the hundreds of civilians who had been killed by his army, because it had become obvious that defeating him without an active outside military intervention was simply not in the cards. The wily Yemeni dictator had worked the tribal conditions of his country superbly.

The document not only allowed for the transfer of presidential powers from Saleh to his vice president, Abd Rabbo Mansour al-Hadi, but just as crucially set a precise and detailed timetable for a process of democratic transition. In accordance with the GCC plan, al-Hadi, now the acting president, was compelled to ask the nominee of the opposition to become the prime minister, and then for the latter to appoint a cabinet of national unity equally divided between the ruling party and the opposition. Both groups were enjoined not to challenge the election of the "consensus" candidate, al-Hadi, which was scheduled to occur ninety days from the signing of the document, and which would launch the second phase of the transition process that would last for two years. During this second phase, a national conference of all Yemeni groups and forces would convene to discuss outstanding problems, and to agree on a process for establishing a constitutional committee tasked with writing a new constitution. The next and final step after the constitution was adopted through a national referendum would be preparing the country for general elections.

The requirements for the first phase of the GCC peace plan were smoothly implemented. A cabinet was quickly formed, and although its membership was made up of the ruling party and the opposition, it appeared to be functioning to some tenets of ministerial responsibility. As stipulated by the agreement, the election of al-Hadi was scheduled for February 21, 2012. *The Economist* brilliantly headlined the event: "One Vote, One Man."[16] While the atmosphere in the streets in no way approximated to electoral fever, nevertheless the majority of Yemenis were generally supportive of the election, not necessarily because they were enthused by the process, but because they were genuinely joyful about Saleh's departure. For the people of Yemen, the election of al-Hadi was more a sigh of relief at the final lifting of the thirty-three-year nightmare of a dictator's rule.

Not that the democratic road was now open, smoothly paved, and laden with cheering crowds. As one politician put it, "If we don't reach an agreement on how to proceed over the next year, the problems are going to [be] worse than they were before."[17] The economy was a major worry. Historically, the fate of democratic transformation has been linked to economic performance, and Yemen exhibited all the signs of a failing economy.[18] Around 45 percent of the population lived under the poverty line. Unemployment stood at 35 percent nationally, and among the young it rose to a staggering 50 percent. With an inflation rate of more than 20 percent, the seventh highest in the world, and a GDP per capita of less than $2,500, giving the country a rank of 178th out of 224 states, the economic indicators did not bode well for a swift democratic transformation.

Strange as it might seem, for al-Hadi and the new political leadership, it was not the economy that was the main concern; the army was. President Saleh had littered command positions in the armed forces with his relatives and clan members. And many of these units, including the best equipped and much feared Republican Guard, under the command of Saleh's son Ahmad, were responsible for much of the violence against protestors and tribesmen. It did not take the new president long to realize that he could not embark on political reforms as stipulated by the GCC plan when Saleh had turned the country's army into a family franchise. On April 6, the new president boldly issued decrees dismissing and

transferring several important army commanders who were relatives and close associates of Saleh. While some complied, others
resisted. The problem for President Hadi was that he did not have
enough firepower to back his legal authority, so he used mediators
and go-betweens, which hardly boosted people's confidence in the
new political order. Indeed, Saleh's son Ahmad sat on the military
commission that was supposed to reassess the place and role of various army units, and reconstitute them into the envisaged national
army. People waited, with a healthy dose of skepticism, for General
Ahmad to decommission himself peacefully for the sake of the
national interest.[19] Equally difficult to visualize was the expectation
of Ahmad Saleh and General Ali Mohsen, whose army divisions
had fought bitter and costly battles for the best part of a year, sitting
next to each other together chewing qat (a narcotic widely used in
Yemeni society), and toasting the birth of a new unified army.

And even if the army overcame all obstacles and reconstituted
itself into a coherent national institution, it would still face the
prospects of fighting debilitating wars against separatist forces in
the north and south of the country. In the north, among the Shiite
Zaydi population, a rebellion had raged for over eight years that
left large swaths of land outside the control of the government
in Sanaa. In the south, Islamist militants linked to al-Qaeda had
taken advantage of the uprising against Saleh and assumed control
of a number of southern provinces and cities, creating Taliban-
style "Islamic emirates." With the urging and help of the United
States, Hadi soon after taking office dispatched troops to the south
under the command of a respected officer, General Salem Qatan.
Using artillery and other heavy weaponry, the troops made steady
progress in pushing the Islamists out of a series of towns. In mid-
June, government successes culminated in the fall of the Islamist
strongholds of Zinjibar and Jaar. The two cities, General Qatan

told the world media, had been "completely cleansed."[20] But only the hopelessly optimistic would declare this to be the end of the radical Islamist challenge to the authority of the Yemeni government. Indeed, less than a week after his military success, General Qatan would be assassinated in a suicide attack.

There can be little doubt that these regional divisions had been exacerbated during the anti-Saleh uprising, widening the gulf that existed before, but that had been somewhat contained even by a less than competent government in Sanaa. In the one-man election of al-Hadi, the average turnout for the whole country stood at 60 percent, but in the north among the Shiite Zaydis it was less than 50 percent, and in the south, less than 40 percent.[21] Admittedly, this happened not just because of regional and sectarian divisions; polling stations were attacked by rebels and separatists. But this only would confirm the titanic task faced by al-Hadi and his national unity government to successfully implement the GCC project, to say nothing of creating the robust and durable institutions of a workable democratic system. And all this had to be achieved in the shadow of a faltering economy, in one of the poorest countries of the world, with almost no resources to speak of.

Regardless of the obstacles ahead, the ouster of Saleh at a minimum brought relative calm to the streets and squares of Sanaa and other Yemeni cities. And much as in the case of Libya, and indeed Egypt and Tunisia, the relative quiet came as a consequence of the triumph of the people who rose against, and were able to dispose of, autocratic leaderships. But the small state of Bahrain supplied a different narrative. Much like the other countries, by the early summer of 2011, Manama, the capital, and other towns no longer saw the thousands of protestors and demonstrators who had filled their streets and squares. A semblance of tranquility had returned to Bahrain, and it indeed was the result of a victory. But this time the victory belonged not to the people but to the autocratic wielders of naked power.

In mid-March 2011, Bahrain's monarch, King Hamad, declared a state of emergency, and requested military help from Saudi Arabia. The entry of some 1,000 Saudi troops, belligerent and well armed, believing they were coming to the aid of a beleaguered Sunni monarchy fighting for dear life against an Iran-supported Shiite majority, forcibly dispersed the demonstrations, removed their encampments from the city center, and allowed the Bahraini security forces to go on a rampage of wholesale arrests. These were followed by detentions and torture, to say nothing of arbitrary and extensive dismissals from governmental and bureaucratic posts.

The main target was the Shiite community. The final toll was appalling: in a country of just over half a million, 34 people were killed, more than 1,400 arrested, and as many as 3,600 lost their jobs. Some forty-three Shiite mosques and religious shrines were destroyed or damaged. One Shiite lawmaker, Mattar Ibrahim Mattar, an influential parliamentarian and political figure, who had been arrested, roughed up, and kept in solitary confinement for over three months, told the late Anthony Shadid of the *New York Times*: "They told me, there are two ways we can deal with you—as a human or as an animal."[22] Mattar belonged to a Shiite political class that since the first demonstrations had become so ostracized and harassed that eighteen Shiite members of parliament felt compelled to resign en bloc, in addition to a number of judges and other Shiite public figures. With their resignations, an essential link between the majority Shiite community and the Sunni power structure disappeared, and the prospects of reconciliation diminished further.

The violent and successful suppression of the protests certainly brought a sense of calm to the tiny country not experienced since demonstrations erupted in February 2011. Indeed, the king deemed the situation to have been normalized enough to lift the state of emergency on June 1. But the calm belied mounting sectarian tensions that threatened to cause irreparable damage to the very fiber of society. Sunnis grew ever more suspicious of the Shiites. Sunni religious figures, encouraged by the regime, organized counter-demonstrations that shouted slogans tying the Shiites to Iran. Programs on television, which is the exclusive domain of Sunnis,[23] questioned the loyalty of demonstrators to Bahrain, and boycott lists of Shiite-owned businesses circulated in the social media. The sharpening of sectarian identity would permeate to one of the most beloved and diverse of all institutions—the football club. The king's son, in charge of an investigating commission, rooted out over 150 Shiite players, staff, and referees from the league.[24] And when in June the king put forth a plan for a national dialogue conference, Sunni figures warned him not to give in to Shiite demands.

The national conference was one of a number of initiatives adopted by the king in the wake of the easing of governmental crackdown. He also announced a by-election for the seats vacated by the eighteen resigning Shiite lawmakers, and dramatically announced the creation of an international fact-finding committee that would be charged with investigating abuses that might have occurred during the suppression of the demonstrations. Things did not go well at the start when, in the wake of the announcement of the national conference of conciliation, the government allocated a mere 35 of the 300 envisaged seats to the opposition groups. In the end the meeting did go ahead, but trust had become the victim of Bahrain's winter of discontent; and so, while people talked, little constructive dialogue took place, and the whole initiative quickly petered out.

The by-election for the eighteen parliamentary seats went ahead on schedule. As the September date approached, Shiite leaders urged the community to boycott the elections, whether in the form of candidates or voters. Those who ended up running, Sunnis and Shiites, had the backing of the government, and in no way would garner even a fraction of the legitimacy of the parliamentarians they were replacing. Four of the candidates ended up running unopposed, and the others partook in a lackluster election, which saw a turnout of around 16 percent. Demonstrations on the day of the election did erupt in some parts of Bahrain, but generally the majority Shiites simply turned their backs on the process, signifying the deepening sectarian chasm that had engulfed the country.

The one initiative that was not dismissed as a work of theater or political malevolence was the appointment of a fact-finding commission. Any fears of a governmental whitewash were alleviated when the king asked a respected American Egyptian international lawyer and academic, Cherif Bassiouni, to head the committee, and gave him total freedom to choose its members. Given the go-ahead at the end of June 2011, the Bahrain Independent Commission of Enquiry, which, in addition to its chair, comprised four other prominent international lawyers and jurists, none with any connection to the Bahraini government, began its work. For the next five months, the commission would interview more than 5,000 people, including hundreds who claimed that they were tortured. The commission produced its final report in late November. To alleviate any suspicion of governmental interference, the report was released to the public at the same time that the committee was presenting it to the king.

In summarizing the 500-page report,[25] Professor Bassiouni first reminded the press and people of Bahrain how unique it was for an Arab government to voluntarily and without international pressure call on an outside group to investigate upheavals within its borders. But after this initial pat on the back, the Bahraini authorities did not fare well in the report. The enquiry found that the security forces had used such excessive force in confronting the demonstrators that their actions violated the principle of necessity and proportionality. Available evidence indicated that on a number of occasions security forces fired into the crowd. Detainees were later subjected to physical and psychological torture; they were blindfolded, whipped, given electric shocks, exposed to extreme temperatures, deprived of sleep, and threatened with rape. The commission did emphasize that it had received 559 complaints about mistreatment of persons in custody; all but nine of these complaints came from Shiites. Finally, the report stated that the evidence presented to the commission by the Bahraini authorities in relation to the involvement of Iran in the internal affairs of Bahrain (which had been used to justify Saudi military intervention) was not compelling enough to establish a discernible link between Iran and the unrest in Bahrain.

Responding to the report's criticisms, King Hamad vowed that he would do everything possible so that "those painful events won't be repeated."[26] He pledged to reform Bahraini laws to make them compatible with international standards to protect basic rights, including freedom of speech. He insisted that officials who abused their power would be sacked, and those Bahraini citizens who were treated badly, or who wrongfully lost their jobs or positions, would be compensated. In explaining and expanding on the king's response, however, government officials seemed intent on decelerating any rampant expectations, drawing attention to the country's polarization, suggesting that it would be a mistake to expect reform to occur soon. Shiite politicians and community leaders applauded the report, but expressed skepticism that it would usher in any real reforms.

To show his commitment to the report and its recommendations, the king created an implementing committee under the chairmanship of a senior lawmaker. A number of reforms were put through; the definition of torture was broadened: it would include not just the usual physical mistreatment but also less visible methods of inflicting pain, such as sleep deprivation, enforced standing for long periods, and exposure to extreme temperatures, as well as the more subtle psychological punishments, such as verbal abuse, threats of rape, and insulting the detainee's religious sect. The arrest powers for security personnel were restricted. Death sentences for two protestors convicted in military court of killing two policemen were overturned, and workers dismissed for political reasons were reinstated.

Some goodwill certainly came the way of Bahrain's authorities with these gestures. But many saw such moves as purely cosmetic, falling far short of addressing the deep structural problems of the country's political and security systems. So while foreign advisers were brought in to retrain Bahrain's police force, the more fundamental grievance of the Shiite community was left unaddressed: the fact that recruitment to the security forces was not open to Shiites. And after months of investigation into the deaths of protestors, five police officers, none of them high-ranking or Bahraini, were put on trial.[27] When security forces felt the need to impose order, they did not seem to give even a second thought to the report's recommendations. Indeed, in December 2011, a mere month after the report was released, the largest Shiite opposition party, frustrated by the lack of substantive communications with the authorities, announced its intention to organize a protest. In response, security forces attacked its headquarters using rubber bullets and tear gas.

More than a year after the suppression of the protest movement, and the efforts at normalization that followed, hopes for peace and reconciliation seemed as elusive as they had ever been. The demands of the majority seemed to be perceived by the Sunni political establishment as a threat not just to its privileged status and power but to its very existence. Yet the Shiites did not show any signs of relenting. And that meant the schisms in Bahraini society would become deeper and more entrenched, and hopes for true democracy would recede further and further.

The one element that brought the Bahraini experience together with those of Libya and Yemen was that a swift shift of direction toward democratic change, as provided by the examples of Egypt and Tunisia, did not materialize. The revolutionary spark either was extinguished very quickly, or took months and months of devastation and loss of life before it was able to sweep out of office tyrants whose behinds seemed to be almost glued to the seats of power. The longer these cruel men fought for survival, the greater the divisions they sowed within the population, to say nothing of the proliferation of groups each demanding its own slice of the rewards of liberation.

Still, the journeys undertaken by these three countries to freedom, which began in the dark winter days of January and February 2011, produced varied outcomes in terms of prospects for democracy. Bahrain, of course, was the least promising, as any move toward political reform would have to come from above. The king's swift success in violently throttling people's demands marginalized any incentive for meaningful concession. Nor were the prospects for true democratic transition that much better in Yemen. True, President Saleh was removed from office, and a new president presided over a cabinet that included a substantial number of opposition figures. The new political leaders had a detailed plan and timeline for the writing of a constitution and the holding of general elections. These were all substantive gains. But there were also many hurdles still to be overcome. Central control over large swaths of land in the north and south of the country was severely contested by hardened and determined insurgents. Saleh, while no longer president, continued to have significant support within the ranks of the military, and among the tribes that he had so diligently cultivated. And these difficult problems had to be tackled against the background of a failing, if not failed, economy.

Perhaps Libya's prospects were the brightest, but that was only a matter of degree. On the positive side, Libya's oil production and its healthy foreign assets, if utilized properly to serve all Libyans, could contribute to the political development of the country. Promises regarding the institution of democratic changes were adhered to, culminating in the enthusiastically supported July 2012 elections. Thus, the outlook for Libya achieving a peaceful and meaningful transition to democracy was better than that of Yemen and Bahrain. But formidable challenges, much greater than those faced by Egypt and Tunisia, remained. The scars of Libya's long and bloody civil war would not be forgotten quickly. Libya's path to stability and democratic peace was not guaranteed.

Serious challenges aside, Libyans, as well as Yemenis, could at least look forward to annual celebrations commemorating the dispatch of their dictators into the trash heap of history, and that eventuality would somewhat temper the immense sacrifices and untold sufferings. But another Arab despot, that of Syria, would prove more resilient.

Syria's political volcano. *Carlos Latuff*

Chapter Six

LIONS AND SAVAGES

Syria

The winter of Arab discontent was no less severe in Syria than in Libya or Yemen, but into the summer and fall of 2011, as the regimes in Libya and Yemen began to flounder, Bashar al-Asad, Syria's autocrat, showed little sign of panic. This was not because, as he would tell everyone willing to listen, his people loved him; it was because, like Qadhafi, he felt no discomfort about butchering his own people, but unlike the case in Libya his army, which was the instrument for the mass killings, stayed on the whole intact and loyal to the regime. Bashar al-Asad in his savagery and callous disregard for human life would remain true to his family name.

In his expansive and generally sympathetic biography of Hafiz al-Asad, the general who ruled Syria from 1970 until his death in 2000, when power was transferred to his son Bashar, Patrick Seale recounts a story, told to him by Hafiz's cousin, Jabir al-Asad, about the origin of the family's name, which in Arabic means "the Lion."[1] Jabir tells of an incident at the turn of the twentieth century, when a Turkish wrestler came to one of the villages in the mountains of northwest Syria, and challenged its menfolk to a wrestling match. A tall and burly man by the name of Sulayman came forth, grabbed the Turk, and hurled him down to the ground. Awestruck by the man's brute strength, the villagers applauded and shouted, *"Wahhish."* Henceforth he would be known as Sulayman al-Wahhish, Sulayman the Savage. His physical strength, a source of much admiration in the prevailing masculine culture, was supplemented by his ability to handle a gun deftly. As a result, his stock would ascend in the village and among its elders and influential clan leaders, so that by the time of his death he had risen to the elevated position of a minor notable.

On Sulayman's death, his son Ali, similarly strong, daring, and a stellar shot, would maintain the increasingly eminent status of the Wahhish family. He fought the French for the Muslim Ottomans, and back in the village he continued the tradition started by his father of mediating disputes and giving protection to the weak. In the early 1920s he distinguished himself by organizing help for impoverished refugees who had streamed out in droves from the parts of Syria that had been ceded by France to Turkey. In recognition of the standing he had established for himself in the community, village elders came to him and counseled a change in the family name: "you are not a Wahhish," they said. "You are an Asad."[2] No longer a savage, now a lion, Ali Sulayman was the father of Hafiz al-Asad.

The son and grandson, Hafiz and Bashar, who between them ruled Syria for over four decades, certainly behaved like lions when administering the responsibilities of governance. Lions get their way because they happen to be the strongest, and they know that their dominion will be challenged at the first sign of weakness. Their instinctual savagery comes to the fore in their defense of their territory. The lions of Syria, both Hafiz and Bashar, have remained true to these primal instincts, first in the way Hafiz leveled a third of the city of Hama in 1982, killing thousands of its inhabitants; and in 2011 and beyond, in Bashar's relentless and merciless assault on his own people throughout the length and breadth of the country.

By the summer of 2011, large demonstrations against the Asad regime were occurring on a daily basis in many cities throughout the country. Bashar, the supposedly urbane, British-educated ophthalmologist, would employ the same tactic in all its operations. Not shy about deploying the army (not police) to attack and disperse protestors, he would dispatch heavily armored units to lay siege to a city, cutting off water, food, supplies, and essential services; send troops in to forcibly break up demonstrations, often shooting into the crowds; then retreat to the encircling line, wait till the next day, and start the same operation again. By banning foreign journalists from entering Syria, Bashar and his killing machine hoped that no reports of atrocities would reach the outside world, a circumstance that had helped his father greatly during his own killing spree in Hama in 1982. However, this time round, not a day would pass without pictures and videos, supplied by Syrians via cell phones and the Internet, appearing on international television screens. These images conveyed not only the depth of people's abhorrence of the regime but also the contemptuous disregard for human life by the troops ranged against them.

Also by the summer of 2011, it had become apparent that the heart of the insurrection against Asad lay in the Sunni community. Totaling some 75–80 percent of the population, and ruled for four decades by an Alawite political and security elite that constituted a mere 12 percent of Syrians, most of the Sunnis had held deep grievances against the regime. This sectarian divide was in fact perpetrated by the Asad clan, which had blatantly privileged its own Alawite community, particularly in the army and state security forces. Still, over four decades of rule, the Asads had created networks of economic advantage that expanded the regime's support base to include important segments of the Sunni community as well as critical minorities such as Christians and Druze. The capitals Damascus and Aleppo—Syria's two most populous cities, and home to thriving Sunni and Christian communities—experienced fewer and less spirited street protests, and when these happened, they tended to be confined to poor Sunni neighborhoods and suburbs. It was only natural that the strongest passions would be felt among the community that believed itself most excluded, the majority Sunni population; but the years of suffocating dictatorship had alienated most Syrians from the regime. Even those Sunnis (as well as Christians and Druze) who did not support the uprising held back not for love of the president or his political order, but for fear of a bloody and debilitating civil war.

At the height of the summer, in July and August 2011, while Asad's troops continued to attack, shoot into, and kill demonstrators in scores of Syrian cities, it was becoming clear that Hama, the very Hama that took the brunt of the Asads' wrath forty years earlier, was yet again receiving the unwelcome attention of the Asad clan. For over two months, demonstrators had gone out onto the streets on a daily basis, shouting anti-regime slogans and pelting advancing security forces with pebbles and stones. They had erected barricades and become adept at burning rubber tires to keep the troops at bay. For weeks, protestors in some of the city's quarters had even managed to oust police and security personnel and take control of their own neighborhoods, experiencing briefly what it might feel like to live outside the straitjacket of despotic rule and breathe the air of freedom. But the Lion in Damascus had other plans for the city.

On July 31, on the eve of the holy month of Ramadan, Syrian tanks and heavy armor smashed through the barricades erected by the demonstrators of Hama, and with little if any restraint attacked entire neighborhoods, demolished houses, and shot at men and women armed with little more than rocks and pebbles. Scores were killed and many more injured. Extolling the regime's triumph against its own citizens, Syrian state television proudly showed videos of tanks rolling through the streets of Hama with their crews brandishing the victory sign to celebrate the triumph of tanks over unarmed citizens.

The death toll in that one day alone was 130 civilians. In the aftermath of the killings, Hama was terrorized by troops that held the city by force for ten days, during which hundreds of soldiers moved from one house to another asking by name for people suspected by the regime of having been involved in the protests. In light of a report released in late August by Amnesty International, about torture in Syrian detentions,[3] those young men from Hama who suffered the misfortune of having been taken into custody by Syrian soldiers might have wished to have joined their fallen comrades instead.

Buoyed by their success in Hama, the Asad clan mounted similar assaults on other main cities, such as Deir al-Zour, Latikiya, and Idlib, employing the same tactics that subdued Hama. Soldiers manning Syrian tanks and armored vehicles smashed their way through whatever flimsy barricades the protestors had erected, and fired their heavy guns at living quarters in neighborhoods believed to be the centers of opposition. The troops thought nothing of firing live ammunition into crowds. Once control was imposed, soldiers and other armed men would roam the streets, terrorizing households and arresting young men at will.[4] The civil disobedience that had brought success to the protestors in Cairo and Tunis seemed not to be working that well in the urban centers of Syria.

No wonder that the character and tone of the protests began to change dramatically by the fall of 2011. It was then that reports started circulating of armed clashes between the army and the opposition. It was not clear who was firing back at Bashar's tanks and troop carriers, but a group called the Free Syrian Army (FSA) began to claim responsibility for mounting military operations against the Asad regime, the most spectacular of which was an attack in November on an air force intelligence complex in Damascus. The FSA was comprised of defectors from the army who managed to slip through security cordons with only light weapons; by the end of the year they would claim to number over 50,000, although in reality a more realistic figure would be around 10,000.[5] Additionally, more and more protestors, who for months had gone out onto the streets with little more than their voices and placards, pebbles, stones, and the occasional Molotov cocktails, were now taking up arms that were slipping through the Turkish and Lebanese borders.

As the uprising approached its one-year anniversary in March 2012, the pattern of the protests had certainly changed. Large anti-Asad demonstrations would burst onto the streets, bellowing insults at the president, and demanding his resignation and the removal of the entire Asad clan. This would be met by the usual firepower from the army, shooting at the demonstrators, and aiming the turrets of their tanks at their houses. But rather than just dispersing (as the demonstrators had done before), bullets would start flying, this time aimed at Asad's troops. Gun battles would ensue, and sometimes would last for days. Few observers, however, thought that the lightly armed FSA, backed by a few protestors with guns, had any chance of inflicting real damage on Asad's regular army. For any decisive shift in the balance of coercive power, thousands more officers and soldiers needed to defect, and much heavier weaponry needed to make its way to the opposition. Meanwhile, the resort to arms by those opposing the Asad regime was used by Asad's propagandists to justify the regime's ferocious assault against its people.

In the midst of the mounting oppression, the president seemed to exist in a parallel universe of self-delusion, deceit, and straight-out lies. This was more than evident in the rare interviews he granted to Western journalists, or in the equally infrequent public addresses to the Syrian people. In October 2011, he told a British journalist that legitimacy associated with elections was inferior to popular legitimacy. Asad explained the concept of popular legitimacy through reference to his personal life. "I live a normal life. I drive my own car, we have neighbors, I take my kids to school," he said, and concluded, "That's why I am popular . . . it's the Syrian style."[6] What need was there for electoral democracy when all that was necessary to be a legitimate and popular political leader was to have neighbors and drive your kids to school? In January 2012, only his third speech since the beginning of the uprising, Asad confidently said that the majority of the people were firmly behind him, and that he ruled "with the will of the people."[7] It may very well be that Asad really believed all this, but he also was adept at outright lying. In an interview with Barbara Walters of ABC News in December 2011, he insisted more than once, without a blink of an eye, that foreign journalists were not banned from entering Syria.[8] This was no ordinary political fib, but brazen, unashamed, in-your-face lying.

Whether the product of delusion or deceit, the Lion's words might have had some resonance inside Syria, but they certainly made no impact on the outside world, where wholesale condemnations pervaded media reports and policy statements. A steady stream of images of regime brutality, passed on by scores of Syrian "citizen journalists" to the Western media, outraged American and European governments and populations alike. Western governments responded with harsh economic sanctions, including freezing the assets of scores of Syrian companies, banning any development loans to Syria, and placing an embargo on Syrian oil, 90 percent of whose exports went to Europe. But they ruled out a Libyan-style military intervention, which seemed to calm the nerves of Asad and the ruling clique. To a Western reporter, he boasted: "The West today is not like the West a decade ago. The world is changing, and new powers are emerging. There are alternatives. We can swim on our own and alongside our friends and brothers, and there are plenty of them."[9] But in reality the friends and brothers were few in number, basically Iran, China, and, crucially to the Asad regime, Russia.

In August 2011, after Asad's troops had pounded and battered the city of Hama into a semblance of submission, and had started a similar campaign against another defiant city, Deir al-Zour, no less a "brother" than King Abdullah of Saudi Arabia demanded a stop to Syria's "killing machine."[10] The king immediately withdrew the kingdom's ambassador, and it did not take long for the other Gulf monarchies to do the same. But then came an even bigger surprise. Three months later, the Arab League, an organization of which Syria was a founding member, and which in the past had been notoriously timid in speaking out against its members, suspended Syria and called on its army to stop killing innocent civilians. In late November, nineteen of the league's twenty-two members voted to impose economic sanctions that included freezing Syrian government assets in Arab countries, halting trade dealings with Syria's central bank, and stopping Arab investment in Syria's public and private sectors. In the meantime, King Abdullah of Jordan became the first Arab leader to ask for Bashar's removal from power.[11] Indeed, in January 2012, the Arab League called for Asad to step down, and for the establishment of a national unity government under a vice president.

For Asad, just as big a headache was the reaction of Turkey, Syria's neighbor to the north, and one of its major trading partners. Throughout the spring and summer of 2011, Turkish leaders had tried to persuade Asad to temper the violence against his people. In August, they seem to have had enough. President Abdullah Gul declared that Turkey had "lost confidence" in Syria's regime.[12] A month later, Prime Minister Recep Tayyip Erdogan went further than anyone else in the Middle Eastern neighborhood in the harshness of his condemnations. "Those who are attacking their people with tanks and guns will not be able to remain in power," he said. "President Asad will eventually have to pay the price for this."[13] In November, Turkey, which had upward of $2.5 billion in bilateral trade with Syria, suspended all financial credit dealings with its Southern neighbor, and froze all its government's assets in Turkey.

While hit hard by international diplomatic isolation and economic deprivation, Asad survived through the support of a few key allies. Iran extended occasional credit to tide him over until the hoped-for final suppression of the opposition. Russia, whose Mediterranean fleet's main naval base is in the Syrian port city of Tartus, continued to give him arms, and intervened tenaciously and effectively in the UN Security Council to prevent resolutions against him. As early as September 2011, the United States and European countries tried to circulate a draft resolution calling for sanctions against Asad, his immediate relatives, and influential associates, but the effort was met with resistance from Russia and China. In October, a mild resolution before the Security Council called for an end to the violence, respect for human rights, and unimpeded entry of media and human rights investigators into Syria. Only if Syria did not comply would the Security Council consider the option of economic and diplomatic sanctions. Russia and China duly vetoed the resolution, parroting Asad's argument that his regime's violence was in response to violence perpetrated by armed anti-government gangs.

Whether the authoritarian leaders of Russia and China really believed the hogwash they were mouthing, or whether acting against one of their own was too painful to contemplate, the consequence was that the savage turned lion would continue to devour his people with impunity. In January and into early February 2012, the city that received the lion's share of Asad's vengeance was Homs, and especially the district of Baba Amr. Syrian tanks and other armor surrounded the district and began a systematic and indiscriminate shelling of Baba Amr with rockets and mortar. More than a hundred snipers were placed on rooftops, and shot at literally anything that moved. Security and army units surrounded hospitals and turned away the wounded and those in dire need of medical assistance, even when these were women, children, and innocent bystanders. Bashar was presiding over the destruction of an entire district, an act that would have made his late father, Hafiz, proud—the *Wahhish* who almost to the day thirty years earlier was meting out the same savage treatment to Hama, obliterating over a third of the city and in the process slaughtering thousands of people.

When in 1982 Hafiz al-Asad leveled Hama and killed its people, no one in the outside world had much of an inkling that a massacre was being perpetrated against the city and its inhabitants. Only later, after the government had regained control of the city, would the world realize that a bloodbath had occurred there. But in 2011–12, Bashar was unable to emulate his father in presenting an unknowing world with a fait accompli. This time round, "citizen journalists" using Twitter, Skype, and other social media outlets, which Bashar simply could not control, continued to furnish the world with detailed reports and moving accounts of the indiscriminate leveling of houses and neighborhoods, and the plight of people with no food or water, electricity or access to emergency medical help. And they did their most poignant work in telling the heartbreaking tale of Baba Amr.

A poor neighborhood of somewhat decrepit homes and buildings compressed together, separated by narrow streets and alleys, Baba Amr was inhabited before Asad's onslaught by a Sunni population of some 50,000. It had gradually become the symbol of defiance to the Asad regime. Baba Amr had led the city of Homs, itself a hotbed of opposition, in the frequency and volume of its protests, and its sons, after being shot at by the Syrian security forces, began to take up arms and shoot back. Army defectors soon joined in the fray, and together they formed the loose military organization they called the Free Syrian Army. The neighborhood quickly became a base of stubborn resistance to the regime. The beginning of 2012 saw a rapid buildup of Syrian armor and artillery around the neighborhood, and by February, regular and indiscriminate shelling of Baba Amr had begun. As the month wore on, the army assault intensified, with the use of mortars and rockets on a daily basis. People who were just hiding from the intense shelling were being killed, and those who ventured outside were hit by sniper fire, kidnapped, or tortured. A video shown on British television after the final destruction of the neighborhood displayed frightful images of brutalized hospital patients, who had been injured while demonstrating and had needed medical attention. United Nations officials testified to the video's authenticity, confirming that they had received similar images and testimony. UN spokesman Rupert Colville said that "security agents, in some cases joined by medical staff, chained seriously injured patients to their beds, electrocuted them, beat wounded parts of their body or denied them medical attention and water."[14] Consequently, injured civilians and fighters in Baba Amr would be treated in homes turned into makeshift rudimentary hospitals by volunteer doctors and nurses. One French surgeon from Médecins sans Frontières, who was smuggled into Syria from Lebanon, said: "I can't really compare Homs to any other war zone I have worked in apart perhaps from Chechnya. The houses in Homs are built in a similar way [to Grozny]. When they are hit, they collapse completely. Also, the ferocity of the attack and the repression are comparable."[15]

And it was the "citizen journalists" who would not allow the carnage that was wreaked on Baba Amr to be buried along with the silent corpses of its dead. Here's one of these journalists, recounting the events of an evening in early February in Baba Amr:

> My plan is to write a simple post from a few reports on the day's events in Homs, the fifth consecutive day of shelling of Baba Amr. Keeping an eye on Skype and Twitter, and my ears turned on to Omar Shakir's live stream broadcast. . . .

People tweet that it seems more peaceful, that the sound of shelling is less intense. Then I notice Omar's latest tweets in Arabic with no hashtags, just cries of desperation. I sense this is Omar the person speaking, not the citizen journalist. I know something is terribly wrong. A few moments later we find out what it was. A different live stream camera had been targeted with a missile. The feed is dead, so are the five people who were manning the camera, including two women. I now realize that Omar had been tweeting about witnessing the explosion of his friends, "A street strewn with limbs. People have become limbs. We have no one but you, God."

Five dead quickly become twenty-nine and another fifty-five wounded. My fresh reports from an hour ago are now obsolete. Baba Amr is under attack, again. . . .

Jaafar, an activist from Daraa messages me on Skype. "I need you to connect me to someone from the media to speak to a doctor in Homs." I tweet [a number of journalists] and we wait. [In the meantime], I speak to Yousef, an activist in Baba Amr who was assisting the doctor. He recounts the day's events: "the shelling started at 5:00 A.M. There are four families buried under the rubble of their homes. The rockets tear through one side of a house and penetrate through the walls into the next. Four days before the shelling, Baba Amr was cut off from the rest of the city. Cut off from bread and food. There is no food. When the Red Crescent (the Arab world's Red Cross) entered, the army took all their supplies before letting them in. And they did not allow them to take any wounded out. . . ." As we speak, I can hear the pounding explosions in the background.

Journalists are responding now. I connect each one to

Jaafar. He's like a media traffic controller, efficient and precise. I listen to him typing while he talks, ordering activists to be ready to speak, in English and Arabic. I listened to [Yousef talking] to the journalists. I could tell that he was getting frustrated. When they ask for the number of dead, Yousef repeats, "Twenty-nine. No, not in the last twenty-four hours, the last four hours." Later, a reporter asks, "What is the condition of the hospital?" He answers, "There are no hospitals. We've made our homes into hospitals. We're treating our wounded in the mosque." She asks again, "Where is the hospital?" He replies in a clipped tone, "It's not a hospital. It's a mosque."

[With that interview], I was hoping my mission was complete. But before I log off, I get a message. An American news network, Jaafar would be delighted. When I tell Jaafar, I notice he is distracted. He tells me there was a loud explosion during [Yousef's] interview. The building was hit. All communication was lost. "Where is the media," he keeps asking . . . "Baba Amr is finished. In a few days, it will be completely gone. Where is the media?" At this point I am depressed as well, and completely exhausted, and I say, "Jaafar, it's not going to change anything. The media can't stop the planes from dropping bombs. It can't stop the army from walking into Baba Amr to finish what they started. The media can't do anything." He is silent and I feel guilty. I had said exactly what he was thinking, but by saying the words aloud, I had rendered us both obsolete. . . .

Before we hang up, I tell him to be safe. I tell him that I'll call him tomorrow. I go to bed only a couple of hours before morning. My head is pounding. Fifty percent of a neighborhood is destroyed. Omar is surrounded by human limbs,

Jaafar is disconnected from his friends, Yousef is missing, the people of Baba Amr are asking for safe passage for women and children before the army enters to round up the men. They are asking for mercy from a merciless regime. . . .

Jaafar is right. What you just read will not save lives. It will not stop the attacks on Baba Amr, or Idlib, or Zabadani, or Palmyra, or Daraa. It will not change what happened this morning, or what will happen tomorrow. It's just a story of what happened, in a place called Syria, while you were sleeping.[16]

While the world slept and when it was wide awake, the indiscriminate shelling of Baba Amr continued. In one of the shelling episodes, two Western journalists who had been smuggled in from Beirut were killed and a number were injured. One of the injured, Paul Conroy, after being smuggled back to Lebanon, described the dire situation he had left behind. "I've done a fair few wars. I've never seen anything on this level," he said. "There are no targets. It's pure systematic slaughter of a civilian population."[17]

At the time that the Syrian army was flattening Baba Amr and killing its residents, Syrian state television showed a beaming president,[18] along with his glamorous, British-born, British-educated wife, who in February 2011 had adorned the pages of the French issue of *Vogue*. The couple was visiting a hospital, where a young Christian boy apparently had been shot by a Sunni classmate. While not directly mentioned, the sectarian subtext was there for all to see. And indeed, the first lady, whose family originates from Homs, had earlier extolled her husband as the president of all Syrians, not just some Syrians. The Lion himself was in particularly good cheer, making jokes and roar-

Baba Amr after Asad and his army finished with it.
Associated Press / Lens Yong Homsi

ing with laughter, as his army feasted itself upon the smoldering ruin of an entire city neighborhood.

In the midst of the carnage, Bashar al-Asad organized a referendum on a new constitution that was professedly advertised to democratize Syria's political system. The main feature of the new document was ending the Baath Party's role as the "leader of the state and society." A multiparty system would be legalized, and other parties would have the "right" to name their own candidate for the presidency, which would be set at a maximum of two consecutive seven-year terms, a stipulation that would allow Asad to stay in power till 2028. The referendum was held on February 26, 2012, had a turnout of 57.4 percent of eligible voters, and was approved by an inspiring 89.4 percent of voters. While the referendum earned the immediate endorsement of Russia and China, Arab and Western countries unanimously dismissed the constitution as meaningless and the vote as "a farce."[19] Claims of massive fraud abounded. *The Economist* reported one incident related to the magazine by a Damascus resident: bus passengers were stopped at one of the army checkpoints ringing the capital and asked to hand over ID cards. After a few minutes, the cards were returned and the passengers were thanked for voting.[20] Even if one were to believe that the impressive percentages were not greatly inflated, the vote, taken without neutral monitors, at a time when the regime was willfully and indiscriminately butchering its own people, was nothing less than a sham. To that effect, perhaps the most biting criticism came from a hitherto good friend, Iraq's prime minister, Nuri al-Maliki. "A national unity government must be formed, freedoms must be given, an impartial election under United Nations and Arab supervision must be held and a national council should be elected to approve the constitution," he said of the Syrian situation.[21] By this time, however, no threat or censure would change the political and military course the Asad regime doggedly and without pity had set for itself. After all, stymied by Russia and China, the UN Security Council had literally given Syria's president the green light.

While Bashar was shelling Homs with rockets and mortar, and surrounding it with tanks and heavy armor, the Arab League, supported by Europe and the United States, brought a resolution to the Security Council in early February that asked all parties, government and armed opposition groups, to stop the violence and reprisals. It called for Asad to step aside, and for an inclusive Syrian-led political process aimed at addressing the legitimate concerns of the Syrian people.[22] This was the second time in four months that a move to condemn Asad's actions had come before the Council. Since the first was summarily vetoed by Russia and China, the second was watered down as a result of many hours of negotiations with the Russians. Still, when it came to a vote, it was vetoed by Russia and China. Apparently no amount of bloodthirsty assaults by Asad's troops on the people, or of the grotesque human rights violations that were being committed, would dissuade the Russians and Chinese from coming to the aid of their authoritarian comrade-in-arms. The fact that the Russians bore the mantle of the last defenders of the Asad regime would hardly raise any eyebrows. After all, Vladimir Putin's meteoric political ascent was built on razing the Chechen city of Grozny to the ground.

Fortified by the backing of his international friends and the heartwarming political support he received from the Syrian population in the February referendum (89.4 percent, lest we forget), Asad decided that the time had come to follow his political triumphs with a momentous military victory. After weeks of softening up Baba Amr—laying siege to the neighborhood, preventing food, supplies, and essential medicine from entering, and shelling it remorselessly—the order was given on February 29, 2012, to finish off Baba Amr once and for all. Foreign television and newspaper reporters immediately realized something dreadful was happening when all connections with the citizen journalists in Homs went dead—Skype screens and Facebook and Twitter pages, as well as YouTube went black, as those who had been manning the stations for months had no choice but to literally run for their lives.

Realizing that they could not win the fight against advancing heavy armor, the lightly armed members of the Free Syrian Army retreated from Baba Amr. Soon tanks began their assault, and army snipers shot at people to keep them indoors, so that security personnel and armed gangs in civilian clothing would go from door to door in search of the men who had defied them. Refugees, mainly women and children, who later were able to cross into Lebanon, came bearing tales of summary executions, horror stories of men having their throats slashed.[23] A close associate of the Damascus regime said, "They want to take it [Baba Amr], whatever happens, without restraint, whatever the cost." He added that defeating the rebels in Homs would leave the opposition without any major stronghold in Syria, easing the crisis for Asad, who remained confident he would survive.[24] Day after day, for an entire week after the entry of Syrian ground troops, desperate pleas from the International Red Cross for its teams to be allowed to go into Baba Amr with medicines and supplies were turned down. Syrian officials said that the area was being cleared of mines and booby traps. But there can be little doubt that revenge killings and mass slaughter had occurred, and opposition activists believed that the delay was to cover this up. When Red Cross volunteers finally were allowed in on March 7, they found a neighborhood that was almost completely deserted, and that had been thoroughly cleaned up by the Syrian army. In the end, piles of smashed bricks, mortar, and concrete would make it hard to believe that the ghost town was once a bustling city quarter where some 50,000 human beings had lived.

Once in control of Homs, the Syrian army moved on to Idlib, another defiant city in north Syria near the border with Turkey, where residents had erected barricades and armed protestors had kept security forces at bay for months. But when tanks, heavy armor, and artillery units arrived after the subjugation of Homs, and rockets and mortars began to rain on the city, even the most optimistic observer would know that Idlib's days of freedom were numbered. Less than two weeks after the obliteration of Baba Amr, the Syrian army captured the city. In the orgy of shelling and shooting, Asad's security forces seemed not to be worried about the supply of weapons and ammunition, and indeed Russia's foreign minister would admit that Moscow was supplying Asad with weapons, but he assured the world that these were not the kind of arms that would be used against protestors.[25] The world must have exhaled a huge sigh of relief.

And to assure the world that, regardless of the violence, political reform was his foremost priority, Asad staged a "multi-party" election in early May for the 250-seat parliament. In light of the wholesale killings that were taking place, the elections, in the words of an activist from the city of Hama, were akin to "a dance on the corpses of dead people."[26] Few took the candidates, or their commitment to democracy, seriously. One Damascene street vendor selling watches was heard shouting: "Authentic Japanese watches, and with every watch you get a candidate for parliament."[27] The results were announced on live television by the head of the electoral commission, who rattled off the names of the 250 successful candidates, but refused to identify them by their political affiliation. Pressed by the few journalists who had been invited to witness the "historic occasion," he would only estimate that Asad's Baath Party and its allies might have won around 70–75 percent of the parliamentary seats.[28] As it turned out, he was not off the mark, since two days later, Syrian state television announced that the Baath Party and its allies won 183 seats out of 250, a 73 percent share of the new parliament.[29] The two opposition parties, who defied a boycott call by anti-regime forces, ended up with only five seats between them.

Beyond the sideshow of the elections, violence would continue. By late fall 2012, more than 30,000 people had been killed, most of them unarmed protestors and civilians. And while the Asad regime was substantially shaken by the vehemence and persistence of the protests, it continued to survive, its posture unbending, its savagery untamed. Well into the second year of the protests, there were few signs that Asad would be forcibly ousted by his own people—somewhat of a surprise given the endurance of the uprising, the fervor and vigor of the protestors, and the immense sacrifices that had been given. But there were a number of factors that could explain the ability of the Asad regime to last longer than those of his fellow dictators in Tunisia, Egypt, Libya, and Yemen.

One was the lack of unity among the opposition groups, which were unable to form an authoritative organization that could organize directed and purposeful resistance and become the acknowledged voice of the opposition internationally. Over twenty separate groups coalesced into the Syrian National Council (SNC) and the National Coordination Committee (NCC), with the two umbrella organizations spending more time hurling insults and recriminations at each other than streamlining opposition to Asad. And it was not as though either of the organizations was a coherent entity; the constituent groups continued to operate in an ad hoc fashion, paying no attention to their leaderships. As one member who quit the SNC in March 2012 said, "There is no Council; it's an illusion. . . . Everyone is working by himself and the whole Council has not met once."[30] The council was divided on matters of religion between secularists and Islamists, on ideological grounds between leftists and free marketers, and even ethnically, with Syrian Kurds withdrawing, accusing the other members of the opposition of Arab chauvinism. A change in the SNC leadership in the summer of 2012 resulted in somewhat less internal fractiousness and better coordination with FSA units. But the council had a long way to go to emulate the role played by Libya's Transitional National Council during the anti-Qadhafi uprising.

200   THE SECOND ARAB AWAKENING

Nor was the Free Syrian Army any more cohesive when it initially took up arms against Asad's army. It did engage Asad's military, particularly in Baba Amr and Idlib, and it did carry out a number of high-profile guerrilla actions against security quarters and installations; but it remained essentially a disparate collection of local groups that had no nationwide organization, to say nothing of a proper command structure.[31] By the fall of 2012, FSA activities had increased as more and more soldiers defected, and as more lethal weaponry, financed by Gulf States, found its way to the rebels across the Turkish border. The FSA engaged Asad's army more frequently in various parts of the country, mainly in highly visible hit-and-run operations that inflicted perceptible damage on government forces. The main impact was psychological as the regime's hitherto invincible image began to be seriously dented, and people began to talk about "civil war," and criticize regime policy more openly. Indeed, in June 2012 the United Nations labeled the Syrian conflict a "civil war," after which Asad conceded that Syria indeed "was in a state of war."[32] While such an admission would raise the spirit of the FSA, even with their increasing strength and confidence, FSA fighters faced a formidable adversary in Asad's army.

More than a quarter of a million strong, the Syrian army was supplemented by a paramilitary militia of over 100,000, an elite special forces division of over 10,000 men, and a Republican Guard that was even larger. And while defections did occur, increasing in number with time, these were nothing like the wholesale defections of entire military units that occurred in Libya and Yemen. Unlike Egypt's military, who early on proclaimed their neutrality in Mubarak's conflict with his people, the Syrian army would remain for a long time solidly behind Asad. This was not surprising, given that more than 70 percent of its officer corps belonged to Asad's minority Alawite community.[33] Driven by more than just tribal and regional ties, the Alawites well knew that after more than four decades of coercive dominion, not only did they stand to lose their privileged status with Asad's demise but perhaps their well-being, even survival, as well.

But it was not just the Alawites who were in Asad's corner. Other minorities, who along with the Alawites make up more than a quarter of Syria's population, plus a proportion of Sunnis who had many economic ties with the ruling elites, and who acted as an important part of the financial backbone of the Asad regime,[34] were hardly sanguine about the possibility of empowered Sunni radicals replacing the secularist status quo.[35] And the regime unwaveringly played to these fears. In its reporting of the opposition's "atrocities," Syria's official media made sure to constantly invoke the feared name of al-Qaeda. These fears were compounded by accounts of brutal killings committed by the FSA against regime supporters.

Still, as the civil war grew larger and uglier, and the opposition continued to fight, showing little sign of fatigue, the solidity of the pro-Asad coalition seemed to crack—incrementally but surely. Asad's supporters found it ever more difficult to justify the carefree devastation of cities and the unspeakable atrocities committed by government forces. And economic sanctions, made more severe with every passing day, began to be felt nationally, particularly by the Sunni-dominated business class. Nor were people any longer confident of government assurances of a soon to be delivered final victory against the "criminals and terrorists."

This skepticism was given credence when on July 18, 2012, a bomb attack on a security building in the heart of Damascus killed a number of senior members of the country's National Security Council, including the defense minister and Asad's brother-in-law. Simultaneously, FSA fighters launched an offensive on various parts of the capital, engaging Asad's forces in fierce fighting. The Syrian army, using tanks, heavy weapons, and helicopter gunships, took more than a week to clear the city of the FSA fighters. But this was a hollow victory. The message was loud and clear—the heavily fortified capital, the seat of Asad's power, where all of the regime's key institutions resided, was no longer immune to the gathering rebellion.

In the Damascus attack, the FSA exhibited a level of tactical coordination not seen before, and this foretold more difficult days ahead for the ever more stretched Syrian army. Indeed, the regime barely had time to bask in its latest "triumph" against the "criminal terrorist gangs" when news came through of FSA units taking over large swaths of Aleppo, the second largest city in Syria, and the country's commercial capital. There again, elite troops with heavy weaponry had to be moved to Aleppo from other parts of the country, and this time the Syrian air force, with its fighter jets, entered the fray. But the rebels were also receiving more sophisticated weaponry, including rocket-propelled grenades, and increasing numbers of foreign Sunni fighters were entering Syria. These Jihadists, contemptuous of the Alawite creed and as unrestrained by human rights norms as Asad's forces, entered the fray determined to kill the dictator's soldiers, even after these were captured and disarmed. Civilians suspected of being on the other side would meet the same fate. At the same time, Asad's ranks were being bolstered by Shiite fighters from Lebanon's Hizbollah. By the fall of 2012, Syria was engulfed in a fully fledged civil war whose undertones were decidedly sectarian.

All this could have been averted had Asad acceded early on to public demands for liberalizing his totalitarian rule, making real concessions and embarking on some meaningful political reforms. But he and the ruling elites contemptuously cast aside people's aspirations for democratic change; instead, he chose the path of unrestrained violence, inflicting unimaginable sufferings and heartbreaks on his people, all of which he intermittently would sugarcoat with empty words and hollow promises. Regardless of the outcome to this tragedy, it would take a very long time for Syria to recover from the human, physical, and psychological devastation wrought on it by the barbarism of a lion reverting to his savage roots.

Cars covered with election campaign posters prior to Iraq's December 2005 first-ever free elections. *Associated Press / Asaad Muhsin*

Chapter Seven

TENTATIVE STEPS ON THE DEMOCRATIC ROAD

Morocco, Jordan, Iraq, and Lebanon

I t was not only the countries that exploded in revolt which were touched by the virus of freedom. The demand for democratic reforms spread to other countries, even if these did not experience the same revolutionary fervor. In some cases, such as the long-established monarchies of Morocco and Jordan, the kings quickly preempted revolutionary eruptions by promising, and acting on, major political reforms. Others, such as Iraq and Lebanon, had already embarked on the process of transitioning to democracy by holding free and fair elections long before the eruption of Arab revolts in 2011. While the experiences of the four countries varied, in no case was the pursuit of democracy marred by willful and widespread state violence. At the same time, in every case, serious questions would remain about the long-term potency of the democratic transition.

In Morocco, youth from the educated urban middle class were highly networked into all the social media avenues that had been so effective in spreading the message of revolt in Egypt and Tunisia, and they had no shortage of grumbles to text-message and tweet:

pervasive corruption, high unemployment, a large gap between rich and poor, and of course a restricted political space. The most virulent criticisms concerned the king's inner circle of relatives, friends, and advisers, labeled *al-Makhzan* ("the depository"), who were said to control a disproportionate share of the country's business activities, and who acted almost as a parallel decision-making institution to the cabinet. There were also complaints that began as murmurs, but grew in volume, about the king's broad constitutional powers, which allowed him to interfere at will in the workings of the cabinet and parliament. Soon, the word had gone round that Moroccans would emulate their Egyptian and Tunisian comrades and hit the streets demanding reforms. The date was set for February 20, 2011.

Some Moroccans might have expected, or hoped for, the Egyptian and Tunisian unfolding of events to be replicated in their own country. But the majority would not have that goal in mind. They would demand reform, but not a total dispatch of the political system. After all, Morocco was very different from the two North African republics with their ousted presidents. It is first and foremost a monarchy; its present king, Muhammad VI, belongs to a dynasty that has ruled Morocco since 1664. This historical longevity is tinged with powerful religious overtones that together endow the king with the kind of legitimacy that is simply not available to republican presidents. The king is at once the secular leader of the country and its "Commander of the Faithful," and until the summer of 2011, the constitution declared him to be "sacred." All this meant, in the words of one Moroccan observer, that "the King has tremendous religious and political capital,"[1] something that neither Ben Ali nor Mubarak had. In addition, King Muhammad, who in 1999 succeeded the repressive and much feared Hassan II, had worked hard at softening the oppressive image of the monarchy;* and had embarked on a number of reforms that won him credit and praise from his subjects.

Typical of the way he would respond to anticipated mass flare-ups, the king tried to preempt the February 20 protests by doubling governmental subsidies on prices of flour, sugar, and cooking oil. He announced his initiative five days before the protest date, hoping no doubt to neutralize one of the most prominent of the protestors' complaints—widespread poverty and the huge and increasing gulf between rich and poor. Whether Muhammad VI thought that the move somehow would exert enough calming influence to stop the protest, or at least significantly undermine it, is not clear; but if he did, he was mistaken.

Thousands of protestors went out onto the streets of Rabat, Marrakesh, Casablanca, and other cities. These were patently peaceful demonstrations, and the police and security forces kept their distance, not attempting to impede their progress. The demonstrators held banners and shouted slogans articulating a variety of socioeconomic demands, such as an end to corruption, creation of jobs, facilitating economic opportunities to unemployed youth, help with the relentless rise in prices, and so on. The ruling elite expected these kinds of demands; what they did not expect were demands of a purely political nature. These were particularly disturbing as they included pointed criticisms of the king and his political order. There was a chorus of chants for limiting the wide-ranging monarchical powers, particularly vis-à-vis the cabinet and parliament, and for reforming the constitution. While not new, such explicitly direct attacks on the monarch were rare in Morocco, and must have given Muhammad VI food for thought. Nor would he take much solace from developments in Tunisia and Egypt during the momentous months of February and March.

Realizing that he should not wait too long, the king went on television on March 9, a mere seventeen days after the February 20 demonstrations, and told the country that the time had come for a comprehensive revision of the constitution aimed at strengthening democratic practices in the country. He appointed a committee with the task of drafting a new constitutional text, which then would be submitted to the people for a referendum within three months. And indeed in June, a draft constitutional document was submitted to the people for a referendum to be held on July 1. If approved, the document would curb some of the king's powers. Whereas it had been the prerogative of the king to select his prime minister and members of the cabinet, the committee recommended that the king would appoint a prime minister, now called head of government, from the party that wins the election. The head of government would then propose candidates for governmental ministries and submit their names to the king for approval. The new constitution also declared the independence of the judiciary, severing all earlier ties to the Ministry of Justice. And the word "sacred" characterizing the king was revised to "inviolable." In all this, according to one analyst, "the king may not have abandoned all his powers, but he seems to have curtailed a significant part of them."[2]

It is not that the king would suddenly become a constitutional monarch in the European tradition, a figurehead, a prized national trophy to be dusted off and brought out on occasions of pomp and ceremony. The new constitution still gave him powers far greater than any other institution, and in the area of policy making, the new "head of government" would not be able to act on anything without the king's consent. Indeed, demonstrations did erupt, denouncing the document, and demanding greater restrictions on the king's powers. But preparations to put the constitutional document to a vote in a national referendum went ahead unimpeded, with all the powers and resources of the palace very much behind the "historic reforms." Here is the account of one eyewitness: "The 'yes' campaign received ample screen and radio coverage [with] anchors acting like town criers rather than journalists. Banners promoting a yes vote were hung at the entrances of medinas and city intersections. Youth [carried] flags and pictures of the king, [and] ads were taken out by major companies saying that they and their employees intended to vote yes."[3] Imams throughout Morocco were instructed to preach in favor of the constitutional reforms.[4] It was no surprise that the referendum was passed by a whopping 98.5 percent. Immediately, preparations for elections, scheduled for November 25, got underway.

Before too long, thirty parties had registered to run in the elections. By October, they could be grouped into four categories. Standing alone was the Islamist Justice and Development Party (PJD), which, very much like Ennahdha in Tunisia and the Muslim Brotherhood in Egypt, saw itself, and was perceived by others as well, as the front-runner. To counteract the PJD, eight other parties formed themselves into the Coalition for Democracy Alliance (CDA). These were parties whose leaders were close to the palace, and who had participated on a regular basis in previous governments. Another three parties joined in a coalition calling itself *al-Kutla* (the Group). These parties had traditionally gained support for playing the role of the opposition, distancing themselves from the *al-Makhzan*, but had operated strictly within the system, never challenging the legitimacy of the monarchical political order, and occasionally accepting ministerial positions. Finally, there were a number of small parties that operated independently, deciding not to join any of the three main parties/coalitions.

Since all of the principal secular parties had been on the political scene for a number of decades, and had participated in governance, few people paid attention to their political platforms, made up of well-worn clichés that had been heard before time and time again— general promises of economic development, providing employment, improving the quality of life, fighting corruption, and so on. These parties were all known quantities. The only intriguing contestant was the PJD. While this was not the first election that the party had entered, it certainly was the first in which, under the new constitutional rules and the promise of clean elections, it had a good chance of being asked to form the government.

Secularists waited to pounce on evidence of the usual Islamist allergy to liberal social rules and behavior, but to their dismay, that did not come to pass. From the very beginning, the PJD presented itself not as an "Islamist" party, but as a party with an "Islamic reference," very much on the lines of the moderate Turkish model. Early in the campaign, the leader of the party, Abdelilah Benkirane, had emphatically fixed the party's position on social issues: "Religion belongs to the mosques and we are not going to interfere in people's personal lives."[5] The party avoided campaigning on such "Islamist" issues as women's head scarves, or the banning of alcohol, or personal status matters. Instead, it came out with detailed proposals that showed it to be business-friendly, yet committed to attacking corruption. It also promised to improve the country's educational system, to find jobs for the unemployed, to cut poverty in half, and to raise the minimum wage by 50 percent.[6] Above all, it repeatedly expressed its fidelity to democratic ideals and practices. All in all, the goal of the PJD was to transcend its Islamist image, and to go beyond its traditional constituency in appealing to the concerns of the country's middle class.

The PJD along with the other parties were fighting for representation in a 395-seat parliament. To ensure that women and youth would be represented, the electoral law reserved sixty seats for women candidates, and thirty for candidates under the age of forty. Unlike the vibrant electoral campaign in Tunisia, Morocco's was relatively subdued. Familiar faces that had been on the political scene for many years and the dearth of new parties did not help, nor did boycott calls from the youth movement and from radical Islamists. It seemed that the chief enthusiasm for the process came from the palace, which placed billboards in main squares and streets urging people to "do their national duty" and to "participate in the change the country is undergoing,"[7] as well as issuing repeated announcements on television.

In the end, voter turnout was not exemplary, but still respectable at 45 percent. The PJD came through with the largest number of votes, mustering almost double the seats won by the next party, the Istiqlal of the Kutla coalition. Coming third with just over half the PJD's votes was a party belonging to the eight-party palace coalition. Indeed, the parties tied to the palace could muster only 30 percent of the total vote cast, leaving the PJD and the Kutla, who presented themselves, and were perceived, as the opposition, with enough votes and seats to allow them to form a coalition with a strong potential majority in parliament. Still, none of the parties, or the palace, would have been too pleased with the 22 percent of the vote that seemed to be purposely spoiled, indicating opposition to the whole process. It was clear that a large number of people, one in every five voters, still did not think the king's reform initiative went far enough.

In accordance with the dictates of the new constitution, the king invited the leader of the PJD, Abdelilah Benkirane, to the palace and tasked him with forming a new government. It took six weeks of hard bargaining with strange potential bedfellows, like old Communists on the one hand and allies of the palace on the other, before Benkirane could form his government. The palace also objected to the appointment to the Ministry of Justice of a PJD member who was a rabid anti-American and a rumored neutral on terrorism, but finally complied on the condition that a friend of the king be put in charge of the critical Interior Ministry. The king also insisted on an independent for the Ministry of Defense. The PJD did end up with twelve ministerial positions, including those of Foreign Affairs, Justice, and Communications. However, women did not fare well. In the thirty-one-member cabinet, the only ministry headed by a woman was that of Family and Social Development, a low-tier ministry, which traditionally received one of the lowest budget allocations. Further, the new minister, a PJD member, had served in parliament before, and her record on issues important to feminists was checkered at best. Regardless, the king formally appointed the cabinet on January 3, 2012—the first Moroccan government led by a political party with an Islamist orientation.

Euphoric as they might have felt, the PJD and its partners could not but recognize the herculean task confronting them. There was of course the general malaise brought about by many years of palace control and the dominance of *al-Makhzan*. As Benkirane announced his government, many Moroccans, especially those who thought themselves neglected and marginalized, wondered whether much would actually change. The question politically was whether the king, still the custodian of substantial constitutional powers, would allow Benkirane to assert the cabinet's independence to pursue an expanded democratic agenda. While they would wish the new prime minister good fortune, not many would hold their breath in the expectation of this happening any time soon.

A more immediate concern was the state of the country's economy. Out of twenty Arab countries ranked by the United Nations' 2011 *Human Development Report*, Morocco placed a dismal fifteenth, with almost 16 percent of the population either living in, or exposed to the threat of, extreme poverty. According to the report, about one in four of the urban youth was unemployed, and among university graduates the figure increased to 40 percent. A month after taking office, Benkirane's government was faced with a reality check when large, angry demonstrations by unemployed university graduates erupted in the capital, Rabat. There was no mistaking the hopelessness felt by a whole generation of educated young men and women who saw little or no prospect of gainful employment in their future. Tragically, three of the despairing demonstrators set themselves on fire, and one died from his burns.[8] The PJD had promised to quickly alleviate the unemployment crisis, but regardless of its pledges during the electoral campaign, delivering on these promises was not an easy matter.

The main problem is the extent to which Morocco's economy is tied to Europe.[9] For starters, Morocco's tourist industry, which brings in more than $7 billion annually in hard currency, and employs upward of 400,000 workers, depends for its survival on Europe, which provides some 80 percent of the country's tourists. The financial crisis that afflicted the eurozone saw a perceptible dwindling of European tourists, many of whom, in 2011 and 2012, had canceled, delayed, or shortened their holidays. Another major hard currency earner is the remittances that flow into Morocco from nationals working abroad. These remittances had contributed significantly to the reduction of poverty, by an astounding 40 percent, between 1991 and 2008, and in 2011 they generated around $7 billion in hard currency income for Morocco. Since the vast majority of these workers find employment in Spain, France, and Italy, remittances shrank significantly because of Europe's financial crisis. Finally, slackening economic growth in the European Union would show in the trade figures. In 2011, European imports of Moroccan goods grew by 7.8 percent, a significant reduction from the 19.8 percent figure in 2010. Most affected was the textile industry, which employs more than 200,000 people. As Europe's Mediterranean countries, Morocco's natural economic partners, proved to be the most vulnerable to the continent's financial crisis, Morocco could hardly escape the resulting economic slowdown.

This was the situation into which the PJD-led government began its much heralded tenure. In the face of high expectations, in part generated by the PJD's own promises, the new government would be hard put even to maintain the unemployment level at its 2011 rate, let alone reduce it as it had pledged. Of course, the economic turmoil was not of the PJD's own making, and much goodwill had accompanied the party's assumption of power. But patience is a transient commodity, especially when it rests on empty stomachs and unfulfilled hopes. Being untarnished by corruption would stand the PJD in good stead, but ultimately it would have to deliver the goods, to meet the minimum demands of the expectant multitude. Otherwise the PJD would be perceived as no different from its discredited predecessors, and that would engender the kind of disillusionment that could close the window of opportunity for broader democracy that came with the November 2011 elections.

Very much like Morocco, Jordan was a quintessential hybrid regime in which the king dominated, but allowed certain political freedoms, such as free elections and an abundance of independent newspapers and magazines. This semblance of openness separated countries like Jordan and Morocco from the murderous regimes of Syria or Libya, or the less violent, but still autocratic, Egypt and Tunisia. So at the time that Muhammad Bouazizi set himself on fire in Tunisia in late December 2010, King Abdullah of Jordan had very few worries about his country's political milieu, or about his unquestioned dominance of the political process.

As in Morocco, the Jordanian king could afford to be tolerant because of the historical and religious legitimacy associated with his monarchy. The Hashemite Kingdom of Jordan takes its name from Hashem, the uncle of the Prophet Muhammad. The Hashemite kings thus benefit from an aura of sacredness that resonates with those segments of Jordan's population, particularly the tribes in rural areas, which still cling to primordial tribal values. To these people, the original inhabitants of the eastern bank of the Jordan River, who traditionally had provided the bulk of the country's army, the king is both a tribal leader and a revered grandee. Other Jordanian citizens, a majority, are of Palestinian origin, most of whom had either left or been expelled by Israel. Tension between the two communities had always existed. It reached a zenith in 1970, when the Jordanian army in a bloody confrontation expelled thousands of Palestinian guerrillas from Jordan. But four decades later, much of the wounds had healed, and the Palestinians were loyal citizens of the Hashemite Kingdom. Urban, professional, and generally affluent, their loyalty to the crown stems from the rapid advancement in their socioeconomic condition, which propelled them to an elevated and influential status in Jordan.

Much like his father, King Hussein, who ruled Jordan from 1953 until his death in 1999, Abdullah believed that the backbone of the regime's support base resided in the rural and tribal domain of Jordan. This segment of the population was privileged not only in army recruitment but also in parliamentary membership, as was evident in the general elections held in November 2010, a mere few weeks before Bouazizi's suicide would render obsolete all assumptions about politics in Arab lands.[10] While the election itself was free, it was not necessarily fair, as the electoral law skewed parliamentary representation in favor of rural areas, leaving urban districts, where Palestinian Jordanians tend to reside, woefully underrepresented. In many tribal areas, each MP represented 2,000–3,000 voters, compared with more than 90,000 voters in the capital, Amman. The only party with any organization to speak of, the Islamic Action Front (IAF), whose main support base was to be found in urban areas, boycotted the elections. The upshot of all this was that parliament would be dominated by tribal candidates whose loyalty to the king was unquestioned.

Not that parliament had that much power. Indeed, its title as the legislative branch of government belied its actual authority and responsibilities. It was the cabinet, not parliament, that initiated legislation, and parliament played no role in the formation of the cabinet; that was the king's prerogative. However, parliament did have the constitutional power to submit a vote of no confidence in the prime minister or individual ministers. In terms of legislation, parliament could only discuss bills that were brought to it, primarily to approve them, but sometimes it was able to veto the occasional bill. Critically, the king had the power to dissolve parliament at will. He did that in 2001, and again in 2009, when he decided that parliamentarians, particularly the Islamists of the IAF, had become too obstreperous for his taste.

At the turn of the year, in the early days of January 2011, on the eve of the eruption of protests and demonstrations in the Arab world, the king could feel comfortable about political conditions in Jordan. He had maintained the system of monarchical dominance through constitutional prerogatives and by designing electoral rules that ensured a pliable and friendly parliament. And apart from worries about the economy (an affliction that struck every Arab country that was not a petroleum producer), the population seemed tolerably content, and more to the point, quiet. But Jordan would not be immune to the revolutionary upheavals that were gathering momentum and spreading to various Arab countries and cities.

The first demonstrations occurred in an unlikely place, the villages in rural areas, among the very tribes on whose unconditional loyalty the monarchy had depended. Theirs were mainly economic and anti-corruption demands, bringing attention to the huge gulf between their own conditions of abject poverty and those of the conspicuous rich in the cities, particularly Amman. The unstated subtext was the belief that many of the affluent accumulated their wealth through proximity to the palace. Rampant rumors that the king had recently bought a yacht as a birthday present for his glamorous wife, Queen Rania, would only extenuate the prevailing mood of discontent.[11] Very quickly, the protests spread to Amman and other Jordanian cities. This time students, journalists, lawyers, and the like went out to the streets echoing the same demands for an end to corruption and for better management of the economy. To the king's alarm, they were joined by a group of retired army generals and security officers. The protests were a relatively mild affair, peaceful, even polite, with demonstrators targeting the prime minister, Samir al-Rifai, thought to be a scion of the wealthy class and its shady ways. But a new element had been added. The protestors were now demanding changes to the electoral law and to the constitutional provisions that gave the king the power to appoint the prime minister and cabinet.

Trying to fob off the protests, and particularly the latest demands for real democratic reforms, the king at the end of January 2011 sacked his prime minister and announced a $230 million aid package that increased wages, lowered the prices of fuel, and further subsidized the country's cooperative stores to reduce the prices of basic foodstuffs and commodities. Neither move seemed to win him much praise. The new prime minister, Marouf Bakhit, was no reformer, and the subsidies were not thought to have gone far enough. As one disgruntled civil servant said, "the government promised [us] a pay raise of $28, while politicians play with millions."[12] Protests would continue, now better organized and usually led by the Islamic Action Front, but they also included leftists and trade unionists. As February progressed, the demonstrators would become more impatient, and their demands for political and economic reforms shriller and less decorous.

Recognizing that he no longer could continue to offer crumbs at the margins of the protestors' central demands, the king announced on March 14 the formation of a fifty-two-member committee of national dialogue, made up of representatives from various political parties (including the IAF), trade unions, women's organizations, as well as journalists, teachers, retired generals, lawyers, and academics. The commission was tasked with producing within three months new laws for elections and political parties. Objections to the committee were immediately raised, as it did not address the protestors' central demand that the appointment of the prime minister and cabinet should be the responsibility of the elected parliament, not the king. But overall, the creation of the committee was seen as a move in the right direction, particularly as the king hinted heavily that future prime ministers should come from parliamentary majorities. Within a month, protests and demonstrations had lost much of their earlier numbers and vigor.

By June, the committee had produced a set of recommendations that were meant to reduce the electoral imbalance between rural and urban areas and introduce a proportional representation system that would better reflect voters' choices. The king applauded the work of the committee, whose recommendations would go to parliament for study and debate, and ultimately would be presented to the king for his signature. But the king cautioned that this should not be a hurried process, that it would take "at least two or three years" to establish the kind of mature political parties able to present and implement meaningful and nationally relevant programs through the electoral process.[13] Given that the IAF was the only party that qualified as a coherent and functioning organization, it was obvious that the king was allowing other political forces a two- to three-year grace period to establish organizational structures and generate bases of popular support that would enable them to compete with the Islamist party. Parliament was also asked to work on amending the constitution to allow for the creation of an autonomous electoral commission and an independent constitutional court.

In the midst of all these efforts at political reform, a disconnect existed in the person of the prime minister, Marouf al-Bakhit, who throughout his tenure had proven very much allergic to change. So immovable had he become that 70 of the 120 members of parliament sent a letter to the king in October demanding that he dismiss Bakhit and his cabinet. Given the overwhelming mood for reform in the country, King Abdullah obliged, and appointed as his new prime minister a respected lawyer, Awn Khasawneh, who at the time of his appointment was a judge and vice president of the International Court of Justice in The Hague.

Khasawneh's appointment was universally applauded. A spokesman for retired military service members, a group of ex-army generals who had been particularly vociferous about corruption in high places, approved of the new appointment, saying, "Awn Khasawneh is known for his integrity, and has no corruption issues in his past like the rest."[14] The new prime minister's legal background would serve him well as parliament and government tackled complex and consequential constitutional legislation. The king told his prime minister that his first priority was "the completion of legislation and laws . . . at the forefront of which [were] the elections and political parties' laws."[15] Even skeptics agreed that the reform laws package would fare better under the new management than it did during Bakhit's premiership.

Although political reform was the issue that dominated parliamentary debates and the public space generally, the new government could not neglect the country's dire economic condition. Jordan's lack of natural resources has endowed it with a perpetually weak economy. In 2012, unemployment was estimated to stand at some 30 percent of the workforce, while a 20 percent increase in the trade deficit in 2011 led to a record fiscal deficit. Recognizing the dangers to a fellow monarch implicit in a faltering economy, the kings and emirs of the Gulf States set up a $2.5 billion fund in December 2011 (with another $2.5 billion going to the kingdom of Morocco) to help finance critical development projects. Europe too made available upward of $1.4 billion dollars in assistance and loans for 2011–13, primarily to encourage the king's political reforms. Such subventions were bound to ease Jordan's immediate economic woes, but the government was well aware that major and difficult decisions had to be made in regard to a non-productive agricultural sector, controlling governmental subsidies of food and essential goods, coming up with solutions to dwindling water supplies, creating jobs in a challenging economic climate, and confronting the incendiary issue of corruption.

While similarly complex and difficult decisions awaited the new government in the political domain, at least the legislative process seemed to be underway, and political reform was being discussed and acted on. Indeed, in March 2012, parliament passed a law for the establishment of an independent electoral commission to oversee and manage elections—the first legislation to emerge from the batch of constitutional reforms being studied and debated in parliament. However, suddenly and in the midst of all the legislative activity, the king dismissed Khasawneh for "delaying key reform legislation."[16] Not many would believe this to be the real reason; the king had grown uncomfortable with Khasawneh's "risky" efforts to bring the Islamists fully into the debate over legislative reforms.[17] In any case, in light of the extensive fanfare that accompanied Khasawneh's appointment a mere six months earlier, the Jordanian public could be excused for beginning to question the commitment of the palace to real and substantive reform. These doubts were not alleviated by the announcement in June of a new electoral law that, to many Jordanians, did little to change the existing electoral imbalance favoring palace supporters.

Much as in Morocco and Jordan, February and March of 2011 were marked by demonstrations in Iraq. But these were comparatively small and lacked the staying power of the ones that toppled regimes and plunged countries in bloodshed. What distinguished the protests in Iraq was the nature of their declared goals. The demands for free elections and new political leaders that had defined the uprisings in other Arab countries were largely absent. This was hardly surprising; the Iraqi government of Prime Minister Nuri al-Maliki had been in power for less than six years, having been put there by the Iraqis themselves in two free and fair elections in December 2005 and March 2010. Instead, protestors were lamenting the abysmal performance of the freely elected Maliki government. The cabinet more often than not was deadlocked, the prime minister increasingly treated with disdain the very democratic process that had put him in office, parliament seemed unable to

discharge its oversight function, and all this meant that few policies were being formulated or implemented—jobs were not created, services were not provided, and security remained elusive.
Things were so bad that the 2012 "Failed States Index," provided
annually by the Fund for Peace organization, ranked Iraq ninth of
181 states. The demonstrators reflected the frustration of the general public; after all, they had done what was asked of them: they
took advantage of the new freedoms, went to the polls in March
2010, and put into parliament fresh faces they thought would produce an effective government. Indeed, at the time, the March 2010
election was seen as the pivotal event that would make Iraq a functioning democratic state. That it did not do so was in no way the
citizens' burden.

Throughout the country's history a Sunni Arab minority (about
20 percent of the population) had monopolized political power
over a Shiite Arab majority (around 60 percent) and a non-Arab
Kurdish community that inhabited the mountainous north and
constituted some 17 percent of the population. The dominance
of the Sunnis attained an emphatic and violent character under
Saddam Hussein's regime, including genocidal assaults against the
Kurds and Shiites. After Saddam's ouster in 2003, followed by the
eruption of ethnosectarian tensions and violence, the first general
election that occurred in December 2005 produced a quintessentially sectarian vote. Shiites voted for Shiite parties, Sunnis voted
for Sunni parties, and Kurds voted for Kurdish parties. The only
party that espoused a secular and non-ethnic electoral platform, *al-
Iraqiya* (the Iraqi) under the leadership of Ayad Allawi, was handed
a drubbing in the elections, receiving no more than 8 percent of
the National Assembly seats.

Maliki, who belonged to the Daawa Party, a member of the
Shiite coalition that won almost half of the parliamentary seats,

became prime minister, and spent the first two years of his tenure beholden to the other powerful figures in the Shiite coalition.
After a terrorist bombing of one of Shiite Islam's holiest mosques
in February 2006, a civil war erupted between Sunnis and Shiites,
turning the country into a bloody and lawless land where the
government could do little to protect citizens. By the end of 2007,
Maliki had become the butt of criticisms domestically and from
abroad. He was belittled for being weak and ineffectual, and for
being totally beholden to various Shiite groups and their grandees.
But things would change starting in the spring of 2008.

Having witnessed the success of the Americans in subduing the
Sunni insurgency through overwhelming force and by coaxing
the Sunni tribes away from al-Qaeda, Maliki decided to take on
the Shiite Mahdi army and its leader, the young firebrand cleric
Moqtada al-Sadr. The Mahdi army had established political and
security control over a large swath of Shiite areas, including the
port city of Basra, Iraq's third largest city, and the Baghdad neighborhood, Sadr City, home to over 2 million Shiites. In March,
Iraqi security forces backed by American and British airpower and
logistical support launched a massive attack on the Mahdi army in
Basra, and by May it had taken control of the city and established a
measure of normalcy. Before long the pattern was repeating itself
in other Shiite towns and areas in the south. But perhaps Maliki's
biggest success was subduing the Mahdi army in Sadr City, when
over 10,000 government troops would enter the Shiite neighborhood, bringing a calm not seen for a number of years.

The state's victory over lawless paramilitary groups brought
Maliki much goodwill among the population. Taking heart from
the widespread popularity that came on the heels of the newly
found assertiveness of the state and its institutions, Maliki formed
his own party, calling it the State of the Law (SOL). He denounced

sectarianism and advocated a vigorous espousal of Iraqi nationalism. Maliki's dramatic transformation from sectarian to nationalist,
from weak to strong, would bear fruits in the 2009 local elections.
Seen as the person responsible for bringing back the authority of
the state, the voters would vote heavily for the SOL, particularly
in Shiite areas. The results showed that the SOL garnered more
votes than any other electoral entity in no fewer than nine of the
fourteen provinces that held elections (the three Kurdish provinces
of Irbil, Sulaymaniya, and Duhok, as well as the disputed province
of Kirkuk, did not hold local elections).

No wonder that Maliki and his party would go into the March
7, 2010, general elections confident of victory. He expected to get
enough votes to be able to dictate coalition terms or even, with
a slight nod from lady luck, to squeeze through with an outright
majority. But to his surprise (and the surprise of others), it soon
became clear that the Iraqi voter had other ideas, and the outcome
was genuinely in doubt. The uncertain result carried on throughout
the election and the vote counting, finally producing an outcome
that would come to haunt Maliki and astound many observers.

The winner this time round was the secular al-Iraqiya, which had
been trounced four years earlier, but which this time ended up with
ninety-one seats, the largest number of seats in the assembly. Maliki
and his State of the Law Party finished a close second with eighty-
nine seats, and the Shiite grouping, the Iraqi National Alliance (INA),
garnered seventy seats, placing third. Not only the political leaders
but the near 80 percent of sitting parliamentarians whom the voters sent packing had learnt their first hard lesson in the meaning of
democracy. The voters were making a point that they would no longer blindly follow their sectarian instincts, that they would choose
representatives whom they thought were the best qualified for the
job, and that they intended to hold their leaders accountable. A *New*

York Times headline, "The Iraqi Voter Rewrites the Rulebook,"[18] summed up the new sentiment.

While the Iraqi voters showed a political maturity that augured well for the country's progress toward democracy, the aftermath would soon temper such hopes. Immediately after the results were announced, it became clear that the increasingly discriminating Iraqi voters would be thwarted by political leaders whose commitment to democracy was contingent on democracy serving their own interests. To many of these leaders, it seemed that the only acceptable prize of the electoral process was the office of the prime minister, not that of the opposition leader.

Foremost among those leaders who thought of "opposition" as another term for failure was the sitting prime minister himself. Maliki simply would not accept the final result of the election which placed him second to Allawi and the secular Iraqiya. He dismissed the results, vowing to sue, and airing his plans to form a new government as the "real" winner. For nine months Iraq had no government while Maliki schemed, cajoled, made promises, and delivered threats, more than once sidestepping constitutional snags, in order to keep the office he increasingly thought of as his by right. Not until late December 2010 did this grueling endeavor finally bear fruit, and Maliki was able to form a government. So many chips had to be cashed that in the end everyone received a portion of the governmental pie. The resulting forty-five-member government inevitably would have little coherence, purpose, or direction. And while in July 2011 Maliki sacked a dozen junior ministers, the cabinet continued to be divided, functioning erratically, and in the process producing very few notable policies. It was incomprehensible to many Iraqis (and to others outside the country) that eight years after the demise of Saddam's rule, in an oil-producing country whose national annual budgets have topped

$80 billion, unemployment stood at more than 25 percent for those under thirty; sewage flowed freely in the streets and into rivers and lakes; and electric grids and plants continued to supply just about half of the demand, and even less during the high demand summer season.

Governmental deadlock and paralysis may have been bad for the country but not necessarily for Maliki. The prime minister exploited the opportunity to make policy independently of the cabinet, thereby centralizing power in his own hands. More often than not, the cabinet's lack of institutional coherence made it easy for the prime minister to block or disregard policies that he deemed to be against his own interests, or that might place some restraint on his unilateralism. Hapless Iraqis soon realized that voting someone into office democratically is one thing; getting him to behave democratically once in office is a different thing altogether.

One incident that would define Maliki's increasing Bonapartist proclivities occurred after the departure of the American forces at the end of 2011. Frustrated with Maliki's unilateral decisions and actions, the deputy prime minister, the Sunni Saleh Mutlaq, called Maliki a dictator in an interview with al-Jazeera, the Arab satellite television station.[19] Incensed, the prime minister dispatched army tanks to surround his deputy's house, creating panic within the household. He unilaterally banned him from attending cabinet meetings, and demanded that parliament fire him for "lacking faith in the political process."[20] For Maliki to equate an injudicious comment with slander against the country's political process—so treasonous that it necessitated the dispatch of armored tanks— would bring back uncomfortable memories of days gone by when Saddam Hussein would equate, as a matter of course, the Iraqi state with his own person. Mutlaq's outburst had come after persistent complaints by al-Iraqiya that hundreds of its supporters had been arbitrarily arrested by Maliki's security forces, detained in secret locations, and tortured to obtain confessions meant to implicate party leaders in terrorist activities and/or planning military coups.

One such "confession" led to the issuing of an arrest warrant on terrorism charges against Iraq's most senior Sunni politician, Tareq al-Hashemi, the country's vice president. Hashemi promptly fled to the Kurdish north, and declared that he was willing to face justice anywhere but in Baghdad. Maliki would respond with the kind of comparison calculated to persuade Iraqis, particularly the majority Shiites, to perceive Sunni leaders as political pariahs. "We gave Saddam a fair trial," Maliki said. "And we'll give Hashemi a fair trial too."[21] The fact that both Mutlaq and Hashemi were not just scions of the Sunni community but democratically elected senior members of al-Iraqiya apparently did not give Maliki pause.

If people thought that parliament would act as the bedrock against authoritarian incursion, they soon would be grossly disheartened. The people of Iraq had delivered in March 2010 what democrats in Iraq and abroad had hoped for. New faces constituted more than 80 percent of the membership of the new parliament, many of them elected on merit rather than on blind sectarianism, and almost all promising to serve the Iraqi "nation," eschewing the narrow ethnosectarian interests that had paralyzed the work of their predecessors. It did not take long for the Iraqi people to recognize what a pipe dream that was. Parliamentarians from Maliki's State of the Law Party behaved as though their only role was to thwart any parliamentary initiative undertaken by al-Iraqiya. On the other hand, members of al-Iraqiya spent much of their time complaining and boycotting sessions. And in the midst of these antagonisms, the Kurdish parties received the applause of the multitude for assuming the role of mediator trying to preserve Iraq;

but in fact they did this only to maintain the special treatment and the wealth of political and economic privileges that came their way since the forcible removal of Saddam.

Parliament did on occasion eschew petty differences and assert its constitutional powers vis-à-vis the executive. For example, it did not comply with Maliki's request to have Mutlaq fired from the cabinet, nor did it accede to Maliki's intense pressure to have the appointment of the head of the integrity commission (tasked with investigating corruption charges) moved from parliament to the prime minister's office. But such acts of parliamentary valor were few and far between. Generally, the institution achieved little, primarily because political deadlock afflicted its internal workings. No wonder therefore that lethargy ensued, and a parliament that many had hoped would be characterized by vigorous debates and a vibrant legislative agenda ended up after not many months with little to show for its exertions, anemic as they were. Time after time, the two-thirds quorum was barely attained, and sometimes not reached at all, and members went on extended breaks while important legislation was shelved.

A few years after the critical, even momentous 2010 elections— years of feeble governance, directed as it was by an increasingly authoritarian prime minister, an ineffective cabinet, and a do-little parliament—the people of Iraq could be forgiven for questioning, and even giving up on, the idea of democracy. Iraqis complained that politicians either had no idea what democracy meant, or used it to get into positions of power in order to serve their own personal interests. They would look at governmental gridlock with increasing dismay and anger, and would end up blaming it on the institutions themselves. When, soon after the capture and execution of Libya's Muammar Qadhafi, an American journalist asked a man sitting in an outside café in Baghdad what advice he had for the post-Qadhafi Libyan regime, the man did not think twice about his answer: "they should have a president who can make all the decisions, and not have all these [parliamentary] blocs like we have now." When reminded that at least he now could express his opinion freely, he and his friends summarily dismissed this right as utterly useless, since the government was not responsive to the public. "Nobody listens to the people,"[22] was the universal lament.

It is true that comparisons with the pre–2003 Saddamist period of slaughter and plunder are utterly untenable. When asked about her opinion of Iraqi politics, a female college student from the Sunni province of al-Anbar, who was demonstrating against the Maliki government, grudgingly admitted that "when Saddam was here, not even one Iraqi could go out in protest because he would be killed."[23] Moreover, politics continued to be conducted within the corridors of democratic political institutions, and while violence persisted, it did not replace dialogue and discussion as the avenues of settling differences and disputes. Yet the truth is that after a decade of transition, Iraq was still making small and uncertain steps on the path toward the democratic goal. The fear is that as frustration, impatience, even malaise, set in and begin to reshape people's attitudes toward the idea of democracy, these hesitant steps might come to a stop, or worse, even begin a backward march.

If Iraq's efforts to transition to democracy were hampered by sectarian loyalties that affected leaders and public alike, Lebanon's democratic struggles arose from similar demographic dislocations. Indeed, these divisions were so sharp and deep that when Lebanon gained its independence in 1943, the country's founding fathers understood that Lebanon's only path to survival was to incorporate these communal divisions into a comprehensive political bargain; hence the birth of Lebanon's "confessional system." In its various incarnations, the latest of which was introduced in 1989, governmental and administrative positions as well as parliamentary seats are allocated to Lebanon's various religious communities in accordance with their population numbers. The president of the republic has always belonged to the Christian Maronite faith (an Eastern Catholic rite), the prime minister to Sunni Islam, the speaker of the house to Shiite Islam, and so on. The 128-seat parliament is divided equally between Christians and Muslims.

For the first three decades of the country's existence, the political situation remained stable, the country's economic performance and outlook was good, and the confessional system worked well. Meanwhile, other Arab countries either proudly declared themselves to be autocratic, or if they felt the need to go through the charade of elections, made sure that they were tightly managed. Uniquely among its neighbors, Lebanon held regular elections that were generally free and fair, and Lebanese politics, while imperfect, were liberal enough to make the country the most politically tolerant in the Arab world. Its temperate weather, Mediterranean beaches, and spectacular mountains added to its easygoing ways, making it the destination of choice for other Arabs looking for a respite from the social and political claustrophobia of their own countries.

Things would take a dramatic turn for the worse in the 1970s. The country's delicate sociopolitical arrangement would begin to strain and eventually break after the large influx of Palestinians into Lebanon—first after the 1967 Arab defeat by the Israelis, and then in the aftermath of the Palestinians' own defeat at the hands of the Jordanian army in 1970. Radicalized by these experiences, and having established bases of operation inside Lebanon, the Palestinians waged a struggle against Israel from Lebanese territory. Israel would retaliate, and retaliate massively, venting its anger not just against the Palestinians but against their host country. As more and more areas of Lebanon felt the devastating impact of Israeli bombing, a schism would occur among Lebanon's communities, with the Muslims generally on the side of the Palestinians and the Christians, on the whole, blaming the Palestinians for Lebanon's misfortune. The fracturing of Lebanon was not long in coming. A bloody civil war broke out in 1975 that was to last till 1990. Thousands were killed, many of them butchered in horrific massacres; whole neighborhoods, including the central commercial district of the capital, Beirut, were destroyed; the infrastructure was ravaged; the army collapsed into sectarian factions; and the government ceased to function. Inevitably, Lebanon became a ready prey to more powerful neighbors: it was invaded and occupied by Syria in 1976 and by Israel in 1982.

After fifteen years of bloodshed and devastation, with no party able to impose dominion on the others, and fatigue setting in, Lebanon's conflicting groups finally agreed on a political settlement that ended the civil war in 1990. The balance of power that had favored the Christians was shifted toward equivalence, and to take note of demographic realities, Shiites were given the same number of parliamentary seats as the Sunnis. A decade and a half of reconstruction followed, its central architect the billionaire Lebanese prime minister, Rafiq al-Hariri. During this period, specifically in 2000, Israel withdrew completely from Lebanon, but Syrian troops remained; a state of affairs hardly palatable to Hariri. It was not surprising that Lebanon's prime minister would fall out of favor with the Syrian occupiers and their new president, Bashar al-Asad; Asad's closest relationship was with Sheikh Hassan

Nasrallah, the leader of Hizbollah, the increasingly powerful Shiite party and militia.

Even though its name means "the Party of God," Hizbollah is not a fundamentalist party that seeks the imposition of an Islamist state in Lebanon. While its original manifesto emphasizes the Islamic identity of the party, it in fact focuses on such political issues as the struggle against Israel and imperialism, and the creation of just rule in Lebanon. It mentions Islamic rule, but emphasizes the necessity of free choice in determining the country's system of government. Over the last three decades, as Hizbollah transformed itself from a small militia to a major political party with a powerful military arm, it followed a two-pronged policy. Domestically, it worked to elevate the political and social status of the Shiite community in the country. Regionally, it waged a relentless struggle against Israel (the "Zionist entity," in Hizbollah's parlance), which meant a close military and political relationship with Shiite Iran and anti-Israel Syria. Hizbollah's weaponry came mostly from Syria and from Iran through Syria; hence the close, even symbiotic relationship with the Syrians.

By 2005, Lebanon was politically split between those who supported Hariri and wanted to see the back of the Syrians, and those led by Hizbollah, who argued for Syria's continued presence in Lebanon. In the run-up to the May 2005 elections, Hariri was working, seemingly successfully, to create an anti-Syrian parliamentary majority. But he would not live to see the fruits of his labor. On February 14, 2005, he and more than twenty of his associates, aids, and bodyguards were killed in a massive explosion in central Beirut so powerful that it blew a crater twelve yards deep.

Lebanon did not join the ranks of the other Arab countries and launch a popular uprising in the winter of 2010–11 because

A Lebanese Christian man kneels in prayer at the grave of the slain Sunni
prime minister Rafiq al-Hariri, February 17, 2005.
Associated Press / Hussein Malla

it already had its own revolution, only five years earlier, in the
wake of the Hariri assassination. The outrage felt in much of the
country then took the form of louder and more insistent demands
for Syria's departure, which was supported by the United States,
Europe, and the United Nations. Pushed into a corner, Asad sought
the help of his client Hassan Nasrallah to stem this rising sentiment. To show the world and the Lebanese that Syria still commanded broad support in Lebanon, Hizbollah arranged for a
pro-Syrian rally in Beirut. On March 8, 2005, half a million people,
mainly Shiite, descended on the capital to show their support for
Asad and a continued Syrian role in Lebanon. But a week later, on
March 14, more than a million people, Christians, Muslims, and
Druze, waving Lebanese flags, and carrying placards and banners

singularly uncomplimentary to Asad and Syria, blanketed the city. Herein lay the proof of what the majority of Lebanese thought of the presence of Syrian "brother" troops in their country. Whatever momentum Asad thought he had built from the boisterous March 8 Hizbollah demonstration had all but disappeared a week later. Not only did Asad's ploy fail, but the March 14 eruption of bitter anti-Syrian feeling, expressed at such an unprecedented scale in the face of thousands of occupying Syrian forces, led to a crescendo of denunciations of the Syrian occupation from the international community. Asad was thus left with little alternative but to order the occupying army to turn around and head back in the direction of the Syrian border. What transpired in other Arab countries in the winter of 2010–11 occurred in Lebanon in the spring of 2005. Expelling the Syrian hegemon, and freeing the country from Asad's stifling despotism, constituted Lebanon's own remarkable uprising.

A month after the Syrian departure, elections were held in Lebanon. Two alliances contested the elections. The first, under the banner of the March 14 Alliance, consisted of the Future Movement, led by Saad Hariri, the son of the slain prime minister; the Progressive Socialist Party (PSP), representing essentially the Druze community, headed by the Druze leader Walid Jumblatt; and other smaller Christian and Sunni parties and independents. Under the banner of the March 8 Alliance, two Shiite parties, Hizbollah and Amal, were joined by the Christian Michel Aoun and his Free Patriotic Movement. It was not on grounds of ideology or principle that Aoun joined forces with the Shiite parties; he simply did not get along with Jumblatt and the young Hariri. The results of the election favored the March 14 Alliance by 72 to 56 seats in the 128-seat parliament. The March 14 Alliance duly formed a government dominated by its members and allies, but with a nod to inclusion gave the opposition five ministries, including that of Foreign Affairs.

The next four years would prove that there is no guarantee that democratically elected governments will function purposefully and competently. From its inception, the cabinet was dogged by virulent Shiite opposition. The initial trigger was the controversy surrounding the assassination of Rafiq Hariri. Suspicion of the involvement of Syria and Hizbollah was rampant, creating an environment of mistrust that brought governance almost to a standstill. The majority might have been with the March 14 Alliance, but the muscle belonged to Hizbollah, the only Lebanese party with its own 10,000-strong militia, armed to the teeth by the Syrians and Iranians. And things would even get worse in 2006 when, without any prior consultation with its colleagues in government, Hizbollah started a war with Israel that would last for over a month, in which Lebanese towns, villages, and infrastructure were ravaged by Israeli bombing.[24] Yet the survival of Hassan Nasrallah, and the fact that the organization was not dismantled as Israel had intended, was turned by Hizbollah's savvy publicity machine into a famous victory for the Shiite organization over the dreaded enemy—a claim that was used to justify Hizbollah's insistent refusal to disarm.

Hizbollah's military prowess would come into play in 2008 in a move that would bring the organization increased political power. The affair began when after a months-long political gridlock caused by Hizbollah demanding veto powers, the cabinet as a whole overruled the minority Shiite members and decided to shut down Hizbollah's illicit telecommunications system. Calling the decision a "declaration of war" against his organization,[25] Nasrallah unleashed his armed militia, who stormed into the Sunni bastion of West Beirut. Fearful that a clash with the Shiite militia would precipitate its own collapse, the army stood on the sidelines. Within less than three days, Hizbollah was in complete control of West Beirut, the governmental and business heart of the capital. Very much embarrassed, the government had little alternative but to answer a call for negotiations from the Gulf state of Qatar. The result was the Doha agreement, which essentially endorsed Hizbollah's demand for veto powers in the cabinet. Henceforth, the March 8 Alliance would have eleven of the thirty cabinet positions, which pushed it above the 33 percent requirement for a veto.

Hizbollah felt energized by its successes, and along with many observers, believed that its position had strengthened in the run-up to the June 2009 general elections. Indeed, as the elections approached, more and more Hizbollah spokesmen were predicting outright victory. In an interview less than a month before the elections, the organization's second in command, Sheikh Naim Qasem, told the *Financial Times*: "I believe that we will take the majority in the parliamentary elections because we have wide support . . . and we believe that these elections will prove that we have this wide popular support." He then went on to expound on the policies to be pursued by the future Hizbollah-dominated government.[26] Western journalists accepted the position hook, line, and sinker, and Western governments began to wonder how to prepare to deal with a government led by an organization labeled "terrorist" by the U.S. Department of State.

American and Western policy makers need not have endured sleepless nights. When the results were announced, they confirmed the voter sentiment expressed in 2005. The March 14 Alliance, with its pronounced pro-Western preferences, scored a decisive victory, garnering seventy-one seats, with the remaining fifty-seven seats going to the Hizbollah-led March 8 Alliance. Voter turnout at 54 percent was the highest since the 1975–90 civil war, and foreign observers attested to the cleanness and fairness of the elections.[27] Hassan Nasrallah went on television and made a gracious concession statement. "We accept the official results in a sporting spirit," he said. "I would like to congratulate all the [candidates] who won [seats], those in the majority and those in the opposition."[28] Words aside, the political reality was that the balance of political forces responsible for the gridlock that plagued the earlier government had not substantively changed. Supporters of the March 14 Alliance might have celebrated a decisive victory, and followers of the March 8 Alliance might have accepted their leader's graciousness in defeat, but few Lebanese believed that a new era of stability and effective governance was finally at hand.

Their pessimism proved right. It took Saad Hariri, the prime minister designate, more than five months to form a government, and he was finally able to succeed only after he agreed to a compromise that clearly favored Hizbollah. The agreement was for a cabinet of thirty members, fifteen of whom belonged to the March 14 majority, ten to the March 8 minority, and five to be appointed by the president. This arrangement made it easy for Hizbollah to veto cabinet decisions (a third plus one). Once again, they had fought tooth and nail for veto privileges, in order to force the cabinet not to accept the anticipated indictment of Hizbollah members for the murder of Rafiq Hariri.

The investigation into Hariri's assassination was conducted by the United Nations Special Tribunal for Lebanon (UNSTL). The tribunal began its work in March 2009 and became a major issue of contention in Saad Hariri's cabinet, as leaks and rumors suggested a shift of culpability from the Syrians to Hizbollah. Opposition from the March 8 ministers grew in shrillness, with mounting accusations that the tribunal was nothing more than an agent for American and Israeli intelligence, determined to sow discord in Lebanon. When, in November 2010, leaked evidence showed "interlinking networks of mobile phones from the vicinity of the blast that killed Rafiq Hariri to Hizbollah's communications center in south Beirut,"[29] the allies of Hizbollah in the cabinet rose up in arms, insisting that Lebanon cease cooperation with the UNSTL and denouncing any forthcoming indictments. Saad Hariri predictably rejected the demand, and the cabinet was thrown into such a crisis that it hardly met over the next two months. Hizbollah's final coup de grâce came in early January 2011. The ten ministers from the March 8 Alliance, joined by a Shiite minister who was one of the five presidential appointees, tendered their resignations, leaving the cabinet with little authority to govern. To add insult to injury for Hariri, the announcement was made as the Lebanese prime minister was meeting President Barack Obama in Washington.

On the collapse of the government, Lebanon's president, Michael Suleiman, asked Najib Miqati, a Sunni billionaire with close ties to Hizbollah, to be the next prime minister. Miqati's candidacy was approved by parliament after the Druze-dominated Progressive Socialist Party switched allegiance to Hizbollah and the March 8 Alliance. But it still would take Miqati a full six months before he was able to form a government. On June 13, he announced a thirty-member cabinet, sixteen of whose portfolios went to the March 8 Alliance. This was precisely what Hassan Nasrallah had been angling for, and it came just in time. Two weeks after Hizbollah ensured its control of the government, the UN tribunal issued four arrest warrants against Hizbollah operatives—in absentia, of course. Nasrallah immediately poured scorn on the arrest warrants, vowing that "no power would be able to arrest the honorable brothers."[30] And indeed more than a year after the indictment, not a single "honorable brother" had been actually arrested.

These machinations were occurring as Lebanese watched the gathering revolutionary storm in other Arab lands. In particular, the Syrian uprising, which began in March 2011, intensified Lebanon's sectarian tensions. Lebanese Sunnis, particularly in the northern city of Tripoli, were vociferous supporters of the Syrian opposition. Indeed, during the assault by the Syrian regime on Homs and Baba Amr, fierce clashes erupted in Tripoli between the city's majority Sunnis and its smaller Alawite and Shiite communities, which cost the lives of at least three people, and left twenty-three wounded. Lebanese Christians said little, but they were no friends of the Syrian rulers. Only the Shiites remained strong supporters of the Damascus government.

Having depended on Syria for long-standing military, logistical, and political backing, Hizbollah and its leader were Asad's most ardent defenders in the Arab world. In May 2011, Nasrallah personally urged the Syrian population to end their protest and support their president. He promised them that "Bashar was serious about carrying out reforms."[31] Many months and thousands dead later, Nasrallah's support for his friend Bashar had not waned. According to the Hizbollah leader, Bashar was leading "a resistance regime," and the opposition in Syria was working with Israel and the United States "to destroy Syria."[32] Hizbollah's influence in the cabinet meant that Lebanon was one of only three of the twenty-two Arab states (the other two were Iraq and Yemen) which abstained from the Arab League resolution condemning the Syrian regime and urging Asad to step down. Unquestionably, the domestic conflict in Syria was an unwelcome element in Lebanon's precarious political balance. But Nasrallah's ramblings aside, Hizbollah did operate within accepted diplomatic parameters, threatening no further strong-arm tactics or maneuvers within Lebanon itself.

Lebanon's democracy, like Iraq's, is hardly robust, and its political institutions are similarly brittle. The country's sectarian divisions are dysfunctional enough, but when one group parades a military force that can intimidate all other groups, including the national army, stability is precarious at best. Yet apart from unleashing its militia in Beirut in 2008, Hizbollah has preferred on the whole to conduct business within the political domain. Even the 2008 incident was more of a threat to extort political concessions than an effort to impose its hegemony by force over the other groups. And when in 2009 the March 8 Alliance lost the elections, Hizbollah accepted the verdict. Similarly, while the governmental crises that plagued Lebanon in 2009–11 did not allow for the efficient functioning of government, they nevertheless were fought under the rules and legitimate tactics of democratic governance. All of Lebanon's forces, including Hizbollah, endeavored to keep the crisis in neighboring Syria from spilling over into their own country. In short, while Lebanon's political system, with its many faults and deficits, is far from being a Jeffersonian democratic model, it is also equally far from the suffocating authoritarianism that afflicted (and in a number of cases continues to afflict) other Arab lands.

Lebanon and Iraq took different routes along the democratic road from those taken by Morocco and Jordan. But the final goal, that of a functioning democratic political system, remains uncertain. In all four cases, there were promising signs. The Moroccan and Jordanian monarchs, responding to the winter of Arab discontent, undertook reforms which, if fully implemented, could nudge the two countries forward along the democratic road. Iraq and Lebanon have had multiple free and fair elections, each of which ended up producing coalition governments that while not particularly efficient, at least emerged from the will of the people.

In none of the four cases, however, can we be certain that the process will continue unimpeded toward a functioning and robust democracy. The reforms in Morocco and Jordan were the products of monarchical impulse, and who is to say that the impetus will not subside, particularly as the two kings continue to retain considerable political power? In Lebanon and Iraq, serious ethnic, religious, and sectarian dislocations, which are replicated among the political elite, constitute a constant threat to the precarious peace and stability of the two countries. A state collapse, or the threat of such a collapse, could lead either to political disintegration, or to a takeover by persons or institutions not necessarily enamored of the democratic ideal.

Carlos Latuff

Chapter Eight

DEMOCRACY AND THE ISLAMIST CHALLENGE

In early March 2012, a mini-scandal engulfed Egypt's Islamist al-Nour Party, which had garnered 28 percent of the vote in Egypt's parliamentary elections. Anwar al-Balkimy, a parliamentarian from the ultra-conservative, Salafist party, reported that he had been attacked on a highway in the middle of the night by gunmen who had beaten him up, leaving him with severe facial injuries, and for good measure they had stolen from him the equivalent of $16,500. Mr. Balkimy, his face heavily bandaged, was shown on television receiving the sympathy and commiserations of many of his colleagues in parliament. The mortified Ministry of the Interior, in charge of the police, conveyed its regrets and promised extra diligence in its efforts to catch the culprits and bring them to justice.

Doubts, however, quickly surfaced. A hospital doctor challenged the account, insisting that it was he who put the bandages on the face of Mr. Balkimy, not to treat lacerations from a physical assault but to cover up plastic surgery on Balkimy's nose. The parliamentarian immediately contested the doctor's assertions, and his fellow MPs took his side, attacking the doctor and accusing him of politically motivated lying. But the doctor and the hospital had a trump card. They produced detailed and damning evidence of the surgery, which apparently had taken place at the very time of the alleged attack. As the hole he was in was getting deeper, Balkimy decided to stop digging, and admit that his claim of an attack was a hoax. His plea that he had fabricated the attack story because of the lingering influence of anesthesia did not sway too many minds, certainly not those of his Islamist colleagues in the al-Nour Party. They were infuriated not just because of the deceit that had embarrassed the party as a whole, but also because of the effrontery of having a colleague go through plastic surgery. Such a practice is singularly reviled among Salafists, who believe that human creation represents the perfection of God and should not be tampered with. The discredited and now abandoned Mr. Balkimy was promptly forced to submit a letter of resignation.[1]

In some ways, Mr. Balkimy's unfortunate episode serves as a metaphor for the larger and infinitely more consequential discussion of democracy's prospects in the Arab world. On the one hand, the rigidity of doctrinal politics, exemplified by the Salafists, and to a lesser extent other Islamists, cannot be comforting to those who wish for moderate politics and policies, whose first requirement is the willingness to compromise and make concessions. The large popular support Islamists have received, not just in Egypt but in free elections in other Arab countries in 2011 and 2012, may not augur well for substantial and substantive democratic change. Yet it behooves us to remember that in earlier times, say under the Mubarak, Ben Ali, and Qadhafi regimes, the good doctor might have thought more than once before coming forward to expose a member of parliament with powerful political connections. And if he had done so, there would be no guarantee that he would escape a thorough going-over by the security forces or by some party thugs. As one blogger, reminiscing on Egypt's past, said: "We always knew that one individual could stick his nose in people's affairs. But this is the first time the people stick themselves in an individual's nose."[2] No doubt much to the distress of Mr. Balkimy, the whole affair was conducted openly. Could it be that, as their roles change from underground opposition to policy makers, in a political environment that demands transparency, unyielding men succumb to discretion and their intemperate ideas get modified?

Political scientists have argued that the creation of democratic institutions has the capacity to change authoritarian attitudes. In this context, it will be particularly interesting to see how the new Islamist political elites deal with issues of principle that are of major concern for liberal democrats: imposing Sharia law, treatment of minorities, restrictions on women's freedoms, tampering with banking regulations, and so on. But this argument is not restricted to Islamists. Secular politicians too have ingrained attitudes, many of them not pristinely democratic. Indeed, whole societies that have lived under authoritarian rule for a long time could be susceptible to authoritarian norms and practices, to say nothing of culturally conservative communities that may not have an issue with democracy's political agenda, but deeply mistrust the myriad social freedoms that come with it.

Observers inside and outside these countries have loudly and passionately applauded, even lionized, the initial steps toward democracy: getting rid of tyrants and holding free and fair elections. But in the midst of the euphoria, it is important not to lose track of Hannah Arendt's definition of true revolutions. To the question of whether the momentous happenings in Arab lands were true revolutions, Arendt would respond with another question: Has democracy emerged as the outcome of these historic developments?

Herein lies the problem. It is so tempting for the observer to become invested in the success of the Arab uprisings that there is always a nagging desire to be on the side of the angels and see only positive developments. And indeed it is not difficult to be optimistic, given the extraordinary changes for the better that have occurred in these countries—the plethora of political parties, free and fair elections, reduction of universal and unrestrained state violence, the ending of state control of the press, and so on. But one need look no further than the faltering democratic experience in Iraq to recognize that consolidating democracy requires much more than just doing away with despots, forming political parties, and organizing free elections. Ranged against these positive developments are a host of alarming political practices and tendencies that might retard the progress of democratic change. Democrats in the Arab world might have avoided one or two potholes on the road to democracy; but it seems there are still a number along the way.

The second Arab awakening is certainly not lacking in impressive achievements. No less than four states—Tunisia, Libya, Yemen, and the Arab world's pivotal country, Egypt—got rid of their long-standing tyrants. In Egypt, Tunisia, and Libya, free elections brought to power new political forces that for decades had been hounded and persecuted. In Yemen, new political arrangements gave the people an opportunity to create representative political institutions. And in Syria, the medieval barbarism of the Asad clan could not silence the brave men and women who demanded freedom. Preempting possible uprisings in their own countries, the Moroccan and Jordanian kings embarked on liberalizing initiatives to reduce monarchical power, modify the constitution, and undertake electoral reform. For the first time in Morocco's history, elections brought to power an Islamist party.

Other countries as well felt the incendiary sparks of the second Arab awakening. Indeed, even in Saudi Arabia, that most unlikely of venues, King Abdullah surprised many when he announced in September 2011 that women would have the right to vote and run in the 2015 municipal elections. Admittedly, for Saudi women this may not have been a life-changing decree: women continue to suffer from a host of social and political restrictions; they still need the permission of a male relative to travel or start a business; they are not allowed to drive a car; female lawyers cannot argue in court; and young women are prevented from participating in sporting activities in public schools.[3] In one international conference, a member of the Saudi Human Rights Commission no less said that the possible implementation in Saudi Arabia of the United Nations Convention on the Elimination of All Forms of Discrimination Against Women made him shiver in fear and worry.[4] Saudi Arabia continues to have no legislative chamber, and King Abdullah has not relinquished any of his absolute powers. In light of all this, allowing women to vote, even to run, in municipal elections might seem a small step on the road to democracy, but a step in the right direction, prompted at least in part by empowering upheavals in the Arab neighborhood.

Yet there is little chance that larger and more concerted efforts at political liberalization will take place in the desert kingdom any time soon. There are many factors that explain Saudi allergy to liberal democracy—the tribal underpinnings of the state, a quiescent middle class that is dependent on the state for its many comforts, a conservative societal culture, and above all the palpable preference of the vast House of Saud for clinging to unbounded power for as long as it can. Saudi rulers consistently use religion to dismiss the need for liberal democratic institutions: what is the need for a civil constitution when the Quran is the country's constitution, and al-Sharia its basic law? This position is defended vehemently by powerful clerics who more often than not are even more rigid than the House of Saud in their opposition to reform initiatives.

Such a mind-set is not confined to Saudi Arabia. It is indeed these very attitudes that became a cause for concern over the political rise of Islamist parties. It was thus hardly surprising that secularists and democrats would watch with mounting alarm as Islamists won electoral victories in Tunisia, Egypt, and Morocco—every free election (apart from Libya) that took place after the eruption of Arab revolts. The high probability of an Islamist victory in Jordan, if elections were truly fair, prompted King Abdullah and the ruling elite to produce a new electoral law that, while an improvement on the old, was still skewed against the populous urban areas where the Islamists had their main support. Even the monstrous brutality of the Asad regime in 2011–12 seemed to be balanced for a number of Syrians—secularists, liberals, and minorities—by their fear of a radical Islamist victory.

The world of Islam, however, is not a monolith of radicalism; it is more complex and its undertones are more nuanced. The months following Islamist victories at the polls pointed to a very obvious conclusion: there was not just one Islamist movement. The winning Islamic groups quickly revealed distinct variations in orientations and policy preferences. And this diversity echoed the intense debates that had raged within the Muslim world about the compatibility of Islamic doctrine with the fundamental elements of democratic life.

There certainly are Islamic beliefs and injunctions which, if taken literally, are difficult to reconcile with democratic ideas. For example, Muslim literalists would argue that the sovereignty of the people, a fundamental democratic belief, is nothing short of blasphemous since in Islam sovereignty lies only with the Almighty. Sharia law, which is based on the Quran and the sayings of the Prophet, and which sets out specific directives about crime, punishment, and family issues, is even more problematic. Such punishments as severing hands for stealing, flogging for unlawful sex, or stoning of adulterers run contrary to accepted behavioral norms in democratic society. Islamic law also dictates entitlements that might have been progressive in the days of the Prophet, but would be challenged vigorously in modern democratic societies. For example, in matters of inheritance, Islamic law entitles a daughter to only half of what a son gets.

Do the issues where Islam and democracy seem to be at odds mean that the two cannot be reconciled? Not necessarily, if a distinction is made between universal themes that hold true for all times and injunctions given to address specific contexts. In this, the role of interpretation is critical: in the end Islam is what Muslims make of it. Taliban rule in Afghanistan typified one model of Islam. But an opposite model is that of Turkey's Islamist Justice and Development Party, which has comfortably adapted Islamic principles within the tenets of secular democracy. Indeed, on a tour of Egypt, Tunisia, and Libya after the fall of their dictators, Turkey's Islamist prime minister, Tayyip Erdogan, enjoined his audiences to adopt the Turkish model, speaking fervently of Turkish democracy, and more pointedly about the need for a secular state. He recommended adopting secular constitutions, and reminded his audience that while he was a devout Muslim and the leader of an Islamist party, he was also the prime minister of a secular country.[5]

The response to Erdogan's remarks would show the diversity of Islamist attitudes in the Arab world. Egyptian mainstream Islamists, Brotherhood and Salafists alike, were cool on the idea of secularism, arguing that the Turkish experience could not be transferred to Egypt.[6] And one leader of the Brotherhood publicly attacked Erdogan for refusing to criminalize adultery in Turkey.[7] In Tunisia, however, there were no such misgivings. Rachid Ghannouchi, the leader of Ennahdha, consistently proclaimed his admiration for the Turkish model, and his disdain for rigid interpretations that are oblivious of modernity.[8] But Ghannouchi is not alone in his liberal Islamic vision. The views of Abd al-Muneim Abul-Fotouh, a former Egyptian Muslim Brother who ran for president of Egypt, are not that dissimilar from Ghannouchi's. And there is an influential liberal current among Libyan Islamists.

In the countries in which they have gained political power, Islamist elites have to move from the comfort of theoretical abstraction; they now are faced with hard political realities, where ideas are transformed into public policy that impacts the lives of millions of people, and that can generate support or provoke resistance, some of which can be vigorous, even violent. Admittedly, a number of years have to pass before appropriate judgment can be made. Still, some reasonable conclusions can be drawn from the Islamists' behavior early in their tenure. In this, Tunisia's Ennahdha and Morocco's Justice and Development Party (PJD), winners of their respective elections, seemed the most flexible and the most willing to compromise. Egypt's Islamists, however, seemed less open to the proposition that politics is the art of compromise.

This diversity among Islamists is best captured in their attitudes on women's issues. Starkest is the contrast between Tunisia and Egypt. In Tunisia, women were encouraged by Ennahdha's promise, reiterated many times, that the Islamist party had no intention to revisit the country's personal status law, which is the most liberal in the Arab world. In the months following the formation of government, civil society and human rights groups did not seem overly concerned that women's liberties and their status in society might be at risk in the new Islamist-dominated political order. Women, after all, garnered 49 out of the 217 assembly seats, and of those, 43 belonged to Ennahdha. During the first year of Ennahdha-led government, there were few complaints from women's groups that the Islamist party would be hostile or indifferent to women's rights.

By contrast, Egypt's Islamists did little to alleviate the concerns of women's civil society groups. Of the 368 Islamists who won seats in the National Assembly, only four were women, and the utterances of one or two of these women betrayed an even more rigid attitude than their male colleagues about women's role in society. Thus, the female spokesperson on women's affairs for the Islamist Freedom and Justice Party (FJP) seemed to condone police brutality against women demonstrators, arguing that women should have stayed at home and left the business of demonstrating to their menfolk.[9] Such a mind-set was easy to dismiss, but potentially more consequential were the Islamists' positions on personal status laws and reforms that women's rights advocates had agitated for and earned under the Mubarak regime. Both the FJP and the Salafist Nour Party insisted on reopening debate on existing laws that had made female genital mutilation illegal, given women the right to divorce and keep custody of their children beyond the ages of seven for boys and nine for girls, allowed them to travel without the permission of their husbands, and given them legal powers to contest discrimination through the office of an ombudsman.[10] The Islamists justified their hostility to these laws by arguing that such regulations undermined the sanctity of the family.

These attitudes in fact reflected a deep conservative strand not just among Islamists but within Egyptian society as a whole. In survey after survey, Egypt exhibits some of the most rigid attitudes in the Islamic world toward social issues and values such as divorce, homosexuality, gender equality, adultery, and so on.[11] Polls have shown that some 60 percent of Egyptians want al-Sharia to be the sole source of law in the country.[12] In articulating socially conservative policies, the leaderships of the FJP and the al-Nour Party are not out of step with the people of Egypt. To most Egyptians, it is the civil society and human rights activists, not the Islamists, who seem intent on sabotaging the wishes of the people. "Is democracy the voice of the majority?" asks an Islamist demonstrator. "We as Islamists are the majority. Why do they want to impose on us the views of the minority—the liberals and the secularists? That's all I want to know."[13]

Herein lies the difference between Egypt's Islamists and those of Tunisia and Morocco. With their overwhelming majority in the National Assembly, the FJP and al-Nour sought to advocate, and tried to formulate, policies that were aligned with conservative majority opinion. Tunisia's Ennahdha and Morocco's PJD were short of an outright majority, and had to enter into coalitions with non-Islamist parties. They had little alternative but to follow a moderate version of Islamic politics. In addition, and in fairness to the leaders of the two parties, Ghannouchi in Tunisia and Benkirane in Morocco had for some time advocated a more enlightened interpretation of Islamic rule. They consequently proceeded not just to follow, but to shape the attitudes of their followers. When in a moment of exuberance the Ennahdha leader (and later Tunisia's prime minister) Hamadi Jebali promised, in the presence of thousands of cheering people, to recreate the religious order of the Prophet and his companions,[14] the party immediately rectified "the slip of the tongue" and insisted that "Tunisia will be a democratic republic with a civil state,"[15] thus quashing any possible nostalgia for an Islamic state among the rank and file of the party.

Liberal and secularist fears that accompanied Ennahdha's election did not materialize, as the party followed a pragmatic approach in its political dealings, and was more than circumspect on social issues. In an address to France's National Assembly in July 2012, Tunisia's president and the leader of the secular Congress for the Republic Party, Moncef Marzouki, assured his audience that Tunisia had not been hijacked by Islamists. "Has Tunisia fallen into the hands of Islamism?" he addressed the question to the French lawmakers. "The answer is no, Tunisia has fallen into the hands of democracy."[16] Indeed, during 2012, Ennahdha's main nemesis seemed to be not the liberals and secularists but the conservative Salafists, who had not participated in the elections, but had evidently expected more from an Islamist governing party. Morocco's PJD was similarly successful in allaying the concerns of the secular urban middle class. It focused on the economy and tackling corruption, and surprised many when it indicated its support for relaxing the country's strict abortion law[17]—another instance of a moderate Islamist party endeavoring to shape Islamic public opinion on a controversial social issue.

Democratic institutions do impose a logic of governance that encourages compromise and pragmatism. In order to govern, Ennahdha and the PJD needed to form coalitions with secular parties. They thus made sure not to impose an Islamist agenda on their political partners or their countries. After proposing to include a reference to al-Sharia in the Tunisian constitution, Ennahdha quickly withdrew it once it became clear that the proposal would prove divisive. And in its first year in power, the PJD behaved in accordance with its leader's promise that government would not interfere in people's private lives. While in opposition, Egypt's Muslim Brotherhood would unfailingly condemn public consumption of alcohol and the showing of flesh on the beaches.

But as parliamentarians, and cognizant of the critical importance of tourism to Egypt's economy, the Brothers found it necessary to moderate their position. A leader of the FJP said the party's priorities were "economic reform and reducing poverty . . . not [fighting] bikinis and booze."[18] Indeed, even the Salafists, who in the past had prided themselves on their absolute unwillingness to concede on crucial issues of principle, quickly compromised on one of those fundamental doctrinal obligations. Salafist beliefs ban them from participating in representative institutions, such as elections and parliaments, since these institutions abide by human-made laws. But after the ouster of Mubarak, the Salafists quickly found a way to moderate their beliefs, and contest the elections.

When it came to the constitution, however, Egypt's Islamists found it more difficult to compromise. After all, the 70 percent of the population that put them in power demanded an Islamic constitution laden with al-Sharia rules and injunctions. And to be able to influence the writing of the constitution, they used their muscle to give sixty-five of the hundred-seat constitutional drafting assembly to fellow Islamists. That is when they got their first major lesson in the imprudence of political inflexibility. Immediately, over twenty members of the assembly resigned in protest over the Islamists' efforts to stack the deck. And in spite of their numbers, the Islamists were unable to restart the process, so that by the time of the presidential elections in May and June 2012, there still was no resolution to the deadlock—an odd state of affairs as a president would be elected without defined constitutional powers. The ensuing paralysis in governmental and parliamentary affairs would be blamed by Egyptians on the Islamists. Only four months after Islamists had triumphantly swept the polls in parliamentary elections their Islamist candidate would barely squeak through to a victory in a tight presidential election. No doubt it was a salutary lesson for the FJP and al-Nour Party that even with a healthy majority the democratic game requires an equally healthy appetite for compromise.

The uproar over the constitutional assembly, and the resulting gridlock, occurred in the shadow of a deteriorating economic situation. The months of revolution had led to a precipitous decline in Egypt's economic activity, which resulted in the government having to support the economy by drawing down reserves and borrowing from domestic banks. By summer 2012, government reserves had dwindled to just over $15 billion, and international investors and lenders were reluctant to put capital in the country until they could see evidence of a functioning government.[19]

And it is not just Egypt's Islamists who would have to contend with a deteriorating economy; Islamists in other Arab countries, particularly the non-oil-producing ones, face huge economic problems—deficits, diminishing capital, unemployment. According to the IMF, the Arab oil-importing countries would grow at an anemic 2.2 percent in 2012, and 3.3 percent in 2013.[20] For the Islamists, this is not just an economic but a hazardous political problem. The patience of the electorate is notoriously fickle. In the next electoral cycle, the Islamists will be judged on whether they delivered the goods. Fidelity to Islamic values will certainly not harm their prospects, but most crucially they will be judged on their performance in the socioeconomic domain: on whether they were able to improve the lot of the poor, and markedly reduce the horrendous numbers of the unemployed. It is indeed intriguing that economic difficulties might end up serving the interests of democrats, as the need to produce results must push the Islamists to pursue compromise and make concessions in order to remain in power and govern effectively.

After the early exuberance that accompanied the Arab revolutions, it is now obvious that getting rid of tyrants is but the first fledgling step toward a democratic future. History has long shown that dictatorship can just as easily be followed by another dictatorship, in some cases with the connivance of some or most of the people. After all, this is what happened in the first Arab awakening. There is, however, a critical difference between the first and second Arab awakenings. The nature of the political environment is markedly different. Authoritarian nationalism is no longer de rigueur; transparent, representative governance is. And while the future is by no means certain, at least the people, after many years of unremitting authoritarianism, have been given another chance to have a say in determining their political future.

Whether true and genuine democracy figures at all in this future rests upon the intentions, proclivities, and performance of the new power brokers in the Arab world. Mostly Islamists, the new political elites will eventually determine the fate of the second Arab awakening. For the democratic project to succeed, the Islamists need to work within the democratic rules of the game, and these rules are not confined solely to winning free and fair elections. Democracy demands a liberal disposition, a tolerance for minority rights and views, and a willingness to negotiate, compromise, and when necessary make concessions for the political process to proceed.

And on this point the jury is still out. It is somewhat ironic that the ultimate realization of Hannah Arendt's simple and elegant formulation, linking the success of revolution to the establishment of democracy, would be left not in the hands of liberals and secularists but in the custody of those professing fidelity to principles whose compatibility with democracy is contested.

NOTES

CHAPTER ONE

1. Council on Foreign Relations, *Obama's Speech on the Middle East and North Africa, May 2011*; http://www.cfr.org/middle-east/obamas-speech-middle-east-north-africa-may-2011/p25049.

2. *Voice of America*, "Gates Says Bahraini Leaders Serious About Reforms," March 12, 2011.

3. Toby C. Jones, "Bahrain, Kingdom of Silence," *Arab Reform Bulletin*, Carnegie Endowment for International Peace, May 4, 2011.

4. Council on Foreign Relations, *Obama's Speech on the Middle East and North Africa, May 2011*.

5. CNN News, June 24, 2006.

6. Al-Arabiya Satellite Television, February 22, 2011; CNN News, February 22, 2011.

7. *The Economist*, May 21, 2011, p. 51.

8. *Wall Street Journal*, January 31, 2011, http://online.wsj.com/SB100014240527 487038332C.

9. Simon Tisdall, "Iran helping Syrian regime crack down on protestors, say diplomats," *The Guardian* (London), May 10, 2011, p. 6.

10. Liam Stack and Katherine Zoepf, "Syria Tries to Placate Sunnis and Kurds," *New York Times*, April 7, 2011, p. A7.

11. *Yahoo News*, March 30, 2011, http://news.yahoo.com/s/nm/20110330/wl_nm_syria/; see also *The Economist*, April 2, 2011, p. 43.

12. http://wikileaks.org/cable/2008/01/08DAMASCUS54.html.

13. Anthony Shadid, "Syrian Elite to Fight Protests to "the End," *New York Times*, May 10, 2011, p. A1.

14. *Yahoo News*, May 24, 2011, http://www.news.yahoo.com/s/nm/20110524/wl_nm/us_syria. *The Economist*, May 14, 2011, p. 60. *Yahoo News*, May 26, 2011, http://www.news.yahoo.com/s/afp/20110526/wl_mideast_afp/syrianpoliticsunrest/.

15. *Yahoo News*, May 26, 2011, http://www.news.yahoo.com/s/afp/20110526/wl_mideast_afp/syrianpoliticsunrest/.

16. Except the Sultan of Oman, who belongs to the Ibadi faith.

17. Hazem Beblawi, "The Rentier State in the Arab World," in Giacomo Luciani, ed., *The Arab State* (London: Routledge, 1990).

18. See Michael L. Ross, "Does Oil Hinder Democracy?" *World Politics* (April 2001), pp. 332–33.

19. See Adeed Dawisha and Karen Dawisha, "How to Build a Democratic Iraq," *Foreign Affairs* (May–June 2003), pp. 47–48.

20. *The Economist*, March 5, 2011, pp. 52–54; *The Economist*, March 12, 2011, p. 32.

21. Fareed Zakaria, *The Future of Freedom: Illiberal Democracy at Home and Abroad* (New York: W. W. Norton & Company, 2003), p. 156.

22. *The Economist*, April 23, 2011, p. 50; Carnegie Endowment for International Peace, *Arab Reform Bulletin*, March 16, 2011.

23. The reference here is to the seventeen sovereign states of the Arab core: the six Gulf Cooperation Council countries plus Yemen in the Arabian Peninsula; the Fertile Crescent countries of Iraq, Jordan, Syria, and Lebanon; and the African countries Egypt, Sudan, Libya, Tunisia, Algeria, and Morocco.

PART ONE

CHAPTER TWO

1. Robert Stephens, *Nasser* (London: Penguin Press, 1971), p. 78.

2. Gamal Abdél Nasser, *Egypt's Liberation: The Philosophy of the Revolution* (Washington, DC: Public Affairs Press, 1955), pp. 21–23.

3. Nasser's interview with the *Sunday Times* (London), June 24, 1962.

4. *Al-Ahram* (Cairo), January 10, 1970.

5. *Al-Ahram*, December 19 1961.

6. His Majesty King Hussein I, *Uneasy Lies the Head* (New York: Bernard Geis Associates, 1962), pp. 110–12 (italics in original).

7. Patrick Seale, *The Struggle for Syria: A Study of Post War Arab Politics, 1945–1958* (New Haven, CT: Yale University Press, 1986), p. 323.

8. The following section is drawn from Adeed Dawisha, *Arab Nationalism in the Twentieth Century: From Triumph to Despair* (Princeton, NJ: Princeton University Press, 2003), pp. 201–3.

9. Anwar Sadat, *In Search of Identity: An Autobiography* (New York: Harper & Row, 1977), p. 152.

10. R. Hrair Dekmejian, *Egypt Under Nasir: A Study in Political Dynamics* (London: University of London Press, 1971), p. 123.

11. Charles Tripp, *A History of Iraq* (Cambridge: Cambridge University Press, 2000), p. 155.

12. Adeed Dawisha, *Iraq: A Political History from Independence to Occupation* (Princeton, NJ: Princeton University Press, 2009), p. 181.

13. Adeed Dawisha, *Egypt in the Arab World: The Elements of Foreign Policy* (London: Macmillan, 1976), p. 82.

14. Phebe Marr, *The Modern History of Iraq* (Boulder, CO: Westview Press, 1985), p. 262.

15. Dawisha, *Egypt in the Arab World*, p. 137.

16. Hannah Arendt, *On Revolution* (New York: Viking Press, 1963), pp. 21–22.

17. Ibid., p. 21.

18. Ibid., p. 55.

19. Quoted in Hans Kohn, *The Ideas of Nationalism: A Study in Its Origins and Background* (New York: Macmillan, 1944), p. 582.

20. Hans Kohn, *Prelude to Nation-States: The French and German Experience, 1789–1815* (London: D. Van Nostrand Co., 1967), p. 254.

21. Abu Khaldun Sati al-Husri, *Safahat min al- Madhi al- Qarib (Pages from Recent History)* (Beirut: Markaz Dirasat al-Wuhda al-Arabiya, 1984), p. 42.

22. Ali Karim Said, *Iraq 8 February 1963: Min Hiwar al-Mafahim ila Hiwar al-Damm (Iraq 8 February 1963: From a Dialogue Over Norms to a Dialogue of Blood)* (Beirut: Dar al-Kunuz al-Arabiya, 1999), p. 213, n. 1.

23. *Egyptian Gazette* (Cairo), May 9, 1966, quoted in Dawisha, *Egypt in the Arab World*, p. 119.

24. Quoted in Roger Owen, *State, Power and Politics in the Making of the Modern Middle East*, 2nd ed. (London: Routledge, 2000), p. 149.

25. See Dekmejian, *Egypt Under Nasir*, p. 147.

CHAPTER THREE

1. See *The Economist*, February 5, 2011, p. 34.

2. The following paragraphs dealing with the institutions of Saddam Hussein's authoritarian rule draw on Adeed Dawisha, *Iraq: A Political History from Independence to Occupation* (Princeton, NJ: Princeton University Press, 2009), pp. 209–41.

3. Ibid., p. 211.

4. British Broadcasting Corporation, *Summary of World Broadcasts, ME/4882/A/3*, April 19, 1975, quoted in Adeed Dawisha, *Syria and the Lebanese Crisis* (London: Macmillan, 1980), pp. 50–51.

5. Europa Publications, *The Middle East and North Africa, 1973–1974*, p. 625, and *1980*, p. 607.

6. Moshe Maoz in an interview with the *Observer Foreign News Service* (London), November 28, 1975, quoted in Dawisha, *Syria and the Lebanese Crisis*, p. 45.

7. Patrick Seale, *Asad of Syria: The Struggle for the Middle East* (Berkeley: University of California Press, 1988), p. 333.

8. Quoted in Kanan Makiya, *Republic of Fear: The Politics of Modern Iraq*, updated ed. (Berkeley: University of California Press, 1998), p. 206.

9. Human Rights Watch, "A Wasted Decade: Human Rights in Syria During Bashar al-Asad's First Ten Years in Power" (July 2010), p. 2.

10. Europa Publications, *The Middle East and North Africa, 1973–1974*, p. 496, and *1980*, p. 490.

11. John Wright, *A History of Libya* (New York: Columbia University Press, 2010), pp. 199–200.

12. M. L. Gathafi, *The Green Book* (Reading, UK: Ithaca Press, 2001), p. 65.

13. See Adeed Dawisha, *The Arab Radicals* (New York: Council on Foreign Relations, 1986), p. 35.

14. Mahmood Mamdani, "Libya Explained," *Huffington Post*, April 12, 2011, http://huffingtonpostunionofbloggers.org/2011/04/12/libya-explained/.

15. Wright, *A History of Libya*, p. 219.

16. *The Guardian,* February 2, 2011, from http://www.guardian.co.uk/media/
    2011/feb/02/wikileaks-exclusive-book-extract.

17. Quoted in Jeffrey A. Coupe, "Tunisia," in Ellen Lust, ed., *The Middle East*, 12th
    ed. (Washington, DC: C Q Press, 2011), p. 711.

18. For the entire cable, see http://middleeast.about.com/od/tunisia/a/tunisia-
    corruption-wikileaks.

19. Tarek Masoud, "Egypt," in Lust, ed., *The Middle East*, p. 399.

20. This was confirmed by Ali Eddin Hilal, the NDP's director of information, in
    an interview with al-Hurra Television Channel, October 21, 2010.

21. David S. Sorenson, *An Introduction to the Modern Middle East* (Boulder, CO:
    Westview Press, 2008), p. 240.

22. Hannah Arendt, *On Revolution* (New York: Viking Press, 1963), p. 21.

PART TWO

CHAPTER FOUR

1. *Al-Ahram Weekly,* October 20–26, 2011, http://ahramweekly.ahram.org.
   eg/2011/1069/ref112.htm.

2. *Financial Times,* September 15, 2011, http://www.ft.com/cms/s/0/582db2a2-
   def0-11e00-9af3.00144feabdc0.html.

3. *The Economist,* October 15, 2011, p. 29.

4. Anthony Shadid, "A Veteran Islamist Imagines a Democratic Future for the
   New Tunisia," *New York Times*, October 20, 2011, p. A10.

5. Ibid.

6. *Tunisia Live,* October 27, 2011, www.tunisia-live.net/2011/10/27/aridha
   .chabiya-popular-petition-shocks-tunisian-politics/.

7. *Al-Ahram Weekly,* October 27–November 2, 2011, http://weekly.ahram.org
   .eg/2011/1070/re4.htm.

8. CNN News, October 24, 2011, http://edition.cnn.com/2011/10/24/world/
   africa/tunisia-elections.

9. *Tunisia Live,* November 19, 2011, www.tunisia-live.net/2011/11/19/opposi
   tion-parties-reactions-towards-talks/.

10. *Tunisia Live*, January 11, 2012, www.tunisia-live.net/2012/01/11/major-tunisian-secular-parties-announce-merger/.

11. *The Economist*, November 26, 2011, p. 58.

12. Rory McCarthy, "Islamism and Secularism in Tunisia," *Open Democracy*, January 14, 2012, www.opendemocracy.net/63668.

13. This was a statement made by Osama al-Saghir, an Ennahdha member of Tunisia's Constituent Assembly, in a conference in Washington, DC, organized by the Carnegie Endowment for International Peace, on April 5, 2012.

14. Ibid.

15. Ali Metwaly, "Tunisian universities face pressure from Salafists," *al-Ahram Weekly*, January 4, 2012, http://english.ahram.org.eg/Newscontent/2/0/30911/world/0/Tunisian-universities.html.

16. David Ottaway, "Tunisia's Islamists Struggle to Rule," Middle East Program Occasional Paper, Woodrow Wilson International Center for Scholars, Washington, DC, April 2012; http://www.wilsoncenter.org/sites/default/files/Tunisia's%20Islamists%20Struggle%20to%20Rule_1pdf.

17. Carolyn Lamboley, "Tunisia's Leading Party Reaffirms Commitment to Arab-Muslim Identity," *Tunisia Live*, March 26, 2012, www.tunisialive.net/2012/03/26/tunisians-leading-party-reaffirms-commitment-to-arab-muslim-identity.

18. Tarek Masoud, "The Road to (and from) Liberation Square," *Journal of Democracy* (July 2011), p. 28.

19. *The Economist*, November 12, 2011, p. 55.

20. Neil MacFarquhar, "Questions Arise on Clout of New Parliament," *New York Times*, November 10, 2011, p. A5.

21. *Ahram Online*, December 9, 2011, http://english.ahram.org.eg/News Content/1/0/28834/Egypt/0/Muslim-Brotherhood.html.

22. *Al-Ahram Weekly*, December 15–21, http://weekly.ahram.org.eg/2011/1076/eg1.htm.

23. *The Economist*, November 26, 2011, p. 57.

24. *Al-Ahram Weekly*, September 15–21, 2011, http://weekly.ahram.org.eg/2011/1064/eg11.htm.

25. The following paragraphs analyzing the goals and beliefs of the leading political parties are summaries of the detailed (and excellent) expositions of all of

Egypt's post-revolution political parties to be found in *Jadaliyya* at http://
www.jadaliyya.com/pages/index3154/freedom-and-justice-party.

26. *Ahram Online*, December 30, 2011, http://english.ahram.org.eg/newscon
tent/1/0/30446/Egypt/0/html.

27. Ibid.

28. *Al-Ahram Weekly*, July 6–12, 2011, http://weekly.ahram.org.eg/2011/1054/
eg6.htm.

29. *Ahram Online,* December 30, 2011, http://english.ahram.org.eg/newscon
tent/1/0/30446/Egypt/0/html.

30. *Al-Masry al-Youm*, September 23, 2011, www.almasryalyoum.com/node/
498598.

31. *Daily Star* (Beirut), November 15, 2011, www.dailystar.com/article.aspx?id/
154079.html.

32. Kevin Connolly, "Egypt Vote: The Weird and Wonderful Party Logos," BBC
News, November 28, 2011, www.bbc.co.uk/news/magazine-15917630.html.

33. Noha el-Hannawy, "Egypt's new People's Assembly swears in today, but
powers are dubious," *al-Masry al-Youm*, January 23, 2012, www.almasryaly
oum.com/en/print/614861.

34. *Jadaliyya*, January 25, 2011, www.jadaliyya.com/pages/index/4160/
welcome-to-the-new-egyptian-parliament.

35. See the excellent piece by Hania Sholkamy, "Why women are at the heart
of Egypt's political trials and tribulations," *Open Democracy*, January 24, 2012,
www.opendemocracy.net/print/63808.

36. http://bikymasr.com/67991/egypt-womens-ngo-takes-pro-fgm-parliamen
tarian-to-court/.

37. *Daily Star*, May 18, 2012, www.dailystar.com.lb/ArticlePrint.aspx?id=17378
9&mode=print; *New York Times*, April 26, 2012, p. 9.

38. http://english.ahram.org.eg/newsContentPrint/36/0/44806/Presidential-
elections-/0/Mursi-holds-last-pre-election-presser-reiterates-pledges-to-
public.

CHAPTER FIVE

1. *The Economist*, June 18, 2011, p. 53.

2. *The Economist*, August 20, 2011, p. 43.

3. *The Economist*, August 27, 2011, p. 22.

4. http://tripolipost.com/articledetail.asp?c=1&i=7348.

5. http://uk.reuters.com/assets/print?aid=UKTRE7AR0QL20111128.

6. *The Economist*, January 28, 2012, p. 49.

7. www.investmentu.com/2012/January/chart-2012-fastest-growing-nations-html.

8. *Washington Post*, February 28, 2012, www.washingtonpost.com/business/industries/libya-boosts-oil-production.

9. http://www.reuters.com/assets/print?aid=USTRE7A941W20111110.

10. http://english.ahram.org.eg/NewsContentPrint/3/0/35371/Business/0/Libya-amending-bank-law-to-attract-foreigners.

11. See, e.g., www.huffingtonpost.com/rajan-menon/libya-post-gaddafi-_b_1397289.html; www.aljazeera.com/indepth/opinion/2012/06/2012614115342445476.html; www.magharebia.com/cocoon/awi/xhtml1/en_GB/features/awi/features/2012/04/15/feature-01.

12. Gamal Nkrumah, "Tripoli's Testing Questions," *al-Ahram Weekly*, July 25–31, 2012, http://weekly.ahram.org/print/2012/1108/re11.htm.

13. *The Economist*, July 30, 2012, www.economist.com/node/21557808/print.

14. *The Economist*, September 24, 2011, p. 57.

15. *Al-Masry al-Youm*, July 4, 2011, www.almasryalyoum.com/en/print/473969.

16. *The Economist*, February 25, 2012, p. 59.

17. Laura Kasinof, "Protestors Set New Goal: Fixing Yemen's Military," *New York Times*, February 28, 2012, p. A8.

18. Figures are from the CIA *World Fact Book*, www.theodora.com/wfbcurrent/yemen/yemen_economy.html.

19. *Al-Ahram Weekly*, February 2–8, 2012, http://weekly.ahram.eg/print/2012/1083/re11.htm.

20. www.pbs.org/wgbh/pages/frontline/foreign-affairs-defense/al-qaeda-in-yemen/yemen-army-recaptures-two-cities-from-al-qaeda.

21. *Ahram Online*, February 25, 2012, http://english.org.eg/NewsContentPrint/2/0/3539/World/0/Deadly-blast-overshadows-yemen-leader-swearing-in.

22. Anthony Shadid, "Bahrain Boils Under the Lid of Repression," *New York Times*, September 16, 2011, p. A1.

23. Scheherezade Farmarzi, "Clampdown in Bahrain," *The Nation*, September 12, 2011, p. 42.

24. *The Economist*, August 13, 2011, p. 45.

25. For a summary of the report, see BBC News, November 23, 2011, www.bbc .co.uk/news/world-middle-east-15861353?print.

26. BBC News, November 23, 2011, www.bbc.co.uk/news/world-middle-east-15850509?print.

27. This and other information in this paragraph comes from *Open Democracy*, January 19, 2012, www.opendemocracy.net/print/63711.

CHAPTER SIX

1. Patrick Seale, *Asad of Syria: The Struggle for the Middle East* (Berkeley: University of California Press, 1988), pp. 3–6.

2. Ibid., p. 6.

3. One of the authors of the report said that the "accounts of torture . . . were horrific. . . . We believe the Syrian government to be systematically persecuting its own people on a vast scale"—see Nada Bakri, "Syria Hunts for Leaders of Protests in Hama," *New York Times*, September 1, 2011, p. A10.

4. See *The Economist*, July 9, 2011, p. 45; *The Economist*, August 20, 2011, p. 44; and the *New York Times*, September 1, 2011, p. A10.

5. *Daily Telegraph* (London), March 7, 2012, www.telegraph.co.uk/news/world-news/middleeast/syria/9129521. See also *New York Times*, October 27, 2011, p. A9.

6. Andrew Gilligan, "Syria's President Assad: 'I live a normal life—it's why I'm popular,'" *Daily Telegraph*, October 30, 2011, www.telegraph.co.uk/news/worldnews/middleeast/8857883/Syrias-President-Assad-I-live-a-normal-life-its-why-Im-popular.html

7. Ian Black, "Syrian President Asad Blames 'Foreign Conspiracies' for Crisis," *The Guardian*, January 10, 2012, www.guardian.co.uk/world/2012/jan/10/syrian-president-asad-foreign-conspiracies/.

8. *ABC News Nightline*, December 7, 2011.

9. Andrew Gilligan, "Syria: The two sides of President Assad," www.telegraph .co.uk/news/worldnews/middleeast/syria/9105638/Syria-the-two-sides-of-President-Assad.html.

10. *The Economist*, August 13, 2011, p. 43.

11. *New York Times*, November 15, 2011, p. A10.

12. *New York Times*, August 29, 2011, p. A8.

13. Bassem Mroue, "Turkey says Syria regime will fall as deaths mount," *Yahoo*

News, September 16, 2011, http://old.news.yahoo.com/s/ap/20110916/ap_on_re_mi_ea/ml_syria_22/print.

14. Australian Broadcasting Corporation, March 7, 2012, www.abc.net.au/news/2012-03-07/un-has-video-of-syrian-hospital-torture/387362.

15. BBC News, February 29, 2012, www.bbc.co.uk/new/world-middle-east-17212781?print=true.

16. This was one of a series of moving blogs posted by Amal Hanano for the electronic magazine *Jadaliyya*, which appeared on February 10, 2012, see www.jadaliyya.com/pages/index/4306/while-you-were-sleeping-again.

17. BBC News, March 3, 2012, www.bbc.co.uk/news/world-middle-east-172 43779?print=true.

18. This information is taken from a blog in Arabic by Salma Idilbi called "Lahdha" ("A Moment"), which appeared in *Jadaliyya* on February 7, 2012; see www.jadaliyya.com/pages/index/4272/bitawqeet-bab-amro (in Arabic).

19. Neil MacFarquhar and Alan Cowell, "Syria Says 90 Percent Approved Constitution," *New York Times*, February 28, 2012, p. A4.

20. *The Economist*, March 3, 2012, p. 60.

21. Nayla Razzouk and Emre Peker, "Syria Shells Protestors' Towns as Assad Enacts Constitution," *San Francisco Chronicle*, February 29, 2012, www.sfgate.com/cgi_bin/article.cgi?f=/g/a/2012/02/28/bloomberg_arti clesM02LWJ6.

22. Security Council, Department of Public Information, Document SC/10536, www.un.org/News/Press/docs/2012/sc10536.doc.htm.

23. *The Economist*, March 10, 2012, p. A60.

24. Alistair Lyon, "Syrian rebels leave embattled Homs stronghold," www.reuters.com/assets/print?aid=USL5E8DB0BH20120301.

25. Fox News, March 14, 2012, www.foxnews.com/world/2012/03/14/2-Syrian-dissidnets-quit-opposition-council.

26. Liz Sly, "Syrians Vote in Elections Boycotted by Opposition," *Washington Post*, May 8, 2012, p. A9.

27. Annas Zarzar and Tamam Abdallah, "Syrian Parliamentary Elections: Cynicism Wins the Day," *Jadaliyya*, May 8, 2012, www.jadaliyya.com/pages/index/5443/syrian-parliamentary-elections-cynicism-wins-the-day.

28. *Al-Akhbar*, May 15, 2012, http://english.al-akhbar.com/print/7372.

29. *Al-Akhbar*, May 21, 2012, http://english.al-akhbar.com/print/7502.

30. www.foxnews.com/world/2012/03/14/2-syrian-dissidents-quit-opposition-council/.

31. *The Economist*, March 10, 2012, p. 60.

32. http://thedailynewsegypt.com/2012/06/28/assad-syria-state-war/.

33. Paul Rogers, "Syria and the Cost of Failure," *Open Democracy*, March 8, 2012, www.opendemocracy.net/print/64597.

34. Bassam Haddad, "The Syrian Regime's Business Backbone," *Jordan Vista News*, March 16, 2012, http://vista.sahafi.jo/art.php?id=2030fb062fbf8cc24bb f201b87411337752fac7.

35. *The Economist*, February 11, 2012, p. 26; see also Rogers, "Syria and the Cost of Failure," *Open Democracy*, March 8, 2012, www.opendemcoracy.net/print/64597.

CHAPTER SEVEN

1. Quoted in Aidan Lewis, "Why Has Morocco's King Survived the Arab Spring?" BBC News, November 24, 2011, www.bbc.co.uk/news/world-middle-east-1585989.

2. Ahmed Benchemsi, "Morocco: Outfoxing the Opposition," *Journal of Democracy* (January 2012), p. 59.

3. Laila Lalami, "The Moroccan Exception: The king says his realm is a beacon of liberalism, but the people demand bread, and roses too," *The Nation*, September 12, 2011, pp. 30–31.

4. *The Economist*, July 9, 2011, p. 46.

5. Valentina Bartolucci, "Morocco's Silent Revolution," *Open Democracy*, January 17, 2012, www.opendemocracy.net/print/63696.

6. *Al-Ahram Weekly*, December 1–7, 2011, http://weekly.ahram.org.eg/print/2011/1074/re4.htm.

7. *The Guardian*, November 25, 2011, www.guardian.co.uk/world/2011/nov/25/morocco-election-low-turnout/.

8. Suham Ali, "The Moroccan government pledges to respect its promise for providing job opportunities" (in Arabic), *al-Magharebia*, February 6, 2012, http://www.Magharebia.com/cocoon/awi/print/ar/features/awi/features/2012/02/06/feature-01.

9. The following details are drawn from *Ahram Online*, February 15, 2012, see http://english.ahram.org.eg/News Content Print/3/0/34640/Business/0.

10. The details below are drawn from Ellen Lust and Sami Hourani, "Jordan Votes: Election or Selection?" *Journal of Democracy* (April 2011), pp. 119–29.

11. *The Economist*, February 5, 2011, p. 32.

12. Al-Jazeera News, February 18, 2011, www.aljazeera.com/news/middleeast/2011/02/201121821116689870.html.

13. www.jordanembassyus.org/new/jib/speeches/hmka/hmka06142011.htm.

14. Ranya Kadri and Ethan Bronner, "Government of Jordan Is Dismissed by the King," *New York Times*, October 18, 2011, p. A6.

15. *Jordan Times*, October 18, 2011, www.jordantimes.com/?news=42382.

16. *Ahram Online*, April 26, 2012, http://english.ahram.org.eg/NewsContentPrint/2/0/40264/World/0/Jordan-king-accuses-outgoing-PM-of-delaying-reform.

17. Robert Saltoff, "Jordanian Premier's Sudden Resignation Points to New Political Strategy," www.washingtoninstitute.org/print.php?template=CO5&CID=3484.

18. Rod Nordland, "The Iraqi Voter Rewrites the Rulebook," *New York Times*, April 4, 2010, p. A1.

19. Dahr Jamali, "Rivals say Maliki leading Iraq to civil war," *al-Jazeera News*, December 28, 2011, www.aljazeera.com/indepth/features/2011/12/2011122881820637664.html.

20. *Al-Ahram Weekly*, January 5–11, 2012, http://weekly.ahram.org.eg/print/2011/1079/re7.htm.

21. BBC News, December 21, 2011, www.bbc.co.uk/news/world-middle-east-16283562.

22. Michael S. Schmidt, "From a Few Iraqis, a Word to Libyans on Liberation," *New York Times*, August 30, 2011, p. A6.

23. Tim Arango, "Iraqi Youths' Political Rise Is Stunted by Elites," *New York Times*, April 13, 2011, www.nytimes.com/2011/04/14/world/middleeast/14iraq.html.

24. http://newsvote.bbc.co.uk/mpapps/pagetools/print/news.bbc.co.uk/2/hi/middle_east/738138.

25. http://newsvote.bbc.co.uk/mpapps/pagetools/print/news.bbc.co.uk/2/hi/middle_east/739160.

26. *Financial Times*, May 12, 2009, www.ft.com/intl/cms/s/0/44f42b66–3ec6–11de-ae4f-00144feabdc0.html.

27. Former president Jimmy Carter, whose Carter Presidential Center was invited to be an election monitor, commended "the election authorities for a successful demonstration of the right of the people to express their will. They did it legally and properly"—BBC News, June 8, 2009, http://newsvote.bbc .co.uk/mpapps/pagetools/print/news.bbc.co.uk/2/hi/middle-east/808928.

28. Al-Jazeera Satellite Television, June 9, 2009, www.aljazeera.com/news/middle east/2009/06/2009681835910848.html.

29. BBC News, January 12, 2011, www.bbc.co.uk/news/world-middle-east-12170608.

30. BBC News, July 2, 2011, www.bbc.co.uk/news/world-middle-east-14004096.

31. Al-Jazeera News, May 25, 2011, www.aljazeera.com/news/middleeast/2011 /05/2011525174748827942.html.

32. Nada Bakri, "Hezbollah Leader Backs Syrian President in Public," *New York Times*, December 7, 2011, p. A8.

CHAPTER EIGHT

1. David D. Kirkpatrick, "Egyptian Lawmaker Forced to Resign Over Nose Job," *New York Times*, March 6, 2012, p. A4; see also Muhammad al-Khawly, "Nose Job Scandal Topples Egyptian Salafi MP," *al-Akhbar*, March 6, 2012, http:// english.al-akhbar.com/content/nose-job-scandal-topples-egyptian-salafi-mp.

2. Kirkpatrick, "Egyptian Lawmaker Forced to Resign Over Nose Job," *New York Times*, March 6, 2012, p. A4.

3. Neil MacFarquhar, "Saudi Monarch Grants Women Right to Vote," *New York Times*, September 26, 2011, p. A1; see also Joshua Jacobs, "The Quiet War in Saudi Arabia," *Open Democracy*, January 15, 2012, www.opendemocracy.net/ print/63673.

4. Eman al-Nafjan, "Saudi Arabia turns a deaf ear to Olympic women," *Open Democracy*, April 18, 2012, www.opendemocracy.net/print/65383.

5. *Hurrieyet Daily News*, September 15, 2011, www.hurrietdailynews.com/ default.aspx?pageid=438&n=pm=erdogan8217.

6. Ibid.

7. Anthony Shadid and David D. Kirkpatrick, "Activists in the Arab World Vie to Define Islamic State," *New York Times*, September 30, 2011, p. A1.

8. Ibid.

9. Hania Sholkamy, "Why women are at the heart of Egypt's political trials and

tribulations," *Open Democracy*, January 24, 2012, www.opendemocracy.net/print/63808.

10. Hana Sholkamy, "Egypt: Will there be a place for women's human rights?" *Open Democracy*, March 14, 2012, www.opendemocracy.net/print/64718.

11. See, e.g., Ronald Inglehart and Pippa Norris, "The True Clash of Civilization," *Foreign Policy* (March–April 2003), pp. 62–70; and "Muslim Publics Divided on Hamas and Hezbollah, Most Embrace a Role for Islam in Politics," *Pew Global Attitudes Project*, December 2, 2010, http://pewglobal.org/2010/12/02/muslims-around-the-world-divided-on-hamas-and-hezbollah/.

12. *The Economist*, October 15, 2011, p. 32.

13. Shadid and Kirkpatrick, "Activists in the Arab World Vie to Define Islamic State," *New York Times*, September 30, 2011, p. A1.

14. *The Economist*, November 26, 2011, p. 58.

15. Sana Ajmi, "Ennahdha Discourse: The Sixth Caliphate or a misunderstanding?" *Tunisia Live*, November 16, 2011, www.tunisia-live.net/2011/11/16/ennahdha-flipflopping-the-sixth-caliphate-a-misunderstanding/.

16. *Ahram Online*, July 18, 2012, http://english.ahram.org.eg/NewsContentPrint/2/0/48078/World/0/Tunisia-has-not-fallen-into-hands-of-Islamists-marzouki.

17. Martin Jay, "New Prime Minister Surprises Moroccans with Support for Abortion," *New York Times*, January 11, 2012, www.nytimes.com/2012/01/12/world/africa/new-prime-minister-surprises-moroccans-with-support-for-abortion/.

18. Khalil al-Anani, "Egypt: The New Puritans," in Robin Wright, ed., *The Islamists Are Coming: Who They Really Are* (Washington, DC: Woodrow Wilson Center Press, 2012), p. 35.

19. Patrick Werr, "Egypt's Brotherhood raises stakes by excluding IMF," *Yahoo News*, April 11, 2012, http://news.yahoo.com/analysis-egypts-brotherhood-raises-stakes-excluding-imf-18445323.

20. Niveen Wahish, "MENA Stalled," *al-Ahram Weekly*, April 19–25, 2012, http://weekly.ahram.org.eg/print/2012/1094/ec2.htm.

INDEX

Page numbers in *italics* refer to illustrations.